WRITTEN IN STONE

WRITTEN IN STONE

A JOURNEY THROUGH THE STONE AGE AND THE ORIGINS OF MODERN LANGUAGE

CHRISTOPHER STEVENS

PEGASUS BOOKS
NEW YORK LONDON

WRITTEN IN STONE

Pegasus Books LLC
80 Broad Street, 5th Floor
New York, NY 10004

First Pegasus Books hardcover edition November 2015

ISBN: 978-1-60598-907-5

10 9 8 7 6 5 4 3 2 1

Printed in the United States of America
Distributed by W. W. Norton & Company, Inc.

This book is for my son James, who has been listening to me talk about Indo-European words for years.

LUBH, PA

Contents

Introduction

Say the word **pu**. Then say **pe**, and think about how your face is moving as you form the syllables. Now say **mei**, and feel the different shape your mouth makes.

This is how language began. The earliest words in our modern vocabulary date back at least 8,000 years, and they describe themselves: we can work out what the words meant by their sounds, and by the shapes our lips form when we say them.

Pu: say it again. Your mouth is pursed, your nose is narrowed. There's an expression of distaste on your face. You are blowing out a breath, as if to dispel a bad smell. In the Stone Age, **pu** meant exactly what it means today – *poo*!

Pe is quite different. It starts with the lips together, and then separates them with a faint pop. **Pe** means *open*. The ancient sound is at the core of the modern word: *open*.

When you say **mei**, your mouth stretches from side to side, before you open wide and show your teeth. **Mei** makes you do exactly what you're saying – it means *smile*. And once again, the old sound is at the centre of today's word: *smile*.

This is how Indo-European, the most successful language in world history, began … with intuitive sounds that really mean what they say.

Hundreds of these single-syllable words used by our ancient ancestors are at the heart of English. These sounds shape our language; the ideas behind them have moulded the modern world. In fact, half the world's population speaks a language that has evolved from a single, prehistoric mother tongue. It was never written down, yet many of its words are unchanged or barely different from their Stone Age sounds.

These words didn't arrive from the source language straight into English. It has been a long journey across many millennia. But whether our modern vocabulary arrived by way of the classics, the Germanic tribes or from the Viking north, all of them share a common root – in a language spoken on the Black Sea steppes, more than 4,000 years before the Roman Empire.

They are the DNA of English: the genetic basis of everything we speak and write.

'… our English tongue, a gallimaufry [*sic*] or hodgepodge of all other speches [*sic*]' is how the poet Edmund Spenser described the language in 1579. Whenever we string a sentence together, we're using words that have been imported from many countries and cultures – from Latin and Greek, from Brythonic, Pictish and other Celtic tongues, from Saxon, from Norse, from French, Spanish, Dutch and German, and even from Slavic, Persian and Indian languages.

But the common ancestor of all these sources was first spoken in Stone Age times, on the steppes of central Asia up to 8,000 years ago. It flourished and evolved for around 4,000 years, even though it was never written down, and spread from the shores of the Black Sea across almost all of Europe and much of Asia.

This ancient mother tongue was spoken by Neolithic tribes who domesticated horses and cattle, invented the wheel and the plough, told stories, grew wheat, made wool and even collected honey. But if they had a name for the language, it has been lost. Archaeologists and linguists refer to it as Indo-European, or sometimes Proto-Indo-European.

Some of their words have survived unchanged to the present day, such as **thaw** and **path**. Many more are virtually the same: **gat** meant to *get*, **halp** to *help*, **dars** to *dare*, **lig** to *lick*, **dran** to make the *droning* noise of a bee, **mur** to *murmur* and **wargh** to *worry*. **Frus** was a *frost*, **mald** was *mild*, **sniw** was *snow* and **sparg** was a *spark*.

Even the most coarse words in English, the ones we sometimes describe euphemistically as 'good old Anglo-Saxon words', are in fact thousands of years older, barely changed since Stone Age man first started cursing.

By discovering these primal words, the building blocks of everything from Latin to Sanskrit and Welsh to Gujarati, we gain an entirely fresh perspective on how we speak and write. The Neolithic syllables have evolved to spawn numerous new words that share common themes, like factions or families within each language.

For more than 200 years, Indo-European has been a subject of intense study for linguists and anthropologists, including the Brothers Grimm and the author of the first dictionary of etymology, Walter Skeat. The origins of the tribes who spoke it are the subject of fervent scholarly debate and scientific literature.

But to the average enthusiast of words and popular science, this entire topic is unknown. Just about nobody outside the arcane world of linguistic archaeology is familiar with the hundreds of prehistoric monosyllables that have been identified at the roots of modern vocabularies – such as **gla**. It means to *glow*, and is re-echoed in *gloat, gloom, gloaming, glower, glory, gloss, gold, gleam* and even *yellow*. After thousands of years we still use **gla** countless times every day. We might not know it, but we're speaking in a Stone Age tongue.

Who were these Stone Age tribes?

We do not even know their name, and a vigorous controversy continues over the question of where they first lived. But their influence is immense: we share so much of their language and their thinking. Whoever they were, these ancient people are at the heart of Western civilisation, because their words shaped our world-view.

Early scholars dubbed them the Aryans, because they were farmers: the word **ar** means to *plough*. But they were much more than just farmers – they were storytellers, travellers, warriors, politicians, inventors, empire-builders, potters, merchants and explorers. The term Aryan took on a more sinister meaning in the 1930s and has long since been dropped, without being replaced.

They invented the wheel – their two words for that crucial technology were **kweklos** and **roteh**. One gives us *wheel* and *circle*, the other *rotor* and *chariot*. They also came up with the *axle*, which they called **aksor** (which is not only the root of *axis*, but in Anglo-Saxon and medieval English meant shoulder, because the shoulders are the *axle* of the arms). And their word for *transport* was **wagh**: that gives us *wagon*.

Today's researchers can't even name them after the place where the culture first developed, because that isn't known either. The most popular current theory links them to the Kurgan culture around 4,500 BC, whose burial mounds are dotted across the Eurasian steppes, in what is now Ukraine and Kazakhstan. There is archaeological data to suggest that they date back even further, to the region of Anatolia in modern Turkey and elsewhere. Most academics agree that they dispersed completely around 2,500 BC, during the early Bronze Age. By that time, Indo-European had evolved so much, in so many different directions, that it no longer existed in its original form. The mother language was gone, and its children had inherited half the globe.

A clearer picture of their day-to-day life emerges from the words that have been passed down to us. They kept sheep and goats, for wool as well as meat – we know, because they had terms for shearing, spinning and weaving, as well as sewing. They drank horse's milk and made cheese and yoghurt; meat broth was a staple, seasoned with wild seeds and herbs. Wild apples and honey were a prized treat. But they also grew grain (**grno**), which they ground into flour and baked as flatbread.

Some tribes were nomadic, and the invention of the wheel transformed their lifestyle. Instead of carrying everything they owned on sleds, pack animals or their own backs, they were able to build carts. That meant they could transport not only their tents and supplies of dried food but water too – an innovation that gave the wanderers the scope to travel much further than ever before.

It's a vivid image: an immense wagon train of families with their herds of sheep, wending across the prehistoric grasslands towards an unknown frontier, carrying all that they needed to survive. Rugged tents. Salted meat. Pots of water stoppered and stacked on carts. Heaps of cloth for making garments or for trading. The younger men would have been on horseback, driving the flocks, while a chain of mares and foals followed the wagons (these horses were bred for their milk). And pulling each wagon at a plod was a world-weary yoked pair of oxen (**uksen**).

We can say with certainty that this culture and its language evolved in northern climes, because it has no words for the exotic animals of the south – no tiger, no elephant, no giraffe, no crocodile. But it does have words for bear, wolf, beaver and otter, for birch, oak, willow, ash and elm. Some are barely different in English today (**as** and **elmo**, for instance).

They wore ornaments made from bone, boar tusk and cattle horn (the word for horn was **ker**, giving us *cornet*, *carrot* and *ginger* … three things that are roughly horn-shaped). They fished with bone harpoons and baited bone hooks; though they were not hunters and rarely killed wild deer for meat, they could use wooden bows with flint-tipped arrows. The bows, especially when fired from horseback, made them deadly raiders.

By studying numerous current languages, as well as their defunct forerunners, linguists can decode the particular sounds these Stone Age people used for different objects and concepts. Scientists call it 'back-engineering' – taking a modern concept and tracing its evolution in reverse, to arrive at the original design.

It's a process of detection that reveals a wealth of history, and teaches us to think constantly in new ways about everyday words.

For instance, the word for plough in medieval English is *ear*. That gives us *arable* today. In Greek, a plough was *aratron* and the Latin word was almost the same: *aratrum*. In Icelandic it is *arthr*, in Armenian *araur* and in Lithuanian *arklas*. The same monosyllable is constant in all; this evidence, and much more, suggests that the Stone Age word for plough was **ar**.

This prehistoric language followed strict rules of grammar that have also lived on. When words changed tense, for instance, they changed their ending: in the past tense, a 'd' was added, just as in English.

Words were combined to create new words: poets were word-weavers, or **wekwom-texos**. The language had a complex syntax, with cases, tenses, moods and voices (nouns could be subject or object; verbs could be past, present or future, passive or active). This was not a stark language but a beautiful one. It used three aspirated consonants that English doesn't use – **bh**, **dh** and **gh**, which are spoken as 'b', 'd' and 'g' with a puff of breath afterwards.

It was so adaptable and effective that it not only travelled with the tribes as they spread out across Europe and Asia – it pushed out and superceded other languages wherever it met them. And as it travelled, it changed, so that it became many regional dialects and, over thousands of years, entirely new languages.

In Europe today, there are few tongues that didn't start with Indo-European (the main examples are Hungarian and Finnish, and Basque). In Asia, the Stone Age words echo from Iraq and Iran to India and Vietnam. By contrast, languages that evolved from other sources – such as the fifteen clicking noises of Xhosa in South Africa, or the nasal sounds of Guarani in Paraguay – seem impossibly alien to Indo-European speakers. It's proof that today's languages didn't evolve across two continents by accident – they developed from a mother tongue that was infinitely more efficient, memorable and flexible than anything the other tribes could come up with.

Whoever these people were, they didn't just invent the physical tools that made travel, warfare and farming possible. They also developed the essential mental tool: a dynamic language.

Language made complex religion possible. The Neolithic farmers, who had numerous words for snow, rain and sunshine, relied on the seasons for their food, and so they worshipped the skies. Their word for the king of the gods was **diw-pitar**, or *sky-father*. To the Romans he was *Jupiter* (which is almost the same word); to the Greeks he was simply *Zeus*.

Who uncovered this Stone Age language? (And were they all barking mad?)

'My leisure hours, for some time past, have been employed in considering the striking affinity of the languages of Europe', wrote the physician James Parsons 250 years ago. He was the first scientist to recognise that English had echoes across the continent and throughout half of Asia, and he had an ingenious biblical explanation for it: the people of the Earth were descended from Noah's three sons, Shem, Ham and Japheth. Clearly, these three boys must have spoken different languages, which spread into Africa, the Middle East and, lastly, to Europe.

No one took much notice of Parsons' 1767 book, *The Remains of Japhet*, because although he was a member of the Royal Society and the Society of Antiquaries, he was better known for his studies of the human bladder and of hermaphroditism.

Yet Parsons was only the first of an extraordinary parade of thinkers, eccentrics and obsessives who laid the groundwork for the study of Indo-European roots – a study that today attracts many of the most brilliant minds in archaeology and linguistics.

The first scholar to be taken seriously was Sir William Jones, who discovered in 1786 that Sanskrit, the 3,500-year-old holy language of India, was closely related to Latin and Greek. Jones was so brilliant as a youth that his hobby during his teens was writing Latin poetry. A political radical who supported the American Revolution, he was a friend of Dr Johnson, and rose to become Chief Justice of the Supreme Court in Calcutta, India.

In a lecture to the Asiatic Society in 1786, Jones highlighted the similarities between Latin, Greek and Sanskrit. They bore, he said, 'a stronger affinity, both in the roots of verbs and the forms of grammar, than could possibly have been produced by accident; so strong indeed, that no philologer could examine them all three, without believing them to have sprung from some common source, which, perhaps, no longer exists.'

That speech marked the start of serious academic research, but not the end of the oddball influence. Indo-European, for some reason, attracts eccentrics and polymaths.

Rasmus Rask, for instance, a Danish professor who spoke twenty-five languages – including Persian, which he learned fluently in just six weeks – travelled from Iceland to Bombay in the early 1800s, studying the similarities between words. And in 1813, Thomas Young, the polyglot who helped to translate the Rosetta Stone and so cracked the code of Egyptian hieroglyphics, coined the name Indo-European for the prototype language. At the time, he was studying translations of the Lord's Prayer in hundreds of languages and dialects.

Franz Bopp arrived in Paris in 1812 determined to devote his life to the study of Sanskrit. For the next five years he spent every waking hour in the city's libraries, completely oblivious to the fall of Napoleon, the return of the emperor from exile, the battle of Waterloo and the restoration of the monarchy; all he cared about was tracing the grammar and inflections of dead languages. He invented the term *Stammsprache*, or source language.

In the middle of the nineteenth century, August Schleicher published the first attempt to reconstruct a forerunner of all Indo-European languages, even using it to write a folk story called 'The Sheep and the Horses'. By the time he was thirty, Schleicher had developed a theory that languages are living organisms that are born, mature, bloom and die. He also discovered the concept of evolution, several years before Darwin published *The Origin of Species* – but applied it to words instead of animals. Schleicher died from tuberculosis, aged forty-seven, in 1868.

The Brothers Grimm, Jacob and Wilhelm, were not only folk-tale collectors: their theories of linguistics explained how words change as they travel. For instance, Grimm's law states that a 'k' sound in the source language always stayed as a 'k' in Latin (albeit written as a 'c'), but became an 'h' in Old German – so the Stone Age word **k'mtom** became *centum* in Latin (and *ekaton* in Greek) but changed to *hunda* in Gothic, and so to *hundred* in English. It's impossible to see the connection between **k'mtom** and *hundred* without those intermediary stages; once Grimm's law is applied, all sorts of links become visible.

The first scholar to write a dictionary of English etymology was Walter Skeat, who devoted much of his life to detective work with words. He traced thousands of origins for his four-volume dictionary, completed in 1882, and included a glossary of 467 root words from Indo-European.

In the twentieth century, Eric Partridge compiled *Origins: A Short Etymological Dictionary of Modern English*, which gathered words onto family trees, tracing the branches back to roots that were usually Indo-European. Partridge, a New Zealander who served with the Australian infantry during the First World War, had become fascinated with slang and the hidden history of words in the trenches, listening to soldiers swearing in ways learned from all over the British Empire.

Finally, Joseph Twadell Shipley was a Brooklyn-born theatre critic who devoted his later years to a vast 'discursive dictionary' of Indo-European roots, into which he shovelled anything that occurred to him – poetry, myth, jokes, folk songs, the periodic table, apocrypha, diatribes and scatology.

All these scholars were inspired and sometimes unhinged by the beautiful implications of Indo-European. Read this book with caution – the contents are mind-altering. You will never think about words in the same way again.

The Stone Age Words

A

Ak, to be sharp or quick

Acute, acid, eager, equine

An, to breathe

Man, animal, animator, sane

Ank, to bend

Ankle, anchor, anguish, England

Ap, to put

Apply, apostrophe, April, inept

Arg, to shine

Argentina, argument, Argonauts, electricity

Ak, to be sharp or quick

Why is an *acrobat* like a horse? The words for both began with a monosyllabic sound used by Neolithic farmers, 6,000 years ago, to signify something quick, sharp or piercing. The sound was **ak** and it has survived into English, with exactly the same meaning, in dozens of words.

An obvious example is *acute*. That word arrived in English with the Romans, whose word for sharpened was *acutus* (the past participle of the verb *acuere*, to sharpen). The Latin for sharpness was *acumen*, a word that has remained helpfully unaltered for millennia.

The Ancient Greeks also used **ak** pointedly. *Akmi*, for instance, meant the point or sharp edge at an object's top – such as a mountain peak. The *Acropolis* was the city (*polis*) at the top. That's why *acrophobia* is a fear of heights (and not vertigo, which is simply giddiness or dizziness).

Akmi came to mean the utmost possible height, the sense in which we use *acme* today. When Wile E. Coyote used *Acme*, of course, it was the brand name of mail-order products for catching the Road Runner, and they never worked properly – since the cartoons first appeared in 1949, the word has become a laughing stock.

The Greek word for pointed was *akros*, which gives us *acrostic*, a poem where the initial letters of each line pointedly spell out a name or message. And they sharpened their blades on *akoni* or whetstones: this might be why another name for the deadly monk's hood plant is *aconite*, since it grows on steep, sharp outcrops of rock. Other names for the flower, with its transparent lilac petals that curve like an ominous cowl, are leopard's bane, devil's helmet and the queen of poisons. It is so toxic that even picking its leaves with bare fingers can be fatal: death begins with a tingling in the limbs, then a numbness, then heart and respiratory failure. Another explanation of its name could be that *a-koniton* is Greek for without a struggle.

An *acrobat*, in Ancient Greece, was originally someone who could walk on the points of his toes, but since that quickly stopped being impressive, *acrobatics* came to include tumbling, rope-walking and flying a biplane upside down.

The **ak** sound is sometimes softened now. *Acidus* in Latin was pronounced 'akkidus', meaning piercing, but it gives us *acid*, and *acidulous*, which is sour-tempered and *acid-tongued*, and *acidimetry*, which involves measuring the strength of acids. Similarly, the Roman word for a needle was *acus*, which they said as 'akkus' – it gives us *accurate* but also *acicular* (the first 'c' is soft), which is needle-like, and *aciculiform*, which is shaped like a needle. You take the point.

In the same vein, the Romans said 'akkerbus', for harsh-tasting and bitter, but it has filtered into English as *acerb* (and *acerbic*), pronounced 'a-surb', and still meaning sour and bitter, like unripe fruit. *Acerbate* means to make something sour, which is why *exacerbate* means to make a bad thing worse.

Sharp, in Latin, was *acrus*, giving us *acrid* and *acrimony*. It also evolved into the medieval English *egre*, which turned into *eager*. The original meaning of eager was acrid and sharp; later, it came to mean keen and even impetuous. So, in Middle English, sharp, tart wine was *vin egre* or *vinegar*. And to goad someone or urge them with sharp words was to *egg* them on – it has nothing to do with poultry.

Horses don't have much to do with poultry either, but they did once provide food. On the steppes during the late Stone Age, the horse became central to tribal life. At first, wild horses were domesticated for meat and milk, like cattle. Later, people discovered they could pull carts and even ploughs. The first man to ride a horse probably did it for a joke, but Neolithic man soon realised that horse-riders moved far faster than any human runner. Archers on horseback could chase down prey; warriors in horse-drawn chariots could cut down foot soldiers.

The original Indo-European word for horse was **ak-wos**, which might be translated as quick animal (a cow was **g-wos**, probably slow animal, because **ga** meant to walk). In Latin, **ak-wos** became *equus*; the Greek word, with the 'k' softened to 'h', was *hippos*. We say *equine* and *equestrian*, but we also say 'horse', from the Germanic word *xorsaz* – and nobody knows where that one comes from. It's fortunate that we didn't adopt the Greek word, because showjumping from the Hippo of the Year show would be frankly bizarre.

An, to breathe

Empty your lungs with a sigh – 'aaah'. Now inhale through your nose – 'nnnn'.

The Neolithic word for breathing, **an**, is simply an imitation of the sound. It's onomatopoeic, but it's much more than that: it defines life itself. Any creature, *human* or *animal*, that is alive must be breathing. Once it stops, life has left it.

The basic word *man* is a combination of two Stone Age concepts: the **m** sound, for me, myself; and the breathing **an** sound. *Man* is my own living-and-breathing self. The word doesn't change in Anglo-Saxon, Middle English, Icelandic, Dutch and Swedish, and it was barely different in Sanskrit (*manu*). The word in Sanskrit for the breath of life is *prana*.

The belief that all things, even rocks and trees, have a living soul is *animism*. The Latin word for the soul is *animus*, but its meaning changed in English – to bear *animus* was to nurture a spirited emotion, usually a hostile one. That leads to *animosity*. If, on the other hand, you bear no grudges, you are blessed with *equanimity*.

When everyone agrees, we are *unanimous*, of one spirit. When a victor behaves nobly, he is *magnanimous*, possessed of great spirit. But when someone behaves in a snivelling, cowardly way, he is *pusillanimous*. (The sound **pu** denotes something boyish or puerile.) Cowards deserve *animadversion* – to be noticed, criticised and punished. So do *animalists*, who believe that we are all no better than dumb beasts and should give in to our sensual passions.

If you are hot-tempered, you are *animous*; if you are lively, the word is *animated*. Anything that is alive is *animate*. To be able actually to bring something to life is a rare gift, usually wielded only by cartoonists, sometimes called *animators*, and mad scientists. Frankenstein's monster was the most famous but, in *Carry On Screaming*, Kenneth Williams played the undead Dr Watt who could revive Egyptian mummies: he was a *re-animator*.

Even the smallest animals are alive. Really small ones are *animalcules* or *animalillia*. The 4.2 million devotees of the Jain religion in India are such strict vegetarians that they try never to harm even a fly. At least you can see flies; if you were constantly worrying about the wellbeing of microscopic mites, you'd go *insane*. The Ancient Greek word for healthy and sound was *saos* – add *saos* and *an* together and, if you're of sound mind, you'll find that you are *sane*.

If you've lost your mind, you should be in a *sanitarium*. If, on the other hand, you're recuperating from a chronic disease such as tuberculosis, you need a *sanatorium*. Anything else would be *unsanitary* – decidedly unhealthy.

The Latin motto *mens sana in corpore sano* reminds us that a healthy mind resides in a healthy body; the two are *consanguineous*, or blood relations. That word contains many components, including the Latin word for blood, *sanguinem*, giving us words like *sangaree*, a spicy drink of diluted wine served cold in hot countries, and *sang-froid*, meaning dispassionate calm – all derived from **an**.

The *sangrail* was the cup that collected Christ's blood from the wound in His side on the cross, more often called the Holy Grail. Whatever you call it, the Grail was *sanguiferous*, an object used for transporting blood. Miraculous statues are believed by many Christians to weep blood, a process called *sanguification*. However the blood appears, it leaves the statue's face *sanguinolent*, or stained with blood.

Blood was one of the four 'humours' of medieval medicine: the bodily fluids that determine our personalities. The three other humours were yellow bile, black bile and phlegm: a phlegmatic person was long-suffering, a black bilious one was evil-tempered and a yellow bilious one was depressive and irritable. But the ruddy-cheeked *sanguine* character was optimistic, cheerful and amiable, as well as having a hearty appetite for food and drink.

If you've got a hearty appetite for blood, on the other hand, you are *sanguinary* – 'bloodthirsty, delighting in carnage, imposing the death penalty freely'. Or perhaps you're a vampire, in which case you are *sanguivorous*: a carnivore who eats only blood. No wonder vampire movies are so full of heavy breathing … it's all about **an**, the breath of life.

Ank, to bend

Morporkian, the language spoken by citizens of Ankh-Morpork in Terry Pratchett's *Discworld* stories, is not an Indo-European language. But Sir Terry's fine instinct for words was working well when he named the city: Ankh has undertones of something twisted, crooked and bent. Most of Ankh-Morpork's inhabitants are all three.

Oddly, the 'Eng' in *England* ought to have exactly the same resonances. And if it doesn't, that's because we've forgotten where the word came from.

The word **ank** meant to bend. It's why *ankle* and *angle* are almost the same sound. The Greeks called a bend an *ankon*, and it must have sounded right for that bony joint at the far end of the leg, because it survived in all sorts of languages. The Germans and Dutch say *enkel*, the Danes and Swedes say *ankel* and the *Anglo*-Saxons said *anklowe*.

Anglo-Saxon was a mixture of Germanic tongues spoken by the Saxons (from Saxony) and the *Angles* (from *Angeln*, a more descriptive and less long-winded name for the province now called Schleswig-Holstein, where the Danish peninsula meets the European mainland). *Angeln* essentially meant *angle-land*, which is exactly what the Angles called the former Roman province of Britannia; once they had grown bored of pillaging its eastern border, they decided to drop *anchor* and settle there instead. Consequently, that coastal area, a bulbous protuberance of fens, flatlands and no sharp angles whatever, is called East *Anglia*.

The most effective way to catch a fish is to bait a hook or V-shaped metal barb, which is why it's called *angling*. By extension, the word means to use wily ways for catching anything or anyone – angling for a spouse, for example. The same word can mean something similar for a different reason: to *angle* your prey is to drive it into a corner and trap it.

Even fish can go angling. *Anglerfish* have worm-like warts, dangling on stalks above their large, upturned mouths. Other fish come to investigate and are snapped up. Anglerfish evolved more than 100 million years ago, so the underwater *anglers* existed long before Sir Isaac Walton published his celebration of fishing and fishermen, *The Compleat Angler*, in 1653.

It isn't just fish-hooks and ankles that bend. Snakes do too, so anything snake-like is *anguine* or *anguineous*, and anything eel-like is *anguilliform*. The Latin for an eel was *anguilla* (literally, small snake); in Tudor times, when noblemen went hawking and treated their falcons' health with a good deal more care than they did their servants', the word for the worms puked up by poorly birds was *anguelle*. A French delicacy, *anguillule*, is small eels in vinegar. But the tiny dried fish served in paste that we know as anchovies have a different derivation, from the Basque word *anchoa* – Basque is not an Indo-European language.

You'd have to be an eel, a snake or, at a pinch, an anchovy to wriggle through an *angust* place. That means straitened or compressed, from the Latin *angustus* or narrow, which itself comes from *angere*, meaning to squeeze.

The concepts of being bent and being squeezed are slightly different, and Neolithic man had slightly different words for them. To squeeze or strangle was not **ank** but **ang** – the root of *angere*, and so *anguish*, *anxious* and *angina*. In the Nordic languages, it became *anger*, the kind of rage that springs from vexation or inner turmoil. In Icelandic, *angr* means war.

One more oddity: the unit of measurement for very short wavelengths is an *angstrom* – about a hundred-millionth of a centimetre long. It was coined after Anders Ångström, the Swedish physicist who produced a map of the frequencies of sunlight. Any wave at those frequencies will contain 20 billion angles every metre, but the name Angström doesn't mean a storm of angles. In Swedish, it translates to 'the stream in the meadow' … possibly a good place for a spot of angling.

Ap, to put

Neolithic language had its own ancestors, perhaps dating back tens of thousands of years. The connection between certain consonants with specific concepts must be a very old one – the idea that 'n' words are negative (no, not, never, negate) or that 'qw' or 'kwa' words are interrogative (question, enquire, which, why, who) is as basic as any language gets.

The tribes at the end of the Stone Age probably didn't invent this idea; they just developed it. The 'p' sound 8,000 years ago and probably much earlier had to do with *place* or *position*. And the monosyllable **ap** suggested a movement – stretching out your arm to *put* something down or *pick* it up.

In English, one close relative to this meaning is *apply* – 'to put a thing into practical contact with another', says the *Oxford English Dictionary* (*OED*) … as in, to *apply* a bandage. Or paint. Or aftershave.

The other sense of **ap**, of grabbing hold instead of setting down, is *apprehend* – to seize, either physically or mentally. You can apprehend a meaning as well as a thief.

In Ancient Greek, the word became *apo*, meaning away from or off – something placed at arm's length. The Latin *ab* has a similar sense; in Sanskrit, it was *apa*. English words with the prefix *ap-* could fill a book, and that's before you include the shortened version, *a-*. That comes from Old French, which elided *ap* to *a* – it entered English and became another common prefix implying distance from. *Away* and *apart* are the most obvious examples. *A + way* suggests something that has gone further down the path or left it altogether – *a-way*. It isn't the opposite of way, it's just at a distance. But *a* + *part* is the opposite of part: it's something that has been cut off from the part – *a-part*. That's why *amoral* is the opposite of moral.

When you start to look this closely at words, they stop acting like mere sounds with meanings. They almost seem to be atomic elements that can bond to each other, becoming molecules and creating chemical structures. Hydrogen and oxygen are gases: combine them and you create water, H_2O. **Ap** and **wagh** are Neolithic words: combine them and you create *away*.

It's hard to have a discussion about English grammar without someone trying to put you in your place about the *apostrophe*. Given its prefix, that's rather *apposite*. An apostrophe indicates where one or more letters have been been missed out (and might have to be put back). You can say, 'It doesn't matter', but you will need the apostrophe if you are going to write that down. An apostrophe stands in for two missing letters when it spells out who owns what: *Jack's book* is short for *Jack his book*. And *Jane's book* is short for *Jane his book*, because unlike French or German, English has only one gender. Everything's male, including Jane.

Apostrophe can also mean a rhetorical trick, where the speaker breaks off to address someone. Comedians do it all the time, talking to the people in the front row – think of Frankie Howerd, chastising a lady for harbouring bawdy thoughts. 'Ooo err missus, ooo nay! Thrice nay!' The audience *applaud*. But it's not just comedians: Hollywood actor Clint Eastwood delivered a speech at the Republican National Convention that was all apostrophe, as he pretended to lecture an invisible President Barack Obama in an empty chair on the stage. The *absent* President didn't *apologise* (that is, put in a good word – *ap* + *logos*).

That's all part of the *ebb* and flow of politics. Ebb comes from the Anglo-Saxon word *ebba*, meaning to recede. It's a reminder that Indo-European words arrived in English through the Germanic languages as well as Latin and Greek.

The Latin word *aperire* means to open: it gives *April* its name, when the earth is opening up shoots and buds. That's *apt* – and apt, meaning well put together, is another English word from a Latin root: *aptus* was the past participle of the verb *apere*, meaning to fit or join together. *Aptus* also gives us *adapt*, and *adept*. With one extra step, we also arrive at *attitude*, from *aptitudinem* … the 'p' has been lost, because the English get their attitude from the Italians (the Italians, like the Old French, didn't feel that the 'p' was worth keeping). *Attitudine* was originally a painter's term in Italian: it meant rightness or *aptness*.

There's no such word as *ept*, but if there were, it would come from **ap**. That's how we get *inept*, after all. The Latin *ineptus* meant improper or foolish, from *in* (Latin for not) and *aptus*. In other words, we're back with those protozoic speech sounds, the 'n' for negative and the 'p' for place – something inept is basically in the wrong place. And should probably be *abolished* (removed from existence, for it has no place here).

Arg, to shine

Arg seems to be one of the later Proto-Indo-European words. It means to shine like sunlight on metal, and so it must date to the Bronze or Iron Age, rather than the earlier Stone Age.

Argent is silver, a word dating back to Tudor English. Originally it meant anything silver; later, it referred only to coins, and was a slang term meaning money, similar to 'cash' today. It is still a word used in heraldry (abbreviated as *arg*), and occasionally by dentists: *argental* mercury is a soft metal mixture once used in tooth fillings. The scientific symbol for the element silver is *Ag*.

There are lots of *argentic* words (ones containing silver) – *argenteous* means silvery, *argentry* is silver jewellery, to *argentify* is to turn into silver and *argentific* means producing silver. If you want to measure exactly how much silver is in *argentiferous* rock, you'll need an *argentometer*. One word is still in common usage: when the Spanish conquistadors landed in South America in the 1500s, they were chasing rumours of mountains made entirely of silver ... so they called the country *Argentina*.

In Latin, the word for transparent is *argutus*, and so to make things clear is *arguere*. To the Romans, *arguing* was about proving truth through debate, not mere bickering and squabbling. That's why a statement that supports a logical proposition is an *argument*. If you have sharp perceptions and you're good at details, you are said to be *argute*; if you quibble about minutiae, that's *argutation*.

Arg Garfunkel … sorry, Art Garfunkel wasn't the first person to sing of 'Bright Eyes'. The Greeks believed that light came from looking: our eyes shone like silver upon everything we saw. This theory might solve the riddle of why a Greek youth called Arestorides was also known as *Argos*. He had 100 eyes, and when he slept, he closed only one pair at a time. The goddess Juno ordered him to keep an eye, or lots of eyes, on her High Priestess, Io. His watch went badly: Mercury, the messenger of the gods, lulled him to sleep with music and killed him. The myth has it that Juno put the eyes of Argos on the tail of her sacred bird, the peacock.

Argos had unblemished eyes, with no *argema* – small white ulcers on the edge of the eye's transparent covering, the cornea. Argema comes from the Greek word *argos*, meaning shining white.

The shining ship built by Hercules for his friend Jason, meanwhile, was called the *Argo*, and its crew of some fifty or more sailors were the *Argonauts*. After the *Argosy*, his voyage to recover the Golden Fleece, Jason beached his ship and dedicated it to the gods – in return, the gods drew its picture in the stars. The second-century astronomer Ptolemy named *Argo* as one of forty-eight constellations in the night sky, and the biggest.

Etymologist Walter Skeat argued that **arg** might be pronounced **ark**. This explains *arc* lamps, of course, but it might also give us the most important word of the modern era: *electricity*. That comes from *electron*, the Greek word for amber – fossilised tree resin that has *electric* properties. If you rub amber with a cloth, a static charge builds up. And if you say electron in a nasal way, it becomes el-*ark*-tron. *Arguably.*

B

Bha, to speak

Ban, telephone, fate, infantry

Bhal, to blaze

Bleach, blanket, flamingo, flagrant

Bher, to bear

Birth, burden, ferret, hamburger

Bhleu, to blow

Bubble, bless, flow, influenza

Bhrag, to break

Brick, fragile, suffragette, osprey

Bhur, to brew

Burn, brandy, brimstone, fury

Bha, to speak

If you have something worth saying, say it out loud. The Neolithic word for speaking has the sense of a proclamation – when a man spoke, others listened. In English, the word that comes closest to this meaning is *banns*, the announcement of a wedding that must be read three times.

In modern English, a *ban* is a prohibition, but in the Old Germanic languages, a *ban* was a call that went out to everyone, a summons to convene or to fight. That's why *banal* means something that everyone does. To *abandon* someone is to leave them beyond reach of the ban, and to *banish* them is to send them so far away that they couldn't hear even if you called.

In Ancient Greek, the sound was softened. *Pheme* meant a voice and *phasis* was speech – so a *euphemism* is literally a good word, though a mealy-mouthed one. *Blasphemy* is speaking against the gods, which might provoke the gods to strike you dumb with *aphasia*, the loss of speech.

A clear voice in Greek was *phone*, which gives us *phonetics*, the symbols that record vocal sounds. If prehistoric man had developed a system of phonetics, we would have a much clearer idea of the grammar that strung these early words together – but history starts when civilisations begin writing things down, which is why the Stone Age tribes of the steppes were prehistoric in the first place.

Thanks to *phone* we have the *telephone*, which enables 'speaking at a distance', and the *gramophone*, which began as the *phonogram* but was preceded by the *phonograph*, literally meaning a clearly written voice. Early gramophone records used to split *symphonies* onto six or eight discs; nowadays, you can cram 1,000 symphonies onto a *mobile phone*.

Alexander Graham Bell's device changed the world; at least, one of them did. He also developed the *photophone*, which used light to transmit sounds. Bell called it his greatest invention; the public was sceptical, and in 1880 *The New York Times* asked sardonically: 'Does Prof. Bell intend to connect Boston and Cambridge with a line of sunbeams hung on telegraph posts, and, if so, what diameter are the sunbeams to be? Will it be necessary to insulate them against the weather?' Though his invention was the forerunner of wireless radio, scientists couldn't find a reliable way to send messages on sunrays. The clouds kept getting in the way.

The Roman word for speaking was *fantem*; the past tense, spoken, was *fatum*. It's obvious that *Fate* is the voice of destiny, but more unexpected is the derivation of *infant*, a child too young to speak – and *infantry*, the common soldiery who fight the battles but have no say in the strategy or politics of war: 'Theirs not to reason why.' Not everything can be expressed in words, of course: some things are *ineffable*.

'Let us now praise *famous* men': that syllable *fa* talks its way into all sorts of concepts. A word before the main speech is a *preface*. A chap who is easy to speak to is *affable*. A story that speaks for itself is a *fable*, and a man *confesses* his sins by speaking them.

A *bandit* isn't likely to confess, but then his etymology is a bit more obscure. He might be *banned*; on the other hand, he might be part of a *band*, and that comes from **bhand** – the original Indo-European word meaning to *bind*.

Thatched roofs are made with *bundles* of straw, but grass and branches can also be woven together by *bending* them. The strip of cloth that ties the bundle is a *riband* or a *ribbon*. Knot a ribbon round your head and it's a *bandana*; tie it around a wound and it's a *bandage*. Wind one round your waist and you have a *cummerbund*.

With a soft 'f' sound, **bhand** is the root of all *faith*, which binds us together, and *federation*, which is a bundle of states or countries all tied up with ribbon … or red tape.

Bhal, to blaze

Bhal is one of Neolithic man's many words for fire. The word conveyed the shimmering, moving, brilliant *blaze*, almost too bright to look upon. If you stare too long at the sun, you'll go *blind*. Most people *blink* first. To a dazzled eye, everything looks *bleached* white, *blenched* and *blanched*, a *blank*.

Because the first cloths to be woven were not dyed, they were white – that's why heavy woollen shawls and bedclothes are *blankets*. White or very fair hair is *blond*.

But fire can transform colours in other ways: sit too close to it and your face will *flush* or *blush* red. Let your blanket catch alight and it will be burned *black*.

In Spanish, white is *blanco*: that word was adopted as a trade name in the 1880s for the powder used by British soldiers to keep buckskin leather gleaming white. In France, white is *blanc*, and linen cloth from Normandy that is woven from bleached thread is still called *blancard*. The French for 'to eat' is *manger*, so if you eat a gelatinous white pudding made from cornflour and milk, you'll find it is *blancmange*. In Slav languages from Czech to Croatian, white is *biely*, *bijel* or something very similar: that sound hasn't found its way into English, but it's a clear example of how closely other modern European language families also cleave to their Stone Age origins.

The initial **bh** was always a soft consonant, and in many of its derivations it is softer still, pronounced *ph* or *f* – the most obvious examples are *flare* and *flame*. The Latin word *fulgere* means to gleam, glitter, shine or sparkle – *effulgent* means radiant, but in medieval English the word was simply *fulgent*. The poet Milton, in *Paradise Lost*, describes the commander of the fallen angels, Beelzebub's boss: 'his fulgent head / And shape Starr bright'. (If you're wondering whether Beelzebub, one of the devil's minions, derives from **bhal**, it doesn't. The word comes from the Hebrew, Ba'al z'bub – the Lord of Flies, worshipped by the Philistines.)

We don't think today of the devil as being burning bright, even though his home is hellish hot – but Lucifer means 'bearing fire' (see **luh** and **bhar**), and it was common slang for a match 100 years ago.

Fulgurant means *flashing* like lightning, and *fulgurate* is an explosive. The Viking god Thor threw thunderbolts around, which is called *fulminating*. There's a grubby by-product to all this fire, so *fuliginous* means sooty.

General Sir Harry *Flashman*, the creation of George MacDonald Fraser, was a Victorian hero, poltroon and ladies' man whose fictional memoirs give first-hand descriptions of battles from the Indian Mutiny and the Crimean Campaign to the Opium Wars and Custer's Last Stand. Flashman was based on the bully in *Tom Brown's Schooldays* by Thomas Hughes, but the word was old slang when the novel appeared in 1857 – it meant a disreputable gentleman, a swell who bet on bareknuckle boxing matches and drank with petty criminals ... a *flagrant* cad.

To *flagrate* is to burn, so a *conflagration* is a huge and destructive blaze. The original meaning of flagrant was blazing or glowing. For the past 300 years or so, it has meant glaring or scandalous – 'flaming into notice', as Samuel Johnson put it. To be discovered *in flagrante delicto* is to be caught in the heat of passion. The Latin for a shameful crime was *flagitium*, so *flagitious* means villainous, or even addicted to *flagrancy* and atrocious crimes – like the third Marquess of Hertford, a Napoleonic nobleman whose life was dedicated to dissipation and infamous living, and who inspired Thackeray's portrait of the vicious Lord Steyne in *Vanity Fair*.

Anything that burns is *inflammable*, but to avoid confusion, the designers of safety symbols prefer to use the word *flammable*, which means the same thing. No one talks of seditious rhetoric as being 'flammatory', though – it's *inflammatory*. And if you've got a rash, that's no mere 'flammation' but an *inflammation*.

Anything *flamboyant* is brilliant or brightly coloured, such as a *flamingo* ... or a dragon with fiery hiccups, which is *flammivomous*.

Bher, to bear

One of the numerous words to descend almost unchanged into English from the Stone Age, **bher** seems to have always had a double meaning – to shoulder a load, or to carry a child. A mother *bears* her baby and then she *births* it. Later she carries the *bairn* in her shawl, which makes it a bit of a *burden*. Let's face it, life is no different today from how it was for our *forebears*.

The Anglo-Saxon word for 'to bear' was *beran*, and the word for a woman's lower body and lap, where a baby would sit, was *bearm*. In the north of England, that word survives in dialect as *barm*.

If you can find yourself a secure place, whether that's onboard a ship or in a safe job, you have a *berth* – a place to bear your weight. And if that safe job involves carting a lot of heavy goods around – bricks, perhaps, or vegetables – you can put them on a *barrow*. That way, you can *bring* more. A strong man can carry more than a weak one, of course – hence the word *burly*. Don't work yourself to death, though, or you'll end up being *borne* away on a *bier*.

In Greek, the blurred initial consonant **bh** was softened into *phor* – a pot for carrying wine or water was an *amphora*. If you're lugging all sorts of stuff around with you, that's *paraphernalia*. When a word or phrase bears a deeper meaning, it is a *metaphor*; when a spirit of joy lifts you up, that is *euphoria*; when the same word or phrase is repeated or carried over in a sentence (like this) the technical term is *anaphora*.

As a suffix, *-phore* implies something conveyed or carried. The most common example is *semaphore*, a system of waving flags to send signals. *Phosphorous* is a chemical element that glows when it comes into contact with oxygen – the Ancient Greek for light was *phos*.

To the Romans, whatever life brought, good or bad, was chance – *fors*. Good luck creates *fortunes* for the *fortunate*.

In Latin, that **bh** was softened further, to become *ferre*. That gives us *fertile*. But as a suffix, *-fer* is used in all sorts of words – *suffer* is to bear pain, *transfer* is to carry a load from one side to the other, *prefer* is to weigh more on one side than the other, *refer* is to hand the burden to someone else, *proffer* is to hold out the burden as a gift, *confer* is to share it with other people, *differ* is to carry it in an unconventional way and *defer* is to put it down with the intention of picking it up some other time.

An object that bears a bad smell with it is *odiferous*. A man whose voice carries is *vociferous*. Rocks that contain copper are *cupriferous*. And something filled with magnificent beauty is *splendiferous*.

Add a 't' to *ferre* and you get *ferret*, a lithe hunter that kills prey in a burrow and carries it out. *Burrow*, if you're wondering, comes from a Neolithic word so similar to **bher** that it seems to be an extension of it: **bhergh** means high land, especially a town built on a height. Perhaps the connection is that the settlement is borne upwards by the rise of the land: at any rate, *bhergh* became *berg*, *burgh* and *borough* – all old names for towns from *Edinburgh* to *Pittsburgh* … not to mention *Hamburg*.

37

Hamburgers don't contain ham, though they might contain horse, but they definitely contain **bhergh**, which also gives us *burglar*, the town thief, who carries away the spoils of his work.

Bhleu, to blow

This word, perhaps more than any other, supplies an insight into the Stone Age mind. **Bhleu** is the way that the earth breathes and life *flows*. A man building a fire *blows* on the burning twigs to make the flames grow; the wind blows across the steppes and the grass grows. That's why *blow* can also mean to *blossom* – after a bud has opened out, it is *full-blown*. When a *flower* opens and *blooms*, when *bulbs* give out shoots, when the river *overflows* and silt enriches the land, when the crops *flourish*, when *blossoms* bring fruit – all of that is natural as breathing.

A strong gust of wind is a *blast*; a feeble shout is a *bleat*. A machine to do the *blowing* for you is a *bellows*, though the earliest ones were simply *blowpipes*: paintings found in Egyptian tombs from the second century BC show a man huffing and puffing at one end of the tube into a furnace at the other.

Blow air into liquid and it will *bubble* and *blister*. Heat the liquid in a *bowl* and it will *boil*. A bowl of hot water is marvellous for chilblains, by the way – in Anglo-Saxon, a *blegn* was a *boil* but it has shrunk now and the *OED* defines a *blain* as a pustule. They are all derived from **bhleu**, as is *belly* – when a woman is pregnant, her belly swells.

Inflate a skin and you get a *ball*, a *balloon* or a *bladder* on a stick – literally, a windbag or, in Latin, *follis*. The *ebullient* jester with his cheeks puffed out is the original *fool*, and his capers are sheer *folly*. Sheets of paper watermarked with a jester's cap are called *foolscap*. The cap has *bells* on it, though they are just the jingly kind … real bells make a loud noise. They *bellow*.

In Latin, a round seal is a *bulla*, which is why papal edicts, sealed with an impression of the Pope's ring, are called *bulls*. Minor edicts are *bulletins*. Precious metal stamped with a seal, such as ingots of gold, is *bullion*. In Low Latin, any form of writing was a *billa*, the diminutive of *bulla*. That's why you have so many *bills*. An even smaller scrap of writing was a *billet* – the *billet-doux*, for example (love letters), or the chit that tells an occupied village that troops are being *billeted* on them. The soldiers will have guns and *bullets*, which were originally roundshot, or little balls.

Latin softened the 'bh' to 'f': the verb *fluere* means to flow. It gives us *fluent*, *fluid* and *flush*, as well as *fluctuate*, which means *flowing* back and forth – that is, in *flux*. There's *confluence*, which means flowing together, *mellifluous*, which means flowing sweetly, and *superfluous*, which originally meant flowing over but has now come to mean wasteful and unnecessary. To have *influence* is to flow through the corridors of power. Then there's *affluent*, which is overflowing with money, or at least with a swimming pool of cash to *float* in – how the rich are *blessed*.

Bless, according to Walter Skeat, also derives from **bhleu**. The early sense of a *blessing*, he conjectures, was 'to consecrate by *blood*', which involved either an animal sacrifice to the gods or a *blob* of blood on the face. The link is that blood is also a **bhleu** word, because it flows and gives life.

Blow air from one end and you can coax a tune from a *flute* or a *flageolet*. Blow from the other, especially if you're *bloated*, and you're suffering from *flatulence*. If the gods breathe softly upon an artist, she will be inspired or experience visions, an experience called *afflatus* – though *afflatus* also denotes the hissing of snakes. Singer-songwriter Joni Mitchell recorded a beautiful album called *The Hissing of Summer Lawns*, a rare example of double afflatus.

There's *inflate*, *deflate*, *conflate* and *reflate*, as well as *exsufflate*, which means to blow away. A dessert that rises like a puff of air is a *soufflé*; a whiff of unpleasant air is *effluvium*. Bad air was believed to carry *influenza*.

Remember that to blow can mean to open out like a flower, and that 'bl' was softened to 'fl'? Wheat, the crop that changed nomads to farmers, produces *flour* – it is the *flower* of cornmeal. *Flora* was the Roman goddess of *flowers*. These days we buy them from rather *florid* shopkeepers called *florists*. A *foil* is a different kind of *foliage*, a thin sheet of metal, from the Latin *folium* or leaf. Each page of a book is a leaf, which is why a volume is called a *folio* and a collection of sheets is a *portfolio*. In architecture, the clover-shaped *trefoil* literally means three-leaved.

Even a simple word like flower can take on unimagined new resonances. As this story shows ...

When the comedy writers Marty Feldman and Barry Took, creators of the anarchic radio sketch show *Round the Horne*, were first trying to sell their idea to the BBC in the mid-1960s, they were summoned to a meeting with the Head of Light Programmes – the forerunner of Radio 2. He was a stuffy and affected man, who always wore a carnation in his buttonhole. Things got heated, the writers got overexcited and Marty plucked the flower out and threw it away. After they staggered out, doubled over with giggles, a friend asked how the meeting went. Barry stopped laughing long enough to say, 'We've just *deflowered* the Head of Light Programmes.'

Bhrag, to break

Like ding, crunch or splash in English, **bhrag** is onomatopoeic. It's the sound of something *breaking*. On the Stone Age steppes, things didn't get a chance to decay quietly. They cracked, shattered and tumbled down. **Bhrag**: it's halfway between a snap and a crash.

A hole in a wall is a *breach*. That can be shored up with *bricks*, which weren't always oblongs of baked clay: the first dry stone walls were built like jigsaws from *broken* bits and pieces of rock, so bricks are rough slabs or blocks that fit into a pattern.

The Gaelic word for an explosion is *bragh*. In Breton, *braga* means to strut about. Both words carry the suggestion that boasting is noisy and destructive – no one likes a *braggart*. A man makes an ass of himself when he *brags*: he sounds like a donkey *braying*.

That sense of a noise that heralds disaster has ribald overtones, which is why we still *break* wind. Badgers smell something horrible, so they are nicknamed *brock*. **Bhrag** gives us *bruise*, meaning to crush a leaf and emit its scent. One meaning of *bray* is to beat flat or to pound in a mortar. In the seventeenth century, a *brayer* was a wooden pestle used to rub down the ink on a printed sheet.

A wine *broker* was originally a *broacher*, because he had to *broach* or pierce the casks, opening them just enough to get the wine flowing. That's why a *broach* or *brooch* is an ornament with a long pin on the back, and we *broach* a subject by introducing it pointedly into the conversation. These days, *broking* means dealing, the way a *stockbroker* buys and sells stocks. A *brochure* was originally a pamphlet stitched together with a long needle; *brocade* is fabric with a raised pattern, often in gold, that is pricked in with needles; *broccoli* is a floret on a needle-like stem – it's an Italian word, the diminutive of *brocco*, which means a stalk.

Latin softens the 'bh' – to break is *frangere*. *Frangible* is breakable, and a *fraction* is a part broken off from a whole number. A broken bone is a *fracture*; a broken piece is a *fragment*; anything easily broken is *fragile* or *frail*. Long folk songs are broken up by words repeated over and over: 'Parsley, sage, rosemary and thyme / Hey, ho, the wind and the rain' – that's the *refrain*.

When people are *fractious*, a fight is liable to break out. Far better to settle things with a vote: the earliest ballots were held with a fragment of stone to represent each vote. That's why votes are 'cast' – the stone was literally thrown into one pile or another. The broken stones give us the word *suffrage*. When the *suffragettes* were chucking rocks through windows, they didn't realise they were doing just what their name implied. They were also being *irrefragable* ... obstinate and inflexible, and hard to break.

The *osprey*, a hawk that can pluck a fish out of the water and devour it, was originally known as an *ossifrage* – literally, a bone-breaker. The Romans brought the word *ossifragus* to Britain: it's the Latin name for the bearded vulture or lammergeier, a big-beaked bird of prey without a bald head from the mountainous regions of Africa, Asia and Europe. Ossifrages earned their name by smashing open tortoises: picking them up in their claws and dropping them onto rocks from a height. Ospreys don't eat tortoises, but they do clutch and carry fish in their talons; perhaps this behaviour prompted the legionaries to call them *ossifraga*. Or perhaps the soldiers just thought *ossifragus* meant hawk: not all legionaries were linguists.

A good many of the troops probably didn't want to be watching the wildlife anyway. They would rather be with a broken woman, which is the literal translation of the medieval English *brethal* ... at a house of ill repute, or *brothel*.

Bhur, to brew

Coffee aficionados complain that the global chains over-roast their beans: the coffee is *burned* to intensify the flavour so that it cuts through the litres of frothy milk and glutinous syrups that are ladled into the bucket-sized mugs. *Burning* and *brewing* aren't the same thing, even though they stem from the same root.

Burn and brew, *bur-* words and *br-* words, can both be traced to **bhur**. The colour of anything burned is *brun* with a long 'u' (in Old Saxon and Old High German), *brunn* with a short 'u' (in Old Norse), *bruin* in Dutch and *brown* in English.

It's not only coffee that tastes stronger for being charred – *burned wine*, or *gebrandet wjin* in Dutch, became *brandywine* or *brandy* in English.

Coffee wasn't drunk on the steppes*, but a hot brew was popular – it probably had the onomatopoeic name **sup** (the original cup-a-soup). We still make it today, all the leftover scraps of meat and vegetables soaked in a pan of water and left to simmer: *broth*. In Tudor times, broth or *browet* had to be made from the juices of boiled meat, thickened by flour.

Broth must *broil*, not burn. If the heat is too high, the stew will bubble and steam like *fury* (with the 'bh' softened to an 'f'). Fury came to mean boiling rage (the Latin for 'to boil' was *fervare*). In Roman mythology, the *Furiae* were three sisters who dwelled in hell and brought divine retribution to sinners on Earth, while the Tricoteuses, the women who sat knitting in the bloodthirsty committees of the French Revolution, were sometimes called the *Furies of the Guillotine*. The Reverend E. Cobham *Brewer* seems to have had a lifelong horror of the

---

* Coffee was allegedly discovered by a holy man called Omar, living in a cave in Yemen during the thirteenth century. Dying of hunger, he tried to eat some brown berries, which were too tough to chew; cooking them didn't improve the meal, but he was able to boil the baked beans to make a drink that was invigorating and reviving. Omar took his discovery to the nearest settlement, a place called Mocha, where the inhabitants were so delighted that they made Omar a saint and gave their town's name to the drink. Centuries later, the Dutch named it *koffie*, from the Arabic *qahwa*, short for *qahhwat al-bun*, meaning bean wine – not burned wine.

French – he was born in 1810, during the Napoleonic Wars. Aged eighty-five, in the 1895 edition of *Brewer's Dictionary of Phrase and Fable*, he was still in a *fervent ferment* about the Furies of the Guillotine: 'Never in any age or any country did women so disgrace their sex,' he complained.

In medieval English, a *brander* or *brandiron* was a trivet, a metal stand for a pot or kettle. Food could be grilled if two branders were laid at right angles, one on the other, to form a grid: when builders placed battens of wood across joists to make a wall or floor, they called it *brandering*.

The old name for sulphur, so highly flammable that it was thought to be the material for Hell's bricks, was *brimstone* (burning stone). Writers of swords-and-sorcery fantasies still refer to their warriors' flashing blades as *brands*, because their steel is forged in flame (ideally, while the young hero watches from the shadows as his taciturn and doomed father hammers the molten metal).

Since a piece of iron taken red hot from the furnace was a brand, it followed that any metal still glowing from the forge was *brand new*. Owners' marks could be *branded* on an animal's hide with the hot metal; when an animal's hide was mottled, as if naturally branded, it was *brindled*.

The word *brand* was first used to mean a trademark, label or logo in 1827, and within thirty years that covered, by extension, the goods themselves: the product was the brand. Now, the brand is the mere concept of the goods, the idea of where and how they should be sold, and who the perfect customers are: ideally, in the case of global drinks brands, people who like their coffee burned.

D

Dam, to tame

Timber, domestic, damsel, madam

Dha, to suckle

Female, fecund, fennel, daughter

Dhar, to hold

Farm, firmament, infirmary, throne

Dik, to point to

Indicate, digit, judge, teacher

Diw, to be bright as day

Divine, Jupiter, journey, daisies

Do, to give

Donate, dolly, data, treason

Dok, to learn

Doctor, auto-didact, documentary, paradox

Drei, to flow

Dry, dram, drowsy, dreich

Dam, to tame

Studies comparing dog and wolf genes suggest they were first *tamed* around 14,000 years ago, several millennia before nomadic hunters began to settle and farm. *Tame* animals predate houses: Stone Age tribes were probably living in yurts and teepees when they began to herd livestock with dogs.

To make something fit for *domestic* use, it must be tamed – not just made dumb and docile, like cattle, but taught to live in safety and obedience with human masters. The first animal truly tamed by Stone Age man must have been the dog – the archaeological proof is there, with dog skeletons discovered at early settlements and dogs' teeth used for necklaces. The language proves it too: the word for dog, **kuon**, is one of the oldest and most basic in the Indo-European vocabulary.*

Man's first use for dogs was guard duty. Hunter-gatherer tribes were so sparsely spread at first that they rarely waged war on each other; raids were uncommon, and the dogs were not

---

* **Kuon** gives us *canine, kennel* and *cynic*, and it also became (with a sound-shift from 'k' to 'h') *hound*. Because of the wild dogs that infested the islands, sixteenth-century sailors called the Atlantic outcrops west of Africa the *Canary* Islands. They brought back small green birds, like finches, that were naturally dubbed *canaries*. Breeders altered the birds' plumage to a brilliant yellow – that was called *canary* too. In the 1700s, a special punishment was reserved for the lowest criminals at Newgate Prison in London: they were chained up in cages hanging outside the jail, for people to gawp and jeer at. These prisoners were called *canarybirds*. You wouldn't treat a dog that way.

kept primarily as look-outs against human attacks. Instead, they were on the watch for bears, wolves and other large carnivores. The dogs had to be safe around people, even children: they were *domesticated*.

Dogs would later have been used for herding sheep and goats, and also for hunting – but certainly not as household pets. A shepherd on foot would struggle to round up half a dozen animals, but with a dog he could herd forty or fifty, according to anthropologist Professor David Anthony of Hartwick College, New York.

Any animal that can be tamed is *domable*, a sixteenth-century word. Being tame is different from being *timid*, but the root is the same. Our word comes from the Latin *timere*, to fear, which is linked to the Sanskrit word for darkness, *tamas*. We've always been afraid of the dark, it seems, or *timorous* of the *tenebrous*.

To feel safe at night, Stone Age man developed his home sweet home. The first *domiciles* as we know them today were made of wood, or *timber* – the material of home-building. Before that, houses were *domes* of curved wood and canvas. The land that the lord of the tribe controlled was his *dominion* or *domain*; the Latin for a lord is *dominus*, which gives us *dominant* and *domineer*. The lady of the house was the *dame* – or the *madam*, in a certain type of house, where there were *damsels*.

Your brain is housed in the *dome* of your skull, and at the side, behind the eyes, are your *temples*. Ancient astrologers *domified* the sky by dividing it into the twelve houses or *demesnes*. The Spanish Inquisition was having none of that and set the *Dominican* Order upon them. This order of monks was founded by St *Dominic*, but their enemies called them the Hounds of God – the *Domini Canes*. These religious attack dogs were not domesticated in the slightest.

Dha, to suckle

Some people will do anything to be famous. There's even a word for it: herostratic – from the arsonist Herostratus, who burned down one of the Seven Wonders of the World, just for the notoriety. The Temple of Artemis at *Ephesus*, built with the fabulous wealth of King Croesus, was destroyed in July 356 BC, supposedly on the night that Alexander the Great was born (the historian Plutarch said that the goddess Artemis herself must have been 1,000 miles away in Thrace, presiding over the princeling's birth; if she had been at Ephesus, she would surely have slain the firestarter with a thunderbolt, and 'herostratic' would mean 'charred to a blackened stump').

Artemis of Ephesus was a remarkable deity, with more cleavage than a bumper episode of *Baywatch*. Artemis had more than forty breasts, hanging like strings of coconuts from her shoulders to her hips. The patron saint of translators, archivists and librarians, St Jerome, gave her the nickname 'multimammia': manyboobs.

Appropriately, the Indo-European word that denoted nipples, sucking and suckling was **dha**, a 'd' sound so soft that it was almost a 'th' or a 'ph'. The Greek word for a nipple was *thele*, and Artemis had dozens of them; that's why the syllable *phe* is at the centre of the word *Ephesus*.

Almost no English words derive from *thele*, except *thelytokous*, which means 'producing only *female* offspring' (the opposite is 'arrenotokous'). But the **dha** sound, softened even further, found its way into Latin as *fe*. *Femina* was a woman, *femella* was an adolescent girl or 'the little woman' … and that gives us *female, feminine, feminist* and *effeminate*. A *femalist* is a man

48

devoted to the fairer sex. *Feminality* used to mean the quality of being a woman, or female nature itself; by Queen Victoria's time, though, it meant a mere female trait, or even just a knick-knack that might please a woman.

In medieval times, *feminie* was all womankind. In law, a *feme sole* is an unmarried woman, and strictly speaking, to kill a woman is not homicide but *femicide*. Abortion is *feticide:* before a child can suckle, it is a *foetus*. *Fawn*, a young deer, is a contraction of the Latin *fetonus*, meaning offspring. A woman exhausted by child-bearing is *ex-foetus*, which gives us *effete* – but if she has had many children, she was at least *fecund*. In Latin, a son was *filius* or, more literally, a sucker: remember that, next time you are invited to sign up for an *affiliate* programme. A different sort of sucker gives rise to *fellatio*.

And a different sort of *fe*-word is the root of fellow. To the Celts and Norsemen, a fee was a sum paid usually in cattle: cows were *feoh*, *fief*, *fehu*, *vihe* or *vieh* in various languages (*fehu* is the basis of feudal). It is possible that these words are connected to the concept of suckling and nipples – one reason for keeping cattle was dairy farming, obviously. At any rate, long before coins existed there were business deals, and a *feolaga* (in Old English) or *felagha* (in Middle English) was a partner; that is, a fellow.

In ancient times, a large family was a symbol of prosperity, good fortune and happiness – all embodied in the Latin word *felix*. *Felicity* is the state of being intensely, blissfully happy; to *felicify* or *felicitate* someone is to render them joyous, *felicitations* are congratulations and a *felicitous* event is one that, by happy coincidence, works out perfectly for all. The Romans called cats *felidae* – hence *feline* – not because they were lucky animals, but because they multiplied so fast: *felis* meant fruitful. We'd say that they bred like rabbits, but the Romans didn't have nearly such a problem with urban rabbits.

Add a consonant to **dhe** and you get **dhugh**, meaning to yield milk. That gives us the coarse medieval word for breasts, *dugs*, but it also gives us *daughter*. In Sanskrit, *duhitri* means 'the girl who milks the cows'. One more bovine connection: the Roman word for cattle fodder is *fenum*. That gives us *fennel*, the name of a herb that smells like new-mown hay.

Dhar, to hold

The first *farmers* did not have *farms*. Nomads shepherded their flocks and herds from one pasture to another, at first on foot and later on horseback. The earliest fragments of riding harnesses have been found by archaeologists in central Europe, dating back more than 4,000 years, and there is evidence that horses and cattle were used to pull carts at least 500 years earlier.

All that was mobile farming, meat on the move. The first plough, called an **ar**, began to be used across eastern Europe around 2,000 BC, and that signalled a different, fixed kind of farming. Cattle can be moved around; crops can't.

Ar seems to be the root of the word **dhar**, which means to hold *firm* without moving. **Ar** is also the stem of the discredited word Aryan, originally a term for the first Indo-European speakers who spread to India, Iran and the West, but taken and corrupted to signify a master race by the Nazis. Arable and agriculture come from **ar**, but **dhar** is much more interesting – it conveys the idea that all power begins with land. A real king cannot be nomadic: he needs a power base.

In Sanskrit, *dharma* was a kind of hunger strike, an extreme method of debt collecting: you sat outside the door of someone who had wronged you, and you held fast, refusing to move or eat until reparation was made. The hunger strike is still an effective protest: Mahatma Gandhi and his followers used it to overthrow British rule in India in the twentieth century. But **dhar** was familiar in a different sense to the empire administrators who oversaw the government and the army in India: titles for native-born officials ended in the suffix -*dar*. A sergeant-major, for instance, was the *jhavildar*, a servant was a *chobdar* and the district governor was the *subahdar*. (The chief of police had the tautologous title of *dharnadar*, the hold-holder).

Dharma in Sanskrit came to mean justice, and *dharmasastra* was the book of laws. In Persia, the meaning was similar – the name *Darayavahush* translates as holding to good, though Western historians shortened it to *Darius*. The emperor Darius the Great seized power in 522 BC after he and six fellow nobles assassinated the king, a thug called Smerdis who had usurped the kingdom himself by force. Rather than provoke a civil war, the seven rebels struck a gentleman's agreement: they would go riding the next day, and the new king would be the rider whose horse neighed first. Darius had a cunning groom, Oebares, who rubbed his hands with the scent of a mare, so that when he led the horse to his master it was whinnying with excitement. Darius wasn't the sort of man to leave anything to chance – after war broke out with the Greeks, he had a servant come to his tent every night as he was going to bed, to repeat the same *affirmation*: 'Remember, O King, to punish the Athenians!'

Feuding, pacts, trickery and betrayal … this is the original *Game of Thrones*, and the Greek word *thronos* means seat of the power-holder. The equivalent in Latin is *firmus*; the verb *firmare* means to make something solid. That gives us *confirm* and *affirm*, and in medieval French, *fermer* was to sign a contract. A signature in Old Spanish was *firmar*, which is why a business is a *firm*. The Queen of England likes to refer to the British Royal Family as *The Firm*.

The opposite of firm is *infirm*, and because in late Latin *infirmans* was an invalid, the *infirmary* is a hospital. 'St James Infirmary' is the oldest jazz and blues standard, a song warning about the perils of consorting with prostitutes. Louis Armstrong, who was brought up in a New Orleans brothel, recorded the most famous version, in 1928. Country music fans know the song better as 'The Streets of Laredo', but it dates back to eighteenth-century English folk music and a song called 'The Unfortunate Rake'. The original lyric ran, 'What should I spy but one of my comrades / All wrapped up in a flannel though warm was the day'; in the Wild West, that became, 'I spied a cowpuncher, all wrapped in white linen / Wrapped up in white linen and cold as the clay.' His *infirmity*, of course, is syphilis.

In church Latin, *firmamentum* was the authority of heaven, and so a byword for the sky. That's why we talk of all the stars in the *firmament*.

In early English, *ferme* became a lease or rent agreement, and so a *fermour* was a tenant, renting land from the feudal lord to grow crops. Finally, the farmer had a farm.

Dik, to point to

When the Colombian novelist Gabriel García Márquez created the fictional village of Macomba in his masterpiece *One Hundred Years of Solitude*, he imagined it at first as a collection of mud huts on a riverbank: 'The world was so recent that many things lacked names, and in order to indicate them it was necessary to point.'

For the original speakers of Indo-European, that is how their universe was. They pointed, and made up names, and in many cases those names have stuck for 8,000 years. But even the act of pointing had to have a word: **dik**. In our civilised era, it's rude to point, so we say *indicate*.

We point with our fingers but we also count with them – that's why *digit* has a double meaning. Toes are digits too: that linguistic quirk carries a strong suggestion that our ancestors used to count on their feet as well as their hands. The paradox is that *digital* machines don't count in tens but in twos, using the binary system of 1s and 0s.

The Gothic word for a foxglove was *fingerhut*, meaning a hat for your finger. The Romans called it *digitalis*, which is the name that the eighteenth-century physician William Withering gave to the heart medicine he extracted from foxgloves after noticing that herbal cures containing the plant helped patients who suffered from dropsy. People tend not to get dropsy nowadays, but that isn't due solely to the effectiveness of *digitalis*: it's also because doctors now call it oedema, or swelling of the extremities caused by congestive heart disease.

Digitation is pointing things out, but when a conjuror misdirects his audience, then – hey presto! You get *prestidigitation*. *Preste* is French for nimble.

A *dictum* is a saying, an opinion set down as an aphorism, and a *dictery* is a witticism. The *dictionary* of Dr Johnson was full of both. Anything beyond the description of words is *indicible*. And the one thing a dictionary doesn't need is an *index*. (How is index a **dik** word? Well, it's Latin, and the plural is *indices*.)

The composer Frederick Delius *dictated* his compositions after he went blind from the effects of syphilis. Delius was a ferociously short-tempered man, and behaved like a *dictator* to his young assistant, Eric Fenby, who ended up nursing the old man through his final illness – an awkward *predicament*. Fenby's faint consolation, apart from having a hand in several great pieces of music (one, *Fantastic Dance*, is *dedicated* to him), was that he had to cope with only one tyrant: it is rare to find a gathering of dictators, but when it does happen, there's a word for it – a *dictature*.

To point something out before it happens is to *predict* it, to countersay something is to *contradict* it and to lay charges against a suspect is to *indict* him – it's pronounced 'indite' because the Middle English word was *enditen*, to write down.

After that comes either *vindication* or a *verdict*. The evidence will be examined by a member of the *judiciary*, who will *adjudicate* or *judge* the case without *prejudice*.

A blessing is a *benediction*; a curse is a *malediction*; a mumble is bad *diction*. That's enough to make anyone *vindictive*, from the Latin *vindicta* ... which in Italian became *vendetta*. The Latin *vindicare* was pronounced *venchier* in Old French – a useful word in the Middle Ages and one that the English adopted eagerly. We used it with a *vengeance* in *vengeful*, *avenge* and *revenge*.

Another Latin word, *predicare*, meant to proclaim or declare, to issue an *edict*. It became *prescher* in Old French, which is where our *preacher* comes from. It is likely that *teacher* is derived in a similar way: the Latin *dicere* is to say, which became *zeikhan* in Old High German and *teikn* in Old Norse. By the time it reached Middle English, the dialect of the Chaucer era, it was pronounced *techen*.

If you want to say something in song, that's a *ditty*. If you want to say it again, that's *ditto*. We could go on forever with this, because it's *addictive*.

Diw, to be bright as day

The earliest prehistoric civilisations had many gods, but all of them worshipped the sun. The Ancient Egyptian sun god was Ra, the Japanese sun goddess was Amaterasu, the Celtic sun god was Lugh, the Aztec sun god was Tonatiuh. To the Ancient Greeks he was Helios; to the Romans Apollo. None of them give us the word 'sun' – that comes from the Norse goddess of the sun, whose name was Sunna.

We can't be sure of the Indo-European word for sun, but we

know the sound that signified a bright, clear, sunny sky – and that word has given us many of our own words for god. *Divine*, *deity*, *dieu*: they all stem from **diw**.

To the Stone Age riders of the steppes, it was obvious where the gods lived. They were in the sky. There were no mountains like Olympus or Fuji to be heavenly thrones, no glaciers to be ice palaces like Valhalla – just the high air above the land. It was the beginning of the notion that heaven is beyond the sky.

In Sanskrit, the god of the sky is *Dyaus*; in Greek he is *Zeus*. To the Romans, he was the father (*pitar*) in the sky: *Diw-Pitar*, or *Jupiter*, whose wife was *Juno*. *Julius* stems from **diw** as well: the name was apt for Julius Caesar, who was declared a god after his assassination. To make a man into a god is *deification*; to kill a god is *deicide*. A woman who gives birth to a god is *deiparous*, and *Deipara* is one of the titles of the Virgin Mary. Anyone who believes in God or the gods, but rejects organised religion, is a *deist*. The two Latin words for a god were *deus* and *divus*; apart from the obvious words, they give us *deodand* and the *divining rod*.

A deodand is a hybrid of a forfeit and a sacrifice: in English law, any possession or object that caused a death could not remain in the family but had to be handed over to God. That meant a bull that gored a man, or a cauldron that fatally scalded a child, had to be given up to the church or the crown. Whatever value it fetched would be donated to a pious cause. The law wasn't abolished until 1846. A *deodate*, conversely, means a gift from God.

A divining rod is a dowser's tool, able in the right hands to locate underground streams or foretell the future … with heavenly assistance.

The Old English name for the god of war was *Tiu*, which gives us *Tuesday*. The Portuguese word for god is *deos*, which is why the incense burned by priests in the East Indies is called *joss sticks*. The Greek god of fertility and wine, *Dionysius*, also takes his name from **diw**: in medieval times, boozers would carry a semi-precious stone, red with black streaks, to prevent drunken blackouts and ease hangovers. It was called *dionise*.

Because the sun doesn't shine at night, a bright sky became synonymous with the *day*, or in Latin *dies*. The Latin word for bad is *mal*, so a bad day is *dies mal* – *dismal*. Animals that are active during the day are *diurnal*; sleeping all day long is *diurnation*. Anything that goes on for many days is *diuturnal*, and lasts a *diuturnity*.

Someone who writes for a *daily* publication is a *diurnalist*, or *journalist*. Writing a daily column is *journalism*, but making daily entries in a *diary* is *journalising*. That's handy if you're travelling, because the distance you can travel in one day is a *journey*.

Journey-work is paid by the day, and often refers to work done badly. A *journeyman* originally meant a qualified artisan or tradesman who had served his apprenticeship, but by Shakespeare's time it meant a shoddy workman, or simply a hired drudge who works from sun-up to sundown.

When the sun comes up, the *daisies* open – so called because they are the *day's eyes*.

Do, to give

Stone Age societies didn't have unemployment benefits, but they have *donated* a useful word for welfare to us: the *dole*. After 8,000 years, we're still relying on Neolithic hand-outs.

'If you want to know what God thinks of money, just look at the people he gave it to,' commented the priceless *Dorothy* Parker, the New York poet and wit. Her jibe is all the sharper when you realise that 'Dorothy' means 'gift of God' – from the Greek words *doron* and *theos*.

The diminutive of Dorothy is *Dolly*: it dates back to the

mid-sixteenth century, when it was common to cut short any name with an 'r' in it by changing the sound to an 'l' – Sarah became Sal, Mary became Moll and Henry became Hal. (These days we do the same with a 'z' – so Caroline is Caz, Jerry is Jez and Terry is Tez.)

Within a century, a dolly was a female favourite or pet, and so a child's toy – a *doll*. Animals and toys both tend to get prettified by their doting owners, hence the Victorian expression 'all *dolled up* like a barber's cat'. *Dollymops* were overdressed servant girls, and *dolly worship* was sarcastic Methodist slang for Roman Catholicism.

In Brooklyn during the Prohibition era, hoodlums had their Tommy guns but rich gamblers and swindlers got the best-looking women … that's why the 1950s musical by Frank Loesser, based on the streetwise short stories of Damon Runyon, is called *Guys and Dolls* (not 'Gangsters and Molls'). But in the 1850s, crooks needed dollies for another reason: illegal pawnshops where stolen goods could be fenced were known as *dollyshops*, because of the black doll hanging over the door as a sign to the underworld that shady business could be conducted within.

Australian and South African men used to call every woman 'doll', the way Cockney lads still call the girls 'dahlin''. In the 1960s, *dollybirds* were ordinary young women who looked like film stars or models when they went shopping in Carnaby Street. But in Polari, the gay slang of the era, dolly meant attractive for quite another reason: many Polari words came from Italian, and dolly was a corruption of *dolce* (sweet, good).

Theodore, a back-to-front version of Dorothy, also means gift of God in Greek. As far back as the Trojan War, around 3,300 years ago, the Ancient Greeks had some funny ideas about religion and presents. One Trojan priest named Laocoön knew this: in Virgil's epic poem *The Aeniad*, as he stares suspiciously at a large and shifty-looking wooden horse that has been left outside the gates of Troy, he warns his neighbours not to wheel it into the city. 'Timeo danaos et *dona* ferentes,' he says – 'I fear the Greeks, even when they are bearing gifts.' He's right, of course: the horse is full of Greek soldiers.

To shut Laocoön up, the goddess of wisdom, Minerva, sent a sea serpent to strangle him. He was about to give the game away – in Latin, *tradere*, which is the root of *traitor*, *treason* and *betrayal*.

Do is the core of several English words that imply a gift or bequest: *dowry*, *donor* and *endow*, for example. A *dose* of medicine is the right amount to give; get it wrong and you'll need an *antidote*. If a doctor accidentally kills his patient with an *overdose*, the victim won't give him a *pardon* for it, even if the courts *condone* it.

And speaking of the courts … remember those Brooklyn hustlers? They were probably looking for a game of *dice*. The word was originally nothing to do with gambling, but instead was printers' jargon: a *die* is a plate with markings that, when inked and pressed onto paper, gives an impression, for the dots on the dice (or *dies*) are indented. The link seems spurious, but a printer's die derives from the Latin *dare*, which means 'to give'.

If that sounds a stretch, consider this: the past participle of *dare* is *datum*, meaning a gift or present. In English, datum is a single proffered piece of information – plural, *data*. *Datum* also becomes *date*, meaning any given day in the calendar. So nerds take heart – you might find it difficult to get a date, but you'll always have plenty of data, and etymologically it's almost the same thing.

Dok, to learn

Do is to give, **dik** is to point out and **dok** is to learn. One of the reasons that Indo-European took hold across half the world was that its words built on each other, like Lego: **dok** is what happens when **do** and **dik** are combined. Through the gift of knowledge, we learn – **dik, do, dok**.

The Greek *doxa* means opinion, and when opinions are asserted loudly they become *dogma*. *Dogmatists* are not animal lovers, just people who love the sound of their own voices, though fans of Asterix and Obelix will remember their yappy little pooch was called *Dogmatix*.

Any sort of *-dox* is a dogma. If it's the generally accepted principle of all right-thinking people, it is *orthodox*; if it is against established teachings, it is *heterodox*; if it contradicts itself, it is a *paradox*. *Doxology* ought to be the study of dogma, but for some reason it is a short prayer giving thanks to God. *Doxie*, the Shakespearean slang for a bad girl, has no theological implications; the word came to Britain from Holland, where *doche* is a doll.

In Latin, *docere* is to teach, which is why a *doctor* was originally any learned man, and why post-graduate students study for their *doctorates*. A *didact* is a teacher, and an *auto-didact* is a self-taught man. A Roman pupil who proved willing to be taught was *docilis*, though schoolchildren don't tend to be *docile* these days. *Docere* in Latin was pronounced 'dokere' with a hard 'c' … that snippet of information is *docent*, or educational.

Docility is a short remove from *docity*, a seventeenth-century dialect word meaning gumption, that combination of common sense and stickability which cannot be taught.

Dockets are labels or tickets, and *documents* are papers, but *documentaries* are television programmes. There are other contradictions: a *doctrine* is a belief or theory that is taught as a truth that should not be questioned, but a *doctrinarian* is a pedant who sticks to the letter of the law without regard for other factors. Japanese commando Lieutenant Hiroo Onodo spent twenty-nine years hiding in the jungles of Lubang, a sparsely inhabited island in the western Philippines, refusing to accept that the Second World War was over. He had been *indoctrinated*.

Disciple might belong under **dik** or **dok** – at any rate, it comes from the Latin *discere*, to learn. A *discipulus* underwent *disciplina*, or military training, and if he didn't toe the line he would face harsh *discipline* and even *disciplinary* charges.

After **do, dik** and **dok,** the next connection is **duk,** which means to lead. That gives us *duct,* and probably *dock.* It also forms the root of *education, aqueduct, conductor, abduction* and *deduction* – all things that lead to places in different ways. There is something philosophically satisfying in the thought that a *duke* and a *docker* spring from the same source.

And then there is **dek,** which doesn't quite have an English synonym: it implies the right education, being well brought up and properly behaved. Perhaps **dek** is to be, as Mrs Thatcher would say, 'one of us'. That involves common *decency,* which is not quite the same as *decorum* – orderly, polite, seemly behaviour.

Decorum comes from the Latin *decor,* an ornament or thing of beauty, and hence a *decoration.* The old and lovely English word *decore* means grace, honour, glory and beauty. Anything *indecorous* is in bad taste.

In Old French, a small but well-formed object was *deintie,* which we spell *dainty.*

The Roman concept of pride and self-worth is summed up in *dignus,* which gives us *dignity, dignified, dignataries* and downright *indignation. Dignus* can also mean fitting and appropriate, which is why a well-deserved punishment is *condign. Dignus* became *deign* in medieval English – the word is usually supercilious, implying that although something is below us, we will condescend to do it. In the Middle Ages, *deignous* meant *disdainful.*

What some people call civic pride, others regard as snobbishness. That's *doxastic* – it depends on your opinion.

Drei, to flow

This is a book about the roots of language, and every root has grown from a seed. In this case, the seed of **drei** is **rei**: both sounds refer to flowing water, but **rei** is much more vigorous.

Rei is *rain* and *river*, and also *rival* – an adversary who lives on the opposite *riverbank*. **Rei** gives us *arrive* (to come by water) and *derive* (to drain off, from the Latin words 'de', meaning 'from', and *riuus*, a stream). **Rei** becomes a *rift*, a cleft in the land (perhaps a chasm caused by a river gorge); a *reef*, which is a *ridge* of rock that seems to cut the sea in two; and *strife*, a feud that divides two people. A rift can also be river rapids, or a cataract or the waves beating on a shore, though those senses have almost died out. In medieval English, a 'rift' was a belch: it still survives in Scots dialect, but this version of the word probably evolved from a different stem, **reug** (the basis of *eructation* and *reek*).

The most select holiday resorts are on the French *Riviera*, and the longest river in Western Europe is the *Rhine*. Before Caesar crossed the Rhine, the Celts in Germany worshipped the river god and offered their newborn children to the waters. If the child swam, he was blessed, but if he sank, he was probably cursed or defective or illegitimate, and in any case not worth the trouble of keeping. Despite what New Age self-help manuals might suggest today, the Celts weren't a nurturing lot – Vandals and Visigoths did not often make caring parents.

The Latin for 'to wash' was *rigare*, from which English gets *irrigate*. **Rei** gives us *rivulet*, and also *riven*, cut in two by the watercourse. To *rive* is to *rip* or tear apart; in German, *riefe* is a furrow, and in Swedish, *räffla* is a groove or channel. That's why a musket with a spiralling groove cut into its barrel, which set the lead shot spinning and made the gun more accurate, became known as a *rifle*. Furrows in water are *ripples*, and in cloth they are *riffles*.

Add a 'd' to **rei** and the word becomes much slower – it is *drip, dribble, driblet, dribs and drabs, drivel, drizzle, droop, dreary* and *drowsy*. All of them carry the sense of a *drop* of water, about to fall. Pour a splash of whisky into a tumbler, and it's a *dram*; take a gulp and it's a *drink* or a *draft*; empty the glass and you *drain* it to the *dregs*. When all the liquid is gone, it's *dry*.

In the eighteenth century, to *drib* was to push or lead an animal little by little, with small steps. That menial skill is worth millions now: the word survives in Premier League football, where the most skilful players are the *dribblers* who can run with the ball at their feet. When coins were made of silver or gold, *dribbing* was a sharp practice, a slang word for defalcation, which meant clipping or trimming the disc to pare away a little precious metal. And in Elizabethan England, to *drib* an arrow was to fire it short of the mark so that it plopped to earth like a *raindrop*.

A *dripstone* is a wedge built over a door or window, like the brim of a cap, to stop the rain from *trickling* down and seeping in. Seep is an abberation: it comes from **sap** ... but otherwise, just about every word you can think of that suggests dampness flows from **rei** or **drei** – in Scots dialect, for example, there's *dreich*, which means overcast, cold, misty and miserable; there's also *dree* or *dreigh*, which refers to anything tedious and uncomfortable that goes on and on. The English equivalent is *drab*.

Add a 'v' sound to **drei**, and you get the idea of something solid that flows slowly like water – a cattle *drive*, for instance, or snow, which *drifts*. Under medieval law, *drof-land* was a yearly payment made by farmers to the landowner for the right of driving their cattle across his land on their way to market or fresh pastures.

E

Em, to buy

Emporium, example, premium, redemption

Es, to exist

Essence, present, pride, soothsayer

Em, to buy

The first trade or bartering began between farmers 10,000 years ago or more, and the currency was corn. Long before the invention of coins, let alone banknotes, the value of wheat crops was well understood, even down to the worth of single seeds – that's the reason that gold, in the smallest transactions, is still traded in grains.

The urge to buy and the satisfaction we get from an armful of designer shopping bags goes back thousands of years too. The Romans had a word for it: *emacitus*, the desire to buy things. The English version, *emacity*, became obsolete in the twentieth century, replaced by less elegant terms such as retail therapy and shopaholics.

The Romans also had a warning, *Caveat emptor*, which means 'Buyer beware!' Getting your money back was no easy matter on the Via Appia: the market traders didn't offer a thirty-day cooling-off period. Goods could not be *redeemed*, or bought back. Anything *irredeemable* cannot be converted into cash – your purchase is beyond *redemption*. Redemption gained a spiritual sense in the Christian world, with the idea that rescued souls had been bought back from the devil. In Middle English it was *redempcioun*, and in Old French *raenson*, which became *ransom* in medieval England: still buying back a soul, but in a rather different way. When Richard the Lionheart, the English king, was captured and held prisoner by the Holy Roman Emperor in 1193, the ransom demand was 65,000 pounds of silver – more than double the amount that the Treasury in London levied in taxes every year. While Richard's mother, Eleanor of Aquitaine, was politicking like mad to raise the money, his brother Prince John (who was running the country while Richard had been off fighting the Crusades) raised about half that sum and offered it as a bribe to the emperor, to keep the king in a dungeon. When he was finally freed, Richard, who had more courage than brains, forgave his malevolent younger brother and even named him as his heir.

A *praemium* was the booty claimed by the commander of a conquering army, the cream of the spoils. By the era of the English Civil War, the word had been co-opted by the earliest insurance salesmen, and now a *premium* is the annual cost of your car insurance. It can still mean the first bonus to be paid out, which is why everyone has a few *premium bonds*.

To buy up every last item in stock was *perimere*, literally to buy right through, and that gives us *peremptory* – decisive, final, beyond all question and even dictatorial.

When a product was readily available, it was *pro-emptus*, which meant that you could get it *promptly*. On occasions, merchants had more stock than they could display, so the bulk of it was kept in a warehouse or *promptuarium*. A well-stocked mind is a treasure house, and if you have trouble remembering facts, you need an almanac or ready reference book, sometimes called a *promptuary*. That's why an actor who forgets his lines can rely on a helpful whisper from the *prompter*. And if that actor abandons the script and starts making up dialogue, he is speaking *impromptu*.

If something was not for sale, it was *ex-emptus* or *exempt*. An outstanding purchase is an *exemplar*, but every sale counts and so everything is a good *example* … until example lost its initial syllable, somewhere in France 1,000 years ago, and became *sample*.

Embezzlement is fraud, usually tampering with documents to steal money. The fraudster Bernie Madoff, a former stockbroker who persuaded investors to give him their life savings and somehow defrauded about $65bn, was sent to prison for 150 years – an *exemplary* sentence, intended to deter copycat criminals.

In Ancient Greece, a commercial traveller with his trunkload of samples was *emporos*: **em** + *poros*, a path. He blazed trading trails such as the Persian Royal Road, which ran from Turkey's Mediterranean coast to modern-day Iran. *Emporium* meant merchandise in Latin; today it's the word for a shop that sells everything. *Emporetic paper* was rough papyrus used for parcelling up purchases, the ancestor of gift wrap and brown paper.

Es, to exist

Everything that *is* must *exist*. 'I think, therefore I am,' said the philosopher Rene Descartes, and so he *was*, but Neolithic man had reached that conclusion millennia before him. That's why **es** had a double meaning – to be, and to be true.

In Latin, to be was *esse*, an *essential* verb. Ancient wisdom held that the universe was composed of four elements – earth, wind, fire and water – but some mystics claimed there had to be something binding and vivifying them all, a life force, a godhead … a fifth *essence*. The Greeks believed it was the air that the gods breathed, permeating all matter. Fifth was *quinta*, so metaphysicians spoke of the *quintessence*. Victorian scientists believed it was an invisible substance that transmitted light and radio waves, and called it the ether. These days, physicists use the word quintessence to cover some unknown sort of dark energy that drives the accelerating expansion of the universe.

Ether isn't there, of course. It is entirely *absent*. *Ab* in Latin means away, so *ab-esse* gives us *absence*. The opposite is to be right in the middle of things, or *inter-esse*, which is an *interesting* thought. Einstein said that compound *interest* was the 'greatest mathematical wonder of all time' and 'the eighth wonder of the world ... He that understands it, earns it. He that doesn't, pays it.' Don't be fooled by his wit: Albert was clever with equations but terrible with cash. To afford a divorce from his first wife, he had to promise her every penny of the Nobel prize money that he hadn't even won yet.

For complex reasons of Latin grammar, *prae-esse*, which means before being, becomes *praesens* when it's a participle. (A participle is a verb that is pretending to be a noun, such as a 'happening' ... as opposed to a participator, which is anyone who loves to join in and is generally a bit of a party animal.)

Praesens means the *present*, the here and now. *Presently* doesn't; it means soon, all in good time; at least that will give us a chance to make ourselves *presentable*. *Presence* can be impressive demeanour and charismatic *presentation*. The *presence-chamber* of a palace was the grand reception room where the king met ambassadors and *representatives* of the people – not so that they could be *presented* to him, but so they could be admitted into his august presence. On the other hand, a *presence* can be something ethereal: an incorporeal being that hovers on the edge of the senses. And in a spookily confusing way, a presension doesn't even derive from the present: it's a foreboding, a pre-sense of what hasn't yet happened.

Then there is *pro-esse*, to be in favour of something, which survives in English as *prowess*. To make the word easier to say, it gained a consonant, became *prodesse* and turned into *prosper* as well as *proud*. *Pride* goes before a fall, because it's one of the deadly sins – and *sin* is an **es** word too. *Esse*, to be, equates to *sinfulness*: thanks to Adam and that apple, our mere existence is a state of *original sin*.

The Greek word for *existence* is *ontos*. It gives us *entity*. *Ontology* is the study of being. The *ontological argument* is a theoretical proof of the existence of God: the very fact that we're here and capable of imagining a supreme deity means that there has to be one. Untology, logically, ought to be the opposite, the study of unbeing and atheism, but it isn't.

Ontologically, existence is truth, because anything that is is truly real. If that doesn't make immediate sense, say it slowly, like a tranced-out hippy ... truly real, man. **Es** is truth, or *sooth*. *Forsooth* means truly, though it always was a sarcastic word, and a *soothsayer* is a charlatan who foretells the future. But a *soothfast* man is loyal and truthful, and to *soothe* was originally to prove a fact. It came to mean the opposite, convincing people that a falsehood was actually true, and by extension *soothing* became flattery and cajoling – which is how it came to mean mitigating pain and calming the nerves.

Because *ontos* was existence, the connected word *eteos* meant reality, and *etumon* was the true or literal meaning of a word. And that is your actual *etymology*.

F

Fri, to love as a friend

Freedom, franchise, France, Friday

Fri, to love as a friend

*F*reedom and *enfranchisement* spring from a Neolithic tribal concept embodied in the root word **fri**. It means to love, but unlike **lubh**, a word that has survived unchanged for thousands of years, **fri** signifies loyalty and family affection rather than erotic desire.

Originally, **fri** was **pri**, but all its English derivatives begin with an 'f'. Only in Sanskrit does the 'p' survive – *priyas* is 'beloved'.

In prehistoric times, the ties between *friends* and extended family were essential to tribal survival. In the modern era, the society is much broader, a family of millions instead of dozens – but we rely on the same values to keep us *free*.

Friends did not own each other; they were not each other's slaves or masters. Their children were *freeborn*. They had their liberty, and were free to go as they wanted. They did as they liked too, acting from *free will*, and were liberal or free with their hospitality – all subtly different connotations of freedom.

In more cynical times, the word becomes a prefix of reproach. Sixteenth-century privateers in search of plunder were *freebooters*. In the argot of Victorian thieves, to free something was to grab it – *freeing a cat* was stealing a lady's hand muff. In 1940s Hollywood, *freeloaders* took advantage of the free food and drink at studio parties: they were after *freebies*. Eighteenth-century *freeholders*, on the other hand, were men of independent means: the word was tavern slang for a drinker wealthy enough to bring his wife out on a spree.

During the Second World War, the *Free French*, led by General Charles de Gaulle, held out against the Nazis. But the term is tautologous: the Free French defended *France*, and France was the *Frankish* kingdom, and the *Franks*, meaning allies, were the Germanic tribes that conquered Gaul in the sixth century, wielding battle-axes called *franciscs*. Thirteen hundred years later, during the Franco-Prussian wars in the 1870s, axes were out and rifles were the weapon of choice: unofficial military clubs of sharpshooters or *francs-tireurs*, wearing no uniforms, harried the Germans, and were executed if captured by the enemy.

During the Crusades, in the twelfth century, the Muslim world regarded any Westerner as basically French. The Arabs called Europeans *Frank-ji*, the Frankish people, and that survives in Hindu as *feringhee*, a contemptuous term for foreigners. But foreign is not a derivation of feringhee: it comes from the Latin *foras*, meaning out-of-doors.

The name *Francis* was made popular by the thirteenth-century saint who preached to his friends the birds; these days, in an oddly circular bit of semantics, anyone called Francis is nicknamed *Frank*.

Frank means free and open; it also means the mark on an envelope that allows it to be sent *free of charge*, or the stamp on a passport that lets the bearer travel *freely*. Originally, in the early eighteenth century, it meant the signature of some official personage with the power to send letters *post-free*.

In Saxon times, the *frilingi* (or *freelings*) were the second tier of people (the *edhilingi* were the aristocratic class, and the *lazzi* were the underclass who avoided work when they could – hence lazy). In medieval England, a *franklin* was a *freeman*, a landowner ranking just below the gentry in social status. When the vote was extended to this class, they were *enfranchised*. Today, the word *franchise* usually refers to a shop trading under the logo of a global brand, but originally it meant freedom – either from servitude, arrest or a specific law or tax.

Freyja and her brother *Freyr* were the most benign of Norse gods. He was the bringer of sun and rain, the lord of fertile crops and of the harvest. She was the goddess of love and marriage, and also of the dead; she had the gift of precognition, able to foresee the future without the power to change it. She travelled in a carriage drawn by a pair of cats. Viking weddings were traditionally held on her day of the week – *Freyja's day*, which became *Friday*. That might be why, in the children's rhyme, 'Friday's child is loving and giving'.

The heart of democracy is not the *universal franchise*, or *freedom of speech* – it's *dress-down Friday*. Any country civilised enough to let its office workers wear jeans and open-necked shirts at the end of the week has evidently evolved beyond feudalism and tyranny.

G

Gar, to call out noisily
Care, gorge, gargle, German

Gel, to freeze
Cold, glacier, gold, yolk

Ghu, to pour
Gush, ingot, fuse, refund

Gn, to beget
Gene, gentle, nation, knew

Gri, to grind
Grain, grease, grotty, engrossed

Gar, to call out noisily

On the golf course, it's good form before playing a stroke to *call* 'Fore!' as a warning to anyone on the fairway ahead who might be at risk of a clonk to the head from a ball. It sounds an old word, a medieval version of 'look out before', but it's actually a Victorian affectation. The earliest known use is 1878, and the game had been played for 600 years prior to that. What golfers did for safety in Renaissance times isn't known – they ducked, probably.

But the Neolithic equivalent of 'fore!' was **gar**! It meant 'Oi, watch out!' and the shout has survived into English, in a sense: we say, 'Take *care*' or 'Have a care'. If you don't, you might succumb to a life full of *cares*, meaning sorrows. The Old Saxon *kara* means grief and lamenting, the loud and woeful shouts of the bereaved – that's why to care can be to feel deep emotion. The same word in Old English was *caerig*, which was pronounced 'charig' and gives us *chary*, meaning *careful*.

In Latin, the bird that calls out at dawn is *gallus*, the cockerel. Turkeys, grouse and pheasants are *galliform* birds – and ostriches too. In fact, the classification *galliformes* applies to any bird that pecks its feed off the ground. Woodcocks are members of the *gallinaceous* family, and the *gallinazo* is a Mexican-Spanish name for the American black vulture. *Gallus* is also the Roman word for Gaul or France, and that is why *le coq Gaulois* or *Gallic* rooster is the French national symbol: it's a visual pun. In fact, the Romans had misunderstood the name that the Gauls called themselves – they were *gallos*, the Celtic word for the strangers. Celts who colonised Ireland used the same, ominous word to describe themselves: the Gaels, speaking Gaelic. The idea of strangers riding in from the east to take what they find, whether it's livestock, land or women, still has a powerful sense of menace today, and has fuelled countless Wild West movies.

The Celtic name for the Gothic tribes east of Gaul was *Germanii*, because their warriors went into battle screeching and roaring. They were the Shouting Men, the *Germans*. Any Roman general who led an army against them was entitled to call himself *Germanicus* – the most famous was a great nephew of the first Roman emperor, Augustus. When the old man died, Germanicus was on campaign in the north and his soldiers proclaimed him their new emperor. Meanwhile, back in Rome, Augustus's adopted son Tiberius was also being declared emperor. To avoid civil war, Germanicus was named Emperor in the East, and parcelled off to the far end of the Mediterranean, where Tiberius promptly had him poisoned. All very *galling*.

An earthenware vase with a long slender neck is called a *gurglet*, sometimes spelled *goglet* or *gugglet*. The word probably comes from the Portuguese *gorgoleta*, meaning a little throat. Gurglets were popular with Europeans in India, because the shape let the contents stay cool by evaporating slowly – handy for keeping water fresh.

A shout comes from the throat, or *gorge*. Too much shouting gives you a sore throat, and you'll have to *gargle*: washing the throat like this was called *gargarising*. Don't try to speak while *gargling*, or you'll get a *gurgle*, and end up *regurgitating*.

The giant with a big mouth and greedy *gullet* in Rabelais's tale was *Gargantua*, which is how anything huge comes to be labelled *gargantuan*. The grotesque carvings on churches that spout water are *gargoyles*, from the Tudor word for the throat, *gargil*. *Gargil* is also the name, now only remembered in pockets of dialect, for a disease of the throat in geese. *Garget*, on the other hand, is an inflamed trachea in cattle, while pigs get a swine of a sore throat called *gargarism*.

75

People who spout a lot of words are *garrulous*. They *garble* a lot of *jargon*, and sometimes talk no sense at all. The philosopher Montaigne coined a word for that: *galimatias*, meaning arrant gibberish. It's a combination of *gallus*, the noisy cockerel, and *ballimathia*, a Latin word for bawdy drinking songs – Montaigne had had argumentative students in mind when he invented it.

Gel, to freeze

One of the joys of a hot afternoon's stroll through an Italian city is the *gelateria*, selling *gelati* or soft ice cream. Frozen desserts are a treat dating back to Ancient Rome, when mountain snows would be brought to the city and stored underground to prevent thawing, before they were flavoured with fruit juices and served at feasts. At its best, ice cream is *gelid* – intensely *cold*, from the Latin word for frost, *gelus*.

The same 'g' to 'c' shift that turns **gel** to cold gives us *cool*, and *chill*. Cold certainly can't come from the Latin *cald*, because that means hot. We caught our cold from the Old English *cyle*, which became both *chele* and *cold* in Middle English.

Clean, a word that has barely changed its sound in 1,500 years of English, might also come from **gel**. The original meaning of clean was something pure and transparent, without imperfections – like ice. It came to mean free from dirt. It is possible too that *cloth* shares the **gel** root, because when we wear *clothes* we are *clad*, and the purpose of *cladding* is obviously to prevent a warm object from getting cold.

If that seems a stretch, the link to *glaciers* is much easier to see. *Glaciation* just means freezing, and *glacious* is icy, but in Old French *glacier* meant to slide, and so the long slopes that acted as killing grounds in castle fortifications were called *glacis*.

A *glacé* cherry is not frozen, just shiny. *Gloss*, *glaze*, *glass* and *glare* are all **gel** words too.

The original meaning of *glib* is smooth and slippery, like ice. *Glide* is a frictionless word, and so is *glissade*. Bald heads are smooth too, or *glabrous* – completely hair-free, from the Latin for smooth, *glaber*. Most bald men can remember when they sported a positive mane: the correct zoological term for an animal that is hirsute when young but bare in maturity is *glabrescent*. The space between your eyebrows is the *glabella*, though not if you have a monobrow.

Think of sunlight shining on ice – that's where we get *glisten* and *gleam*, *glimmer* and *glance*, *glimpse* and *glint*. All that *glisters* is not *gold* ... it might just be a *gilded* glacier mint.

That idea of dazzle and shine gives us *glee* and *glad*, which originally meant to be in bright spirits. But the connection to *gilt* also gives us gold coins such as *guilders*, and even *yolk*, the *golden* part of an egg. Stranger still, **gel** is the root of *glair*, the egg white. But the next logical step takes us even further from the root sense: the 'g' to 'y' shift from gold to yolk, which is easy enough to see, then becomes *yellow*. Ice isn't yellow – sunshine is, and sunshine melts ice. But the link is beyond question, especially when you remember that the German word for yellow is *gelb*.

Gelt can mean money of any coin, and *geld* was tax in Old Norse. The levies that Viking raiders extorted from Saxon villagers along Britain's east coast were called *Dane geld* – the first payment of more than three tons of silver was made by the English king Aethelred the Unready, whose advisers told him to pay up rather than risk further defeats in battle, after he was trounced at Malden in Essex in 991. Unready doesn't mean he wasn't ready to fight – it means *unredey*, or ill-advised. Kipling certainly thought he was – 900 years later, he wrote: 'We never pay any-one Dane-geld / No matter how trifling the cost; / For the end of that game is oppression and shame, / And the nation that plays it is lost!'

In 1904, scientists hit upon an 8,000-year-old word to describe the '*jelly*-like coagulation of a colloidal liquid'. They called it a *gel*, not deliberately harking back to **gel** or even *gelus*, but simply taking the first syllable of the scientific word for jelly, *gelatin*.

Gel is ideal for ointments and poultices, but an inventor named Alfred Nobel had developed a different kind of *gelly* a few years earlier, in 1875, when he patented *gelignite*. An explosive mixture of gun cotton, saltpetre, wood pulp and nitroglycerine, its name described it perfectly: it stayed cool and stable until it was detonated, when it burned with a short burst of devastating energy. **Gel** + *ignis* (the Latin for fire) wasn't Nobel's only invention – he held 300 patents including one whose name came from the Greek word for potential force, *dynamis* ... dynamite. On top of that, Albert was the boss of Bofors, the armaments company that built the heavy artillery of the First World War. All those explosions are the reason Alf left his considerable fortune to fund a series of philanthropic prizes, the Nobels: he had a guilty conscience.

Ghu, to pour

Joseph Eichar could have been the richest man in history, except that he was born at the wrong time. The American pioneer was digging for salt in a creek bed in Ohio, in 1815, when he struck oil – a *gusher* that sent a plume 30 metres (100 feet) into the air. If he'd made the discovery eighty years later, at the dawn of the automobile era, Eichar's oil would have been priceless. Instead, it was worthless.

That was America's first *oil gusher*, but the phenomenon had been known for millennia – in Iceland, underground pressure forces water to erupt from the ground in boiling columns. The Vikings discovered one of these superheated waterspouts in a valley in south Iceland, where it blasted thousands of gallons of steam and spray up to 67 metres (220 feet) into the air, four or five times a day. They called it *Geysa*, meaning *Gusher*, after a water giant whose daughter had married a god; these days, all waterspouts are called *geysers*.

That's got nothing to do with geezer, Cockney slang for an ordinary bloke. Wellington's troops adopted the word during the Peninsula War in Spain around 1810, from the Basque word for a man, *giza*.

The Old English word for intestines was *guttas* – perhaps because the Saxons loved to pour food and drink down their *gullets* and into their *guts* until it came *gushing* out again. *Gut* became the word for a mould: smiths poured liquid metal into a *goten* to make an *ingot* – *in* + *goten*. As the meaning became lost, this *gutteral* word changed to a *ningot*, then a *nigget* and now a *nugget*.

In Ancient Greek, *khumos* is plant *juice* and *khemeia* means extracting juices for medicine. Arab doctors were fascinated by this quasi-magical process, and called it *al-khemeia*, a word that came back to us as *alchemy*. That was the nearest thing we had to science for hundreds of years, and then we lost the 'al' and learned *chemistry*. As any biochemist knows, food in the large intestine turns to acidic pulp called *chyme*, before passing to the small intestine where it is broken down into the milky fluid called *chyle*. *Chylopoetic* doesn't mean verses about vomit, but merely anything that produces chyle.

The 'kh' sound was softened in Latin to an 'f'. *Fundere* is to *found* or cast metal, which is *fundamental*. The die-cast blocks of metal used by printers are called *fonts*: this used to mean a particular type style and size. An example is 12pt Helvetica, in which letters without ascending or descending strokes (such as 'a' and 'e') are the height of 12 full stops, or points, stacked on top of each other. On tabloid newspapers, the 'splash' headline can be 120pt capitals, or even larger. Since the rise of desktop publishing on computers in the late 1980s, font and typeface have merged their meanings: early Apple Macs came preloaded with *fonts* named after cities such as Chicago and Geneva, which could be scaled to any size on screen.

The past tense of *fundere* is *fusus*, which is why molten metals *fuse* together, and your lights go out when the *fuse* blows. *Fusil* means made liquid by heat, but fusillade, a hail of red-hot metal, might not be related – it appears to be part of the 'focus' family of words from the Indo-European root **bhok**, a hearth, which includes fuel, foyer (a heated room) and curfew (when all fires had to be put out).

What is more sure is that *futilis* in Latin means *free-flowing*. By the seventeenth century, it meant leaky – and there's nothing more *futile* than carrying water in an empty bucket.

The Romans applied prefixes to *fundere* with their usual merciless efficiency. There was *confundere*, to pour together – that gives us *confound*, and *confusion*. *Effundere* is pouring out, or *effusion*, and *diffundere* is pouring all over the place, which is *diffusion*. *Infundere*, of course, is pouring in – that's *infusion*. *Transfundere* is pouring across, or *transfusion*, and *suffundere* is to pour below, giving us *suffusion*.

Refund comes from *refundere*, which means to pour back into the bottle. The past tense of that one is *refusare*, or rejected – that is, *refused*. *Refuse* became a noun in the Middle Ages, signifying the debris that people couldn't use and threw away: broken pottery, perhaps, or wood shavings. There wasn't much a medieval peasant couldn't use; these days, supermarket *refuse* bags are brimming with less-than-perfect produce that we *refuse* to buy. We have a *profusion* – which comes from *profusus*, or lavish. Now there's a *profound* thought.

Gn, to beget

In the *beginning*, there was either *Genesis* or *genes*, depending on your views about human *origins*. What is certain is that the Indo-European root **gn** has *generated* hundreds of words about creation – far more than can be examined here.

Take the three dozen words ending with *-genesis* as a suffix: there's *oogenesis*, the process by which an egg is formed, and *schizogenesis*, which is reproduction by splitting in two like an amoeba, and *palingenesis*, which literally means born again – *palin* means again in Ancient Greek: hence, a *palindrome* is a word that reads the same backwards and forwards, such as eve or rotor (but not Bolton. As Monty Python's John Cleese told Michael Palin, 'A palindrome of Bolton would be Notlob … it don't work!')

There are even more words that simply end in *-gen*. *Allergens* produce allergies, *hallucinogens* produce hallucinations and *gasogens* produce gases … but the exception to the rule is *hydrogen*, which produces water, not hydras. When everything produced is the same, it's *homogeneous*.

In the Book of *Genesis*, Adam begat Seth and Seth begat Enos, and that was the *genealogy* of mankind … it's bad luck on Seth, who is everybody's ancestor, that he's overshadowed by his more famous brothers, Cain and Abel. The British aristocracy had the same problem with *primogeniture*: the oldest son inherits the title, even if he's a *degenerate*, while the younger ones are pushed to the side. The *original* meaning of *gentle* was the first-born: in Latin, *gentilis* meant from a respectable family, and *gentil* was an Old French word that survives in English as *genteel*. A *gentleman* was a son of good breeding, a member of the *gentry*. A lady, strictly speaking, doesn't have to be well-born, so long as she's good at baking bread: the word is derived from the Old English *hlaef-diger*, meaning loaf-kneader.

In *general* (from the Latin *genus*, a group of things), **gn** starts everything. It's in our *genetics*, which come from our *progenitors*; even our *gender* is proclaimed by our *genitals*. *Pregnancy, progeny, congenital, indigenous*: **gn** is *regenerated* whenever language plays the *Generation Game*.

But it goes far beyond that. Our *genius* is the spirit that attends each one of us from birth – it is rarely intellectual, and much more likely to influence our moods, desires and destiny. Far more of us have a genius, say, for idleness or gluttony than for cinema, which is why for every great movie there are 20 bad ones in the same *genre*.

In French, *gens* are people, so *gens d'armes* are men-at-arms – and *gendarmes* are policemen. The Latin *gens* means a clan, and the word was adopted in Hebrew. That's why non-Jews are *Gentiles*: they are foreigners, not part of the group.

Ingenuous is a **gn** word: *in gens* is within the clan, and so trustworthy, frank and honest. An *ingenue* in the theatre is an artless, innocent girl. *Ingenuity* is another **gn** word, signifying a native wit bred in the bone. But genuine is a wholly unrelated word. Like genuflect, it's all about the knee. The Roman word for a knee was *genu*, and *genuinus* meant that certainty a father feels when he sits his own son on his knee. It takes an expert to identify what's authentic, but everyone possesses a natural instinct for the genuine article.

As with gnats and gnus, the 'g' in front of the 'n' is sometimes silent. That's why *gnaive* and *gnatal* are not the accepted spellings, and why the angels didn't sing '*Gnoel Gnoel*' at the *Gnativity*; they are all **gn** words, though. The 'g' disappears in *nation, native, nature* and *innate*, but it stays stubbornly in place at the end of *benign*, even though we don't pronounce it. Benign used to mean well born, and *malign* was the opposite – the 'g' makes itself heard in *benignant* and *malignant*.

That errant 'g' comes and goes in words based on the Greek *gnosis*, meaning *cognition* – the higher thoughts that are born in the mind. *Agnostics* use the 'g', for example, but *gnostics* don't; *prognosis* and *diagnosis* do, and *knowledge* doesn't. The verb to *know* has two senses: it can mean mental comprehension but also sexual familiarity. 'Adam *knew* his wife, Eve, and she conceived' … and we're back to Genesis.

Gri, to grind

The next time you're weary of the daily *grind*, remember that the *grindstone* made civilisation possible. There was no point in harvesting crops unless the *grain* was *ground* to fine *granules*. Inevitably that was going to require a bit of elbow *grease*. It's all *grist* to the mill …

Grist, in fact, can mean the corn itself, or the act of *grinding* or the flour that results. A *grist-cart* was an Elizabethan wheat wagon, and in the early days of the American West, a grist meant very many – perhaps as many as there were grains on an ear of corn, or in a sack. J. Fenimore Cooper, who wrote *The Last of the Mohicans*, once described a swarm of bees as 'an onaccountable grist'.

Grit is particles of sand or gravel. *Grits*, on the other hand, is a sort of porridge, popular in the Southern United States, and sometimes served with fried catfish or prawns (shrimp in American English). *Hominy grits* make a filling meal – Virginia's *Charleston Post & Courier* declared in 1952, 'Given enough of it, the inhabitants of planet Earth would have nothing to fight about. A man full of [grits] is a man of peace.'

Grits were called *groaten* in Old English, a word that survives in dialect as *groats*. *Groat-sugar* is coarse-granuled. *Groats*, the medieval coins, are also **gri** words, but by a different route: *grote*, like grist in America, meant many. Then it became *great*. *Grote pennies* were thick silver coins, weighing an eighth of an ounce (3.5 grams), and worth about four copper pennies. Groats were taken out of circulation in 1662, after the Restoration.

A *gross* also means many: specifically, 144, or a dozen dozens. A *great gross* is a dozen gross, or 1,728. These days anything *gross* is plain horrible, but it used to mean coarse and thick. Grotesque, which stemmed from the Italian *grotto* (and originally from the Roman *crupta*, a crypt) meant decorative at first, but it sounded so gross to English ears that the meaning changed, to distorted, exaggerated and then downright horrible. That's etymology in reverse: it wasn't a **gri** word to begin with, but it became one. In the 1960s, it spawned the Liverpudlian slang *grotty* – George Harrison of The Beatles presented it to the nation when he called some clothes 'dead grotty' in the 1964 movie *A Hard Day's Night*. The word was also a favourite of the Monty Python team, who dubbed the Canary Islands *Lanzagrotty*; in the 1970s, *Grotsend-on-Sea* became a generic name for faded seaside towns.

A *grote* in Edwardian criminal slang was an informer; it too was probably short for grotesque. The rhyme with 'scrotum' changed the word to *scrote* by the 1970s – it still meant a horrible little man who couldn't be trusted.

To be *engrossed* is to be utterly absorbed, but in military terminology, to engross an army was to reckon up its numbers; it also meant to perform a defensive manoeuvre, drawing a battalion of men into a compact group. Napoleon thought the British were a nation of *grocers* – the word was coined in the fourteenth century, when it meant not a shopkeeper but a wholesale merchant who bought imports in bulk: it was spelled *grosser*.

Grogram is a coarse fabric of wool and mohair, woven with silk. In the eighteenth century, Admiral Edward Vernon was called *Old Grog* by his men, bacause he always wore a *grogram cloak*. He was a disastrous naval commander: he lost 1,400 sailors in a storm off the Isles of Scilly in 1707, and thirty years later he led an assault on Spanish forces in the Caribbean, in an operation so huge it would not be exceeded until D-Day two centuries later. The Battle of Cartagena de Indias was a catastrophe, with 50 ships sunk and 18,000 casualties, many of them killed by disease as yellow fever swept the navy. Old Grog's reputation endured, though, because he introduced the tradition of a watered-down rum ration, the sailor's *grog*. By keeping the men *groggy*, he kept them happy.

Grog was soon popular on land too. But it was rough stuff: drink too much of it in a *grog-shop* and you would get *grog-blossom*, red pimples on the nose. Grog-shop was also bare-knuckle-boxing slang; a punch in the 'bread basket' was the stomach, one in the grog-shop was the mouth.

I

Ieh, yes ... **Neh**, no
Yeah, OK; nay, negative

Iug, to join
Yoke, yoga, jugular, joust

Ieh, yes …

When Paul McCartney and John Lennon first played 'She Loves You' (*Yeah* Yeah Yeah) to Paul's dad, James, he complained about the Americanised slang: 'Why don't you sing "*Yes* Yes Yes"?' he said. But the form 'Yeah' is much closer to what the word was in early Indo-European languages, as well as to other modern versions – for instance, *oui*, *ja*, *da* and *haa* in French, German and its Nordic cousins, Russian and its Slavic cousins and Hindi.

Some English scholars believe that 'yes' began as the emphatic form of *yes*; a simpler affirmative was *yea*. Many languages do this: for example, the insistent version of *oui* is *si*. These days, at least in southern England, if you want to underline a yes, you have to become verbose: 'Oh, but absolutely! Definitely! Certainly!'

In Scots and northern English dialect, *aye* is much more common – and if you're being emphatic, *och aye*, which is 'Oh yes'. There are many spurious explanations for the derivation of *OK*, from the unlikely (it comes from the Choctaw Native American *okeh*, meaning it is so), to the improbable (it's a Bantu word from West Africa, *waw-kay*, meaning yes indeed) and the downright ridiculous (it's an acronym for Orl Korrect, a favourite saying of US president Andrew Jackson, who was a famously bad speller). But by the mid-nineteenth century, OK was rapidly becoming the most popular word in America. It still is. The Choctaw, on the other hand, were busy being oppressed to the point of near extinction, and slavery was still practised in many states – neither an indigenous nor an African word was likely to become the fad of the New World.

It seems much more probable that the 'och aye' of the Scots settlers summed up the spirit of the pioneers; it was boiled down to a pair of initials as it swept the nation. OK?

… Neh, no

Nay is the opposite of aye, because it's *not aye*. In German it's *nein*, in Norwegian *nej*, in French *non* and in many Slavic languages such as Croatian it's *ne*. In fact, from Japan (where it's *nai*) to Spain (where it's *no*), **neh** words are *negative*. Ever becomes *never*, one *none*, owt *nowt*, either *neither* and ought (meaning anything) *nought* (*nothing*).

The Latin for wickedness was *nefas*: *ne* was *not*, and *fas* was divine law – so *nefarious* is villainous. *Nefandous*, on the other hand, means unspeakable and abominable, because *fandus* was Latin for 'to be spoken'. And the Roman word *negliger*, or *neglect*, gives us *negligee*, a nightdress that is *negligent* about what it covers.

To go back on your word is to *renege*; to claim you never said it is to *deny*; to go over to the other side is to become a *renegade*. That's not *nice*, which originally meant foolish: it compounded *ne + scrire*, to know. But being nasty is sometimes *necessary*, from *ne + cedere*, to give up. Nasty isn't a **neh** word – it comes from the Indo-European word for dirt, **nask**.

All these Latin words suggest that the Romans were tireless people, forever expanding their lexigraphic frontiers. Actually, the administration of empire got in the way of the day's serious business, which was sitting around relaxing. This is revealed by the roots of *negotiation*, which is *neg + otiari*, the opposite of being lazy (*otiari* is leisure). They were evidently trying to be *nonchalant*, or appearing not to care – that's *non* plus the French *chaloir*, being concerned.

Almost any word can be *negated* by non. *Nonpareil* is having no equal – although it is also a size of type, a rose parakeet, a gorgeously coloured finch found in the Southern United States and several kinds of moth. A *non sequitur* is a conclusion, like this one, that doesn't follow from what was said before.

Nonsuch Palace was the most ambitious, not to say megalomanic, of Henry VIII's architectural whims. He wanted it to dwarf Hampton Court in scale and imagination, and he demolished a village in Surrey called Cuddington to build it. The work cost more than £100m in today's money. It remained a royal palace for 130 years, until Charles II made a gift of it to his mistress, Barbara, Countess of Castlemaine. She pulled the place down and sold it off brick by brick, to pay off her gambling debts.

At the trial of another royal in 1820, Queen Caroline, who was accused of having an affair with her secretary Bartolomeo Pergami, all of the Italian witnesses replied '*Non mè*' to every question. The Georgian equivalent of 'I plead the Fifth Amendment', it was short for '*Non me ricordo*', or 'I don't remember'. For years afterwards in English slang, a *non me* was a lie.

Iug, to join

A thousand years ago, before the Norman Conquest, a Saxon smallholder had basic needs, and it was the duty of his lord to see that they were met: 'A farmer ought to be given for the occupation of his land two oxen, one cow, six sheep and seven acres sown … and let him be given the tools for his work and the utensils for his house.' These were his boor's-right – not birthright, but the bare essentials due to a boor, or countryman (it's a bad thing to be an English boor these days, but like the Dutch *boer* it simply meant farmer in the eleventh century). This was all enshrined in a document drawn up during the reign of Edward the Confessor, called the *Rectitudines Singularum Personarum* or *The Rights of the Individual*.

Those minimum requirements to keep a farm viable had hardly changed for millennia. In particular, one fact stands out: the farmer needed only one cow for milking, but two oxen for ploughing. A pair made the work much easier and faster – if they worked together, and not against each other.

But that was impossible for the Neolithic ploughman. It was hopeless to rein two bullocks separately to an **ar**, or a scratch-plough made from a stout branch, and hope that both animals would have the same ideas about where they wanted to go. Then some bright spark invented the *yoke*.

A yoke is a pair of wooden collars for cattle, connected by a chain. It makes them *jumentous* beasts, linked in harness. In Hindi, a *yojan* is the distance a ploughing pair can traverse before they have to be unyoked. It's not an exact measurement … somewhere between four and ten miles.

The yoke became a symbol of domestication and then *subjugation*. Roman prisoners captured in battle were yoked and led in triumph like livestock. In the Middle Ages, milkmaids carried their pails on a yoke across their shoulders, which is probably how *yokel* became a sneer at country folk.

The Latin *iungere* became *joindre* in Old French: they both meant to *join*. That created *joint* and *conjoin*, *junction* and *conjunction*. A *joiner* is a woodworker and his craft is *joinery*, more ornamental than mere carpentry – but a *jointer* was a Victorian builder's mate, who used bent iron rods to strengthen the corners of walls or who, later on, wired up the electrical connections in the *junction box*.

In law, a *jointure* is a *joint tenancy*, often shared by husband and wife. If the man dies, his widow becomes the *jointress*. *Rejoinder* is also a legal term, the name for the defendant's response to the plaintiff's claim, though it now means any sort of reply, especially a sharp one. To impose a rule, especially on yourself, is an *enjoinder*.

The composer Franz Liszt's piano recitals were so dramatic and filled with such extraordinary flourishes that women wept and fainted. No recordings exist, but his amazing musical dexterity is attributed to the flexibility or hypermobility of his hands: his fingers were *double-jointed*. A phenomenon dubbed Lisztomania swept northern Europe in the 1840s – wherever he appeared, fans fought to touch him, snatched souvenirs such as discarded gloves and broken piano strings and begged for locks of his hair. One lady-in-waiting at a royal court wore a cigar butt that Liszt had stubbed out in the street. She hung it in a diamond-studded locket … apparently, it stank.

The *jugulum* in Latin is the collarbone, where a yoke sits, and so the main vein in the throat is the *jugular*. *Jugulation* is another word for strangling. And in Latin, *iuxta* meant next to, close enough to be touching. Of course that gives us *juxtapose*: to place side by side. But it is also the root of *jostle* and of *jousting*, where two knights tilt at each other on horseback. (The *OED* lists *joust* as a variant spelling; it prefers *just* and *justing*. The poet Edmund Spenser spelled it *giust*, and since he lived in the golden age of tournaments, perhaps he's the best authority.)

In Sanskrit, there are four ages of history or *yuga*, yoking the years together. *Yoga* was the discipline of mind and body that joined the *yogi* with the divine, achieving holy union. Marriage is another holy union, the *conjugal* rite.

The Greek for a yoke was *zeugos*, which survives in scientific terminology such as *zygote* (a cell created when two gametes bond), but also in the figure of speech called *zeugma*.

Zeugma takes a verb and yokes it to two nouns. The more different the nouns, the more elegant the zeugma. Schoolchildren used to be taught this one: 'He bolted the door and his dinner.' Now, the most popular example comes from *Star Trek*: 'You are free to execute your laws, and your citizens, as you see fit.' That seems apt for a cabal of army officers forming a government … that is, a military *junta*.

K

Kad, to fall away
Caddy, catarrh, cataract, catastrophe

Kap, to seize hold
Copper, occupy, deceit, princess

Kar, hard, strong
Carbon, crayfish, chancellor, harsh

Kard, heart
Cardiac, core, courage, quarry

Kas, cut
Castration, chestnut, castle, cheese

Ker, to turn
Circle, carriage, succour, bicycle

Kiv, to lie down among friends
Civil, kip, citadel, home

Kru, gory
Cruel, crucial, crook, lacrosse

Ku, to swell
Cave, curve, succumb, hull

Kwa, interrogative pronoun
Who, what, where, which

Kwi, to live
Quick, viable, viper, hygiene

Kad, to fall away

Kad is the start of *cadence*, which arrived in English from the Latin word for 'to fall', *cadere*. When a voice or an instrument slides down the musical scale, that's a *cadence*. The tendency to fall, especially when frailty is caused by old age, is *caducity*. In astrology, when a planet is *cadent*, it is descending through the nightly skies.

But *cadency* is a different sort of descent – it follows the generations of a junior branch on a family tree. That leads to *cadet*, a younger son or brother. Boys who join the army are called cadets, because of the tradition among the nobility that, while eldest sons inherited the title and the estates, and middle sons went into law or the church, the youngest of the male line entered the armed forces, without a commission, to learn the fighting trade and to forge a glorious career. Or be killed, of course; youngest sons weren't much missed.

The word came to mean a student at an army or naval college, or any schoolboy receiving military training. It was also given a twist to become *caddy*, an eighteenth-century word for any lad or man who hung around on the off-chance of getting odd jobs. By 1857, it meant the boy on a golf course who carried the players' clubs.

For the Ancient Greeks, **kad** became a prefix: *kata-*, meaning down. That survives in all sorts of English words – a *cataclysm*, often misused to mean any kind of disaster, is a deluge, a down-rushing of waves. *Catacombs* are a network of subterranean caves, connected by tunnels down under the ground. A *catabatic* fever goes down by degrees, and *cataleptic* seizures cause the sufferer to fall down, while *cataplexy* is a state of stupefaction or feigned death brought on by terror. A *catadromous* fish, such as the eel, swims down to the sea to spawn. A cold in the head gives you *catarrh*, which is rheum (that is, mucus) flowing downwards. *Cataracts* are waterfalls, *catastrophes* are severe downturns in the course of events and a *catasta* was the platform on which prisoners stood before being sent down into slavery.

The prefix *kata* also gave the Romans a name for a waterfall in Egypt, and the English a folk expression for a heavy downpour.

'Raining cats and dogs' is a phrase that had its beginning in Homer's epic of the Trojan War, *The Iliad*. The Greek poet, 2,750 years ago, compared the deafening clash of swords and spears against shields to the crash of forest trees felled by axes. The noise comes *kata doupos*, 'down like thunder'.

The Roman historian Pliny the Elder named the great Nile waterfall *Catadupa*. Close to the border of Egypt and the ancient kingdom of Nubia, where Aswan and its dam stand today, the waters of the Nile still crash down torrentially there – it's the only *cataract* remaining on the river. The people who lived beside the waterfall were called *catadupae*, and they were assumed to be deaf.

Such arcane allusions were common knowledge to any Englishman who knew his Latin and Greek, in Tudor and Jacobean times. But most people in the sixteenth and seventeenth centuries couldn't read, much less speak dead languages. When swanky academics or priests remarked, during a deluge, that the rain was pouring *kata doupos*, or perhaps that it was raining like Catadupa, the rest of the population had to invent a translation.

Lots of unlikely explanations have been back-engineered for the apparent nonsense of 'raining cats and dogs'. The *OED* ties it to the phrase 'cat and dog' (as in, 'Those two are always arguing like cat and dog'), and adds that a children's game, played in Napoleonic times, used a stick called a cat and a wooden club called a dog. Another, more gruesome idea was that, when heavy rain flooded the streets, the animals would drown; credulous people would see the floating carcasses and assume that it had been literally raining cats and dogs. The playwright Richard Brome, in his 1653 comedy *The City Wit, or The Woman Wears the Breeches*, used the expression, 'It shall rain dogs and polecats'. A century later, Jonathan Swift, in *The Complete Collection of Genteel and Ingenious Conversation*, commented: 'The populace has other amusements, and very rude ones; such as throwing dead dogs and cats and mud at passers-by on certain festival days.'

Brewer's *Dictionary of Phrase and Fable* has a less revolting explanation: cats, in Norse folk stories, were weather spirits. Sailors still say that a frisky cat 'has a gale of wind in her tail'. Dogs and wolves, meanwhile, were the companions of Odin, the Viking god of storms – so gales and downpours together were caused by cats and dogs.

Kap, to seize hold

Screenwriter William Rose woke up one morning in the early 1950s with a classic movie in his head. He had dreamed the whole plot: how a gang of crooks rent rooms in a shabby boarding house, run by an eccentric old woman, because the building overlooks a railway station where they are planning a security van heist. Darkly comic and constructed around a criminal fantasy, it eventually starred Alec Guinness and Peter Sellers, and became celebrated as the perfect *caper* movie: *The Ladykillers*.

Caper as a word was a classic bit of Victorian underworld punning. In the English sense, it meant 'to dance or leap in a frolicsome manner'. But in Dutch, *kapen* meant to rob or plunder, and a *kaper* was a pirate. Combined, the word implied a robbery that was also a bit of fun.

Kap is to *cop* hold of something in your hands. It can mean to *catch* a ball or to *capture* an enemy. Money in your hand is *cash*. *Caught* by the *coppers* after a caper, a thief generally ends up in *captivity*. The *captor* makes the *capture*; the *caitiff* is the prisoner, though the original word expanded in the seventeenth century to mean any miserable wretch or petty villain.

To be *capable* is possessing the skill to take matters into your own hands. Lancelot *'Capability'* Brown, known as England's greatest gardener, won his nickname in the eighteenth century not because of his practical talents but because of his salesmanship: he would tell potential clients that their acres possessed great 'capability' for improvement.

The Latin for a box is *capsa*, of any *capacity* – it could be as small as a *capsule* or as big as a *sash* window frame or *casement*. A portable box is a *case*, whether it's a small one for papers or a big one for clothes, a *briefcase* or a *suitcase*. If it's really big, it's *capacious*. Put anything in a box and it is *encased*. A trunk containing ammunition or explosives is a *caisson*.

Kap worked its way into the middle of many words, always with a sense of taking or holding. There's *occupy*, which is seizing control; *recuperate*, which is holding on to health; *participate*, which is taking part; *anticipate*, which is seizing hold of an event before it happens; *disciple*, which is a student who holds to his master's teaching; and *reciprocate*, which is making a gift in return for taking one. Because *manus* is Latin for hand, *emancipate* is to free somebody, to take them out of their enemy's hands.

All those words come from the Latin *capere*, to take hold: the verb changed, depending on its prefix. *Ad* + *capere* became *accipere* – literally to take to yourself, in English it became *accept*. *Con* + *capere* became *concipere*, to take together – it gives us *concept.* The prefix *de-* means down from, like something falling down from the sky or from a tree: *de + capere*, to take down from, was the root of the Roman word *decipere*: at first it meant catching birds or animals with a trap, and then it meant using any sort of *deception* or *deceit*.

Ex is out of, so *excipere* (from *ex + capere*) meant taking things separately – we make *exceptions*, especially when the reason is *exceptional*. *Incipere* was the opposite, and gives us *inception* and *incipience*, which both mean a beginning.

The man who holds first place is *primus + capere*, or *princeps*. Augustus Caesar named himself *princeps* when he became emperor: it seemed more tactful than 'dictator'. *Princeps* is the root of *principal* (foremost) as well as *principle* (fundamental law), but it also creates *princes* and *princesses*.

Little *princelings* are not really created, of course, not even by the Florentine schemer Machiavelli, who wrote the rule book for autocrats in *The Prince* in the early 1500s. They are born, sometimes with the help of hot water (one word for hot in Latin is *formus*) and tongs called *forceps*, which seize hold of the emerging child. Queen Victoria's eldest grandson, Wilhelm, was a forceps delivery, dragged out of the womb so roughly that the midwife damaged his left arm. All his life it was weak and stunted, which gave Wilhelm an inferiority complex: that's probably why, when he became the warmongering Kaiser Bill, he was so irritable and *captious*.

Kar, hard, strong

The *hardest* natural substance on earth is crystallised *carbon* or diamond, but for most early farming communities, it was the discovery of another type of rock-hard carbon that changed the world and spelled the end of the Stone Age. *Charcoal*, the almost pure residue of carbon that results when wood is baked dry, burns far hotter than ordinary logs – hot enough to smelt bronze by mixing molten tin and copper, which requires furnace temperatures of more than 1,000 degrees centigrade. When communities learned how to make charcoal, around 7,000 years ago, they could begin to work metal. By 3,000 BC, the Egyptians were using charcoal to smelt iron, and within another 1,000 years they were able to blow glass; meanwhile, bronze-working was common in Britain by 2,000 BC, around the time that Stonehenge was built.

Charcoal technology had probably been brought to the British Isles, along with the Indo-European language, by the Bell Beaker tribes of northern Europe. The Beaker folk take their name from the distinctive shape of their pottery: they had also discovered charcoal ovens, to make *ceramics*.

Charcoal is not coal, the fossil fuel found in *carboniferous* rock. The word coal comes from the Indo-European **gual**, meaning something that burns. But the Romans referred to both coal and charcoal as *carbo*, from **kar**, the hard stuff. *Carbunculus* meant a small lump of coal, and that brings us back to diamonds, and all other gemstones: a *carbuncle stone* is any gem with a fiery colour. Hard red spots or pimples on the face, often caused by excessive boozing, are also called *carbuncles*.

The Latin for prison was *carcer*, perhaps because the convicts were doing hard time while *incarcerated*.

Napoleonic cavalry carried *carbine* muskets, short-muzzled guns that would not get tangled with their legs as they rode. The weapon's name reflects its deadly effectiveness: the gun-toting horsemen were *carabins* or *scarabins*, the French name originally given to the men with carts piled high with corpses, who trundled through plague-stricken towns shouting, 'Bring out your dead!'

The scarabin carters were so called because they looked like dung beetles, rolling a ball of dead matter. French dung beetles were *scarabees*, from the Greek *skarabeios*. In Greek, any kind of hard-*crusted* beetle was *karabos*. The *crab* was *kharkhinos*; in Latin it was *cancer*. Whether it's the *kernel*-like hardness of the tumours, or the pincer-like pain of the disease, *carcinogens* and *carcinomas* are derived from the image of a crab. *Kankar* in Sanskrit has a different meaning: it's *gravel*.

Another *crustacean* with an armoured *carapace* is the *crayfish*. Like the crab, it *crawls* and *gropes* on the seabed.

The Romans used the word cancer for the cross-struts of a trellis, perhaps because the crab moves sideways and the mesh of a lattice is diagonal rather than vertical. To make a lattice was *cancellare*, which came to mean thoroughly crossing something out, or *cancelling* it.

To emphasise their status, medieval officials would sit behind criss-cross wooden screens – for instance, in the *chancel* of a church. Their position conferred a title upon them: *chancellor*. The court of the *Lord Chancellor* is called *chancery*; the post was introduced by Edward the Confessor, in the eleventh century. This dignatory is also called the Lord High Chancellor or the Chancellor of England, the highest judge in the land. In Tudor times, when Archbishop Wolsey and Sir Thomas More both held the position, the Lord Chancellor was styled 'the keeper of the King's conscience'.

Kar is the root of another kind of status. Because it could mean strong as well as hard, it formed the English suffix -*cracy* – *bureaucracy*, *democracy* and *autocracy* literally mean governmental rule through offices, through the people and through dictatorship. *Plutocracy* is rule of the wealthiest; *ochlocracy* is rule of the rampant masses – sometimes called *mobocracy*.

The charcoal-burners of Naples were the front for a secret political movement in the early 1800s: calling themselves the *carbonari*, they wanted to overthrow the Neapolitan king and establish a republic. Spaghetti cooked in olive oil with eggs, cheese and bacon was a cheap dish beloved of the Italian charcoal-burners: that's why it is called *carbonara* or, in the States, 'coal miner's spaghetti'.

While we're discussing nineteenth-century history, a *carburettor* was patented in 1886 by Otto Benz. By mixing air with liquid *hydrocarbon* (i.e., petrol), the device creates a combustible gas for powering a motor car (but car is short for carriage, not carburettor).

The hard 'k' became softened to an 'h' in Germanic languages, so that **kar** gives us *harsh*, *hardy*, *hardware* and *hearth* … where coal is burned.

Kard, heart

The Indo-European term for the *heart*, **kard**, has its own basis in a wordless sound that meant to vibrate: **krr**, a root that is probably onomatopoeic. **Krr** sounds like the noise a taut rope makes when it is twanged. Stone Age man must have understood that the inner throb of the human *heartbeat* is the essence of life. Perhaps he also imagined, as medieval anatomists did, that the great blood-filled organ behind the ribs was held in place by tendons called *heart-strings*, and that we experienced emotions when these trembled and resonated.

The heart can signify six different things, according to the *OED*. It's the part of our internal anatomy, of course, that keeps the blood circulating – though as late as Tudor times, the heart could mean the stomach, because that was the body's largest organ. A *hearty* meal is a filling one. We still say, 'My heart was in my mouth' when we mean that our stomach gave a lurch. *Next the heart* meant 'on an empty stomach': in 1542, Erasmus recommended 'a newe founde diete, to drink wine in the morning nexte the *harte*' – clearly, Monty Python's 'Philosopher's Song', that claimed all the great thinkers had been notorious drunkards, was true.

The heart can also be 'the seat of feeling, understanding and thought', or anything that is central, such as the *Heart of England* – the euphemistic phrase coined by the UK Tourist Board for the West Midlands. It can be a term of endearment or praise: a favourite affectation of Noël Coward was to call his friends *dear heart*, while every self-respecting pirate called his crewmates *me hearties*.

The heart can be the essence, as in Graham Greene's *The Heart of the Matter*, in which the hero, a burned-out spy called Scobie, realises that if he could grasp the sheer *heartlessness* of God's scheme for the universe, the planets themselves would deserve pity (it's a wonderful novel, but not exactly *heart-warming*). And finally, a heart can be nothing but a shape, on a Valentine's message or a playing card. But playing cards aren't called 'cards' because some of them are hearts. The root to cards is **kar**, meaning hard, because card is stiff paper.

The Greek for heart was *kardia*, and hence *cardiography*, *cardiology* and all other kinds of *cardiac* medicine. The muscular substance of the heart is the *myocardium*. The two main arteries that carry blood to the brain are the *carotids*. Pressing on them can quickly cause blackouts, which is why the Greek for a stupor was *karos*. Oysters don't have hearts; their *cardines* are the hinges of their shells.

In Latin, the heart is *cor*, and so the centre of both an apple and the world is its *core*. Generous, warm people are *cordial*, but the wise and prudent are *cordate*. Anything heart-shaped is *cordiform*.

The French changed *cor* to *couer*, which gives us *courage*. *Take heart* means be brave. Richard the Lionheart spoke French, and so he was really Couer-de-Lion. *Encourage* and *discourage* are obvious developments, but so is *discord* – the arguments that ensue when not everyone is of one heart. The opposite is *concord*, a word that gave a name to the most elegant symbol of international *accord* ever designed … the supersonic airliner *Concorde*.

To *record* a detail is to write it on your heart, or memorise it. *Misericord* is heartfelt compassion, but an *accordion* is a squeeze-box that you hold across your chest as you play.

In a hunt, the heart of the prey is given to the dogs – that's why it is called the *quarry*.

The **krr** root could have spawned another word, **karn**, for meat, probably the bloody internal organs – giving us *carnage*, *carnivore*, *carcass*, *carrion* and *charnel house*. In Latin, the entrails are *corata*. Because *crows* are carrion birds, **krr** could be the origin of their name – though it might also be an imitation of their caw-caw call. Either way, *cormorant* means *sea-crow*. *Carnal* means fleshy, even though it's mainly used now in a sexual sense, as in *carnal desires*. *Carnival*, the festival of flesh, was originally a binge before the forty days' fasting of Lent, leading up to Easter. And Easter signifies *reincarnation* – coming back in the flesh.

Carmine is crimson, and a *carnation* is flesh-coloured, while *incarnadine* means dyed *scarlet*. This may well be why *cardinals* in the Vatican wear red.

Kas, cut

Alessandro Moreschi was the only classical *castrato* ever to be recorded. The Italian soprano, born near Frascati south-east of Rome in 1858, was castrated aged seven when his parents realised he possessed a fine voice: for a boy from a poor family, this was one of the few hopes for a lucrative career of any kind. In his teens, Alessandro became a star, dubbed the Angel of Rome, and was the First Soprano in the Sistine Chapel choir for thirty years. He was famous for the emotion rather than the purity of his tone, and the way he made every note sob.

Alessandro enjoyed fame. 'He paraded himself among the crowd like a peacock,' wrote one contemporary, 'with a long, white scarf, to be congratulated.' But before he was fifty, his career was over: the new Pope Pius X decreed that all church sopranos must be boys.

Most boys would prefer to be playing conkers, with horse *chestnuts*, or *castaynes*. The Latin for chestnut is *castanea*, probably because a pair of conkers look like gelded testicles cut off in their prime (since **kas** is cut, *casnuts* or chestnuts means much the same thing). The pairs of wooden shells that Spanish dancers rattle are *castinettas* or *castanets*. They don't have to be *castaneous* – that is, chestnut-coloured.

In Ancient Rome, *castration* implied innocence, and so *castus* meant pure. The opposite, *incastus*, meant soiled or defiled; since the most common way for a young girl to have her *chastity* spoiled before marriage was with a member of her own family, *incastus* signified *incest*. To be *chaste* can mean virginal or merely celibate, or perhaps just decently monogamous.

Akaterina in Greek became *Catherine* in English: it means pure, and was the name of a saint from Alexandria who enraged the pagan Roman emperor Maxentius by converting his wife to Christianity. She was sentenced to death by the breaking-wheel – her body would be tied to a spiked cartwheel before she was bludgeoned to death with clubs as it spun around. As soon as she touched the wheel, though, it disintegrated, which tells you something either about the power of faith or the standard of fourth-century Roman workmanship. Maxentius, by now thoroughly disgruntled, had her beheaded. We remember her with the spinning firework called a *Catherine wheel*.

Chastening and *chastising* are two different things. The first is a purifying punishment, often delivered by God. The second is a stinging rebuke, frequently involving corporal punishment: it hurts, and it might bring about a sharp improvement in behaviour, but there's nothing cleansing or spiritual about it. *Castigation* is different again: it's just a good telling-off.

Castus could also mean conforming to religious rules and rites. It's the origin of *caste*, the Indian system of class that organised Hindu society in a pyramid of privilege, through the 'purity' of their bloodline: at the top, the Brahmins or spiritual aristocracy; below them, the ruling officer class of Kshatriyas; next, the middle class of merchants and officialdom called Vaisyas; under them, the working class called Sudras; and at the bottom, the Harijans, sometimes called Pariahs or Untouchables.

When words have been cut from a piece of text, a *caret* is inserted: this symbol ^ appears above the 6 on a standard keyboard. In Latin, *caret* literally means, 'It is missing'.

Roman military camps were entrenched, with ditches cut around them for fortification. These *castra* were the foundation of many English towns, including *Lancaster*, *Gloucester*, *Doncaster* and *Manchester*. A small *castrum* was a *castellum*, which gives us *castle* as well as *chateau*. The obsolete English word *castellan* is the governor of a castle, the *chatelain*; a *chatelaine* in English is a handy ring, worn at the waist, with all the items that a Victorian housekeeper might need – her keys, scissors, penknife and darning kit.

Castrum crossed into Arabic, and came back to Europe with the Moors, around the tenth century: *al-kasr* meant the castle, and in Spanish, and then English, it became *alcazar*, a fortified palace.

A beaver in Ancient Greece was a *kastor*, because of its incisors. By the time the word reached medieval France, it was any kind of rodent. The Greeks used a musk called *kastorion* to treat stomach pains; it was obtained from the dried pineal glands of beavers. These days, *castor oil* doesn't involve killing any semi-aquatic mammals – it's made from vegetable seeds.

None of these products of **kas** was nearly as important to the early farmers as their own *kasi*, or *cheese* – so named because it was milk you could cut. *Casein* is the basis of cheese, *caseation* is the conversion of diseased tissue into a cheesy substance and *cassata* is a Neapolitan ice cream that looks like soft cheese.

Ker, to turn

Two innovations enabled the first Indo-European speakers to spread their infectious language across the Old World. One is obvious, and the other seems equally basic now ... but was far from straightforward at the time. First, the domestication of horses brought mobility. Whole villages could load their goods onto pack animals and ride away to new settlements, astride a handy source of meat and milk. And then there was the invention of the wheel.

The trouble was that one wheel wasn't much use. Early farmers had been using sleds probably for thousands of years, loading them up and dragging them, or hitching them behind horses. Russian peasants used the same method of transport right up until the nineteenth century. Adding a wheel to a sled doesn't help: it turns it into a wheelbarrow, which is difficult to pull and heavy to push. It's also more prone to tipping than a sled.

The real genius of human history was the man (or woman) who invented the axle and, by connecting a pair of wheels, created the first *cart* – about 5,400 years ago. That brilliant concept spread so fast that archaeologists can't begin to guess where it began: evidence of the innovation has been found in southern Iraq and Denmark, Armenia and Austria, Ukraine, Poland and Turkey, all of it dating within a few centuries if not decades. All that seems certain is that this was the period when the Proto-Indo-European grammar and words really spread out.

The word for wheel was **kwel**, and the word for axle was **aks**, but the term that really caught on was the one that described what wheels on an axle did. They turned around, **ker**, in a *circle* – and they turned a sled into a *carriage*. A wheeled wagon was easier to haul, even when it was *carrying* much more weight. It could be loaded with mountains of *cargo* and still go *careering* along the track. Building *caravans* of wagons became a full-time job for some craftsmen – the *carpenters*, which literally means *cartwrights* or *cart-makers*. And if the turning wheels took a tribe to some region where the locals seemed less than pleased to see them, horse-drawn *chariots* were even more effective than cavalry for subduing the natives.

In medieval times, a *cark* was a load of between three and four hundredweight (15,250–20,300 kilos), though it came figuratively to mean a burden of worries. To *cark* a wagon was to load it; to *charge* it had the same meaning. That's why a warhorse and a big plate are both called a *charger*, because they carry a burden. These days, we charge our phones by loading them up with electricity, and charge our glasses with wine before a toast.

It wasn't only wheels that turned. A plough turned the soil, and in medieval times a *carucate* was as much land as could be tilled by one ploughman with a team of eight oxen in a year; the annual tax on that land was called *caruage*. In Wales, the little wheel-shaped boats that turn upon the water are *coracles*, from the Welsh *cwrwgl*; in Gaelic, the word is *currach*.

In the eighteenth century, a *caroome* or *caroon* was a licence from the Lord Mayor that let London tradesmen use a cart on the streets. A *carrack* was a sea-transporter.

In Latin, **ker** became *currere*, to run. That's the root of *current* and *recurrent*, *course* and *recourse*, *occur* and *recur*. To *concur* is to run together or agree; a *concourse* is an assembly place were everyone runs into each other; and *concursion* is rushing together. *Decurrent* means running down, *percurrent* means running through and *excurrent* means running out (while an *excursion* is just a run out in the country). *Cursory* means brief, at running speed. In *cursive* handwriting, the letters run into each other, as people do in a *corridor*. When a child runs to her mother, she wants *succour*, which originally was protection: *sub-cur*, to run under.

A *caricature* is a satirical drawing, loaded with meaning. *Circumlocution* is a round-about way of saying things. *Circum-navigation* is going by *carriole* or *caroche* or *corsair*, not to mention the *motor car*, right around the world. And that's before you take advantage of two-wheeled transport derived from the Greek word for a circle, *khukhlos* ... such as a *bicycle*. In fact, enough words spin off from **ker** to fill an *encyclopedia*.

Kiv, to lie down among friends

The most *civilised* thing in the world is a weekend lie-in, which is appropriate, becase sleep is the basis of *civilisation*. One of the oldest words in the Indo-European vocabulary is **ki**, which means to lie down to sleep. We hear echoes of it in *coma* and *cemetery*, the sleeping place of the dead. In the church, *cimelia* are treasures laid down in storage, and the *cimeliarch* is the archivist.

Because sleepers need peace, and don't make a lot of noise themselves, **ki** is also the root of *quiet* and *tranquil*, as well as *requiem*. *Quiescere* in Latin means to lie still and *quiescent*. It gives us *acquiesce*, meaning to lie down rather than fight. RIP doesn't stand for Rest in Peace but for *Requiescat in Pace* ... which does translate to rest in peace. *Quietus*, the Latin word for quiet, became *quei* in Old French. By the time it reached English, it was *coy*, meaning too shy to speak up. For 500 years, *quietus* in English has meant a peaceful release, either from debts or from life itself. To be let off your punishment was to be *quit* of it: quit originally meant freed or at liberty to leave, and *acquit* has a similar meaning now.

Early man could sleep safely only among friends. **Kiv** meant to lie down, or later to settle, in a place where people trusted and respected each other, where you could go to sleep without being afraid that you'd wake in the morning with your possessions stolen and your throat cut. That's still the definition of a civilised society.

A *kip* in Old English was a place for lying down but not sleeping, and certainly not a place to trust the inhabitants: it was a brothel. Its meaning in underworld slang changed, first to a lodging house and then to a bed, before it came full circle with its modern sense, a short sleep.

The Latin *civis* means *citizen*: a man's home, the place where he slept, was part of a community. It implies he is a peaceful fellow, a *civilian*. A *civil* person made a good citizen, and *civility* was politeness, decency, good manners; all the things that keeps existence bearable in a *city* – which is short for *civitatem*. It means *city-state*, a self-governing region with a town or *citadel* as its centre.

Nowadays, the *civil service* is the administrative arm of government, but the phrase was coined in 1785 for the non-military employees of the East India Company. This firm, the most powerful private business in history, was initially called the Governor and Company of Merchants of London Trading into the East Indies, and was given its charter by Elizabeth I in 1600. Set up to handle imports from China and India, it became the chief buyer of tea, silk, cotton, saltpetre (the chief ingredient of gunpowder) and opium; owned by private stockholders, its profits ran to billions. By the eighteenth century, it controlled India through its private armies, and kept control of the subcontinent for 100 years, until the Indian Mutiny of 1857. After the British government took over, India was run by the *Imperial Civil Service*: a staff of around 1,000 senior 'covenanters', almost all from wealthy British families, held sway over 300 million Indians. It was a far cry from *civicism*, the principle that all citizens share equal rights and duties.

In the Germanic languages, **kiv** became *hiv*, and *hivo* meant the man of the house, the husband. *Heim* was a house where a family lived – in English, *home* still has that sense. A thousand years ago, it was pronounced *ham*, and that word survives in hundreds of English placenames. *Hampstead*, for instance, simply means *homestead*, and *Hampton* was a town of homes. *Newham* was a new home, *Shoreham* was a home on the shore and so on: a millennium before postcodes and AA road maps, the average medieval town planner saw little need for great creativity in naming settlements.

Because *heim* was house, *Heinrich* meant ruler of the home. The English version is *Henry*. The Old French *hanter* meant to dwell in a place, and that's why ghosts that decide not to stay in the cemetery return to their old *haunts*.

Kru, gory

Our ancestors who developed the Indo-European tongue lived in a harsh climate and harsher times – arctic winds and sudden blizzards could freeze the land, and violence was commonplace. We know this, not from the archaeological remains, which are inconclusive, but from the language.

The multiple shades of meaning in the syllable **kru** are part of the proof: a word that starts by meaning bloody and gory, comes to mean vicious and then bitter, raw cold. And all those meanings are echoed in modern English **kru** words.

The obvious one is *cruel*, via the Latin *crudelis*: literally, it means delighting in blood. The Roman word for blood itself was *cruor*, and *cruentus* was bloody – the English spelling is *cruentous*, though it is a rarely used word. *Cruentation* is a medical term for the ooze of blood when a corpse is cut open. To start bleeding again is *recrudescence*. A *cruet* was originally a small bottle that held the wine that is changed to blood during Mass; it came to mean any vial, and then, somewhat parochially, a holder for salt or pepper.

The *crux* or *cross* was an instrument of torture and slow execution long before the *Crucifixion*. The first *crosses* were probably two tree trunks, lashed together in an X-shape: prisoners would be lashed upright with their arms and legs splayed, and they would die of thirst if the weight of their own bodies didn't suffocate them first. *Cruciation* is *excruciating* torment.

Anything *cross-shaped* is *cruciate* – it's *crucial* too, though that word usually means leading to a critical decision between two options. Anything branded with a cross is *crucigerous*, or *crouched*. *Crouchen*, the medieval word for bent double, gives us *crouching*.

In Old French, *crosier* meant a *cross-bearer*, but it became the name for a bishop's staff with its curlicued head. A shepherd's *crook* is a less exalted version. The word became less respectable still, because a *crooked man* would be lame and usually a beggar with a *crutch*, and a *crook* was a downright thief.

In French, *croc* was a hook, perhaps a weapon of bloodshed, and *crochet* was a little hook, like the ones used by needleworkers. *Croquet* is a game played with a hooked stick (or an upturned flamingo, if you're in Wonderland). When the French saw Native Americans playing a game that was like croquet with racquets, they called it *lacrosse*.

Crux in Spanish became *cruz*, so an evangelical war was a *crusade*.

A *crucibulum*, in medieval Latin, was a light burning before a *crucifix*. Often the flame burned in a bowl hanging by chains, and a *crucible* became any pot that could be heated until the contents melted or burned. Later, the Old English for all kinds of earthenware pot was *cruce*, which gives us *crockery*. An *old crock*, originally a cracked and battered dish, is now a broken-down motor car.

In Greek, *khreas* meant flesh – *creophagous* is another word for carnivorous. The *pancreas* is a major organ in the stomach: it was supposed to be able to digest 'all flesh', or *pan* + *khreas*. *Creosote* got its name because it was supposed to preserve flesh, though you'd be safer painting it over your garden fence than on a flitch of bacon.

Ku, to swell

Bronze Age cultures across Europe and Asia honoured their dead with elaborate tombs, sometimes single mounds but often in clusters. Many were used more as temples than family sepulchres: some were reopened on ceremonial dates for hundreds of years, new skeletons were interred and the bones of ancient ancestors taken out to be venerated. In Britain we call these tombs barrows or tumuli. On the central Asian steppes, they are called *kurgans*, and they are so numerous that some archaeologists have named their builders the *Kurgan* people.* They left nothing behind but these burial sites: the shape gives them their name, like swellings on the land – **ku** for kurgan.

Within the kurgan there is a *cave* or *cavity*. The Latin *cavus* means hollow, so to *excavate* is to hollow out a *cubby*-hole. A large underground vault is *cavernous*, but if a surface is pitted with minute *cavities* it is *cavernulous*. Animals with hollow horns such as goats and *cows* are *cavicorns*.

---

* These people later became the Scythians, from the root word **skeud**, to shoot. They were highly proficient with a bow and arrow from horseback. We'd call them the Archers. Trace the roots of English back far enough, and it turns out that our Indo-European heritage began with a prehistoric version of radio's favourite soap opera …

Curvus in Latin means bent or *curved*. In geometry, a *curve* is defined as the arc traced by a moving point that constantly veers away from a straight line. Einstein made geometry redundant when he proved that straight lines are curved too – everything is, even light, and space and time. Pop physicists on scientific TV shows usually explain this by describing space like a trampoline distorted by a heavy weight, which like most analogues spun by professors on television makes no sense at all when you stop to think about it; the trick, of course, is not to stop and think. Before Einstein, and before television, curves were easier to understand: the Victorians had the *curvograph* and the *curvilinead*, handy instrument for drawing *curvated* lines.

In the ancient world, when people stretched out on couches to talk or eat, their bodies were *curved*, because they reclined on one elbow. The Greek for elbow was *kubiton*. A *kubos* was a vertebra, one of the square bones in the back. That's where *cube* comes from – Rubik's Vertebra would probably not have been nearly so popular.

In Latin, *cubare* meant lying down, and a *concubina* was a woman who lay down with a man. *Incubara* meant lying down on top of something, which is what birds do to hatch their eggs. *Cubare* became *couver* in French and *cover* in English, as well as *covey*, which is a brood of newly hatched partridges.

An *incubus* was a demon believed in medieval times to lie on top of sleepers and squeeze the breath out of them – for most peasants, sharing your house with livestock and your bed with the whole family probably didn't help the respiration either. Much better if you have your own *cubiculum* or bedroom; these days, though, *cubicles* are used as changing rooms or workspaces, where sleeping is discouraged.

The word for lying down at the dining table, incidentally, is *accumbent*. To be *decumbent* is lying ill in bed, and simply to be flat on your back is *recumbent*. If duty lies heavy on you, it is *incumbent*, and if you give way under the weight, you *succumb*.

Problems that mount up are *cumulative*; they *accumulate*. A Roman *cumulus* was a heap, like a kurgan. If you want a heap of money, put a quid on a string of bets, gambling all the winnings each time: it's called an *accumulator*, though the *cumulation* of the venture will probably be that you lose your pound.

In Greek, anything swollen was *cyma* – such as a curved brass bell or *cymbal*. In medieval English, that was a *chimbe*; the word now is *chime*.

A hollow pot in Greek was *kumbos*; this extension of **ku** must be very old, because it's almost the same in Sanskrit – *humbos*. The 'k' has changed to 'h', which it also did in Germanic languages. *Curvus* became *hyf* in Old English: many *beehives* are just boxes now, but the traditional curved shape can still be found. *Hyf* is also related to the Old Norse *hufr*, which meant a ship's *hull*. If hull is a **ku** word, it is likely that *hole* and *hollow* are too.

Cupa in Latin was a tub or a cask, and that's why a barrel-maker is a *cooper*. With the 'k' sound changing again to 'h', he's a *hooper*, making *hoops*.

To *hop* is to leap up, making a curve through the air. The Old English *hopian* suggests a different sort of leap, when your spirits spring up – that feeling of *hope*.

Kwa, interrogative pronoun

I nvestigative journalism and poetry are rare bedfellows, but Rudyard Kipling brought them together: 'I keep six honest serving-men (they taught me all I knew); / Their names are *What* and *Why* and *When* / And *How* and *Where* and *Who*.' In fact, Kipling had just the one servant, doing many jobs: **kwa**, the word that starts every *question*. **Kwa** is *ubiquitous*. The first Indo-European speakers had several subtly different variations on the basic, all-purpose **kwa** (or as we'd say, *huh?*) – **kwoivos** was what, **kwaut** was *which*, etc. The 'k' sound vanished in later Germanic languages but was retained in Latin.

Kwa is the root of every *query* from a *quest* to a *questionnaire*. *Quotations*, *quizzes* and *inquisitions*, they are all **kwa** words. So is *quoth*, the archaic version of said. Quoth became *cwethan* in Old English, meaning to confirm something in precise language, particularly in a legal document such as a will – and so *becwethan* became *bequest*.

In Rome, a *quaestor* was a criminal lawyer, a sort of classical Perry Mason. When a Roman asked for something, he usually got it. *Conquirere* meant to seek and *acquire*, which gives us *conquer* and *conquest*. The *conquistadors* were explorers and mercenaries who claimed swathes of the New World for the Portuguese and Spanish empires. The European troops earned a reputation for ruthless slaughter, because they killed men in battle; the tradition among the Aztecs of Mexico, in contrast, was to take prisoners alive, to be human sacrifices. But the numbers who died in combat were trivial compared to the millions of native central and south Americans killed in epidemic waves of smallpox, measles and typhus, to which the indigenous people had no immunity.

Both Karl Marx and his fellow nineteenth-century economist Adam Smith regarded this genocide as the most colossal event in human history. Rock musician Neil Young must agree, because he wrote a sprawling epic of a song, describing the coming of the conquistadors: he called it 'Cortez the Killer', and live versions can stretch to twenty minutes or more. But other archaeological studies have shown that Mexico suffered years of drought before the invasion, and a home-grown plague was rife – cocoliztli fever, a viral haemorrhaging sickness spread by mice and rats. It had wiped out four-fifths of the population in some places before Pedro de Cieza de León,

Hernando Cortés and others set foot in the Americas. As always in history, a deeper *inquest* reveals hidden causes.

Exquirere meant to search out. In Pepys and Milton's time, *exquire* was a useful English word with a similar sense – to go out and look for something. It's sadly obsolete now, but there is a related word: the past tense in Latin was *exquisitus*, meaning something special that someone had taken the trouble to seek out. In English, *exquisite* can mean precious in every sense – so gorgeous, it's pretentious. *Exquisitism* is another word for dandy foppishness.

Quotare was the medieval Latin term for numbering (answering the interrogative 'how many?'); it gives us *quota*, *quotient* and *quotidian*, which means of an everyday character and thus ordinary.

Aesop, a Greek slave who lived 2,600 years ago, is attributed as the author of animal fables that might really have been told for many hundreds of years before he lived … assuming, of course, that he did live and that his own story isn't a fable itself. This is one of his briefest animal parables: a vixen with a newborn litter sneered at a lioness, 'Only one cub?' – and the lioness roared back, 'Only one – but he will rule as king!' Aesop was pointing out the importance of *quality* over *quantity*: the first word comes from *qualis*, which is Latin for 'what kind?', and the second from *quantus*, 'how big?'

Qualis is also the root of *qualify* and *disqualification*. *Quantus* gives us *quantify*, and *quantum*, a word for packets of subatomic energy: it's a completely misleading name, because *quanta*, according to *quantum theory*, have no bigness at all.

Anyone with constant *queries* can sound like a moaner, which might be why the Latin *queri* means to utter plaintive cries. *Querulous* is complaining, whining and whingeing; if you want to bicker about it, you can also say *querulent*, *querulental* and *querulential* – they all mean the same thing. But there's no point quarrelling about which is right: that would be sheer *querulity* (or *querulation*, or *querulosity*). *Quibble* if you must – that word comes from *quibus*, meaning from whom, as in 'from whom did you get this *questionable* information?' And if you can't answer, you're in a *quandary* ... which is not really a word at all but a Latin phrase, *quam dare* – literally, 'how much to give?' *Quasi*, meaning as it were, can be prefixed to almost any noun to make a sort-of-thing, a *quasi-thing*. It is also a condensed Latin phrase: *quam si*, as if.

Kwi, to live

To get the first fact over with *quickly*: *quick* doesn't only mean fast. Its original meaning was alive, and it's that sense which we invoke when we talk about being *cut to the quick* – right to the heart and down to the soul. The quick is also the tender skin at the base of the fingernail, the place where the cuticle stops and living flesh starts. In pregnancy, *quickening* is the stage when the unborn child first starts to kick.

'He shall come to judge the quick and the dead,' warns the Book of Common Prayer, and that implies that everyone, living and dead, will face the heavenly accounting procedures. The phrase became a favourite of cowboy pulp novelists, who took it to mean that there were two kinds of gunfighters ... Louis L'Amour, the biggest-selling Western writer ever (200 million copies and rising) named one of his novels *The Quick and the Dead*; it was also the title of a cowboy movie with Sharon Stone in 1996.

When a dry stream *quickened*, it began to flow; *quick* coals were burning; a quick mind was lively; a quick disposition was hasty and hot-tempered – and it was not until the mid-1500s that quick came to mean rapid or swift.

The greatest *quick-change* performer ever was Leopoldo

Fregoli, a Victorian music artiste who could swap costumes so fast that he had to allow journalists backstage to prove his act was not done with identical twins. He could run off one side of the stage in the rags of a street musician and, in the time it took him to emerge on the other side, be transformed into a drag act wearing full lace and bustle. A rare delusional condition called Fregoli syndrome is named after him: sufferers believe that various people are really one and the same, cunningly disguised.

In Latin, the 'w' sound is hardened, and **kwi** became 'vi'. *Vivus* meant life, and in Romance countries (that is, former Roman colonies where Latin was spoken) a shout of *viva* still means long live. *Viva voce* meant by word of mouth. Anything that can support life is *viable*. Living creatures can be nurtured in a *vivarium*, which nowadays are glass cases where colonies of fish or insects are bred for study. The Romans used *vivaria* to fatten up fish and fowl, right up to the moment when they landed fresh on the table.

Some snakes lay eggs; others give birth to live young, which is called *viviparation*. That's where *vipers* get their name from. Viper is also a name for the lowest kind of human being – but not because snakes crawl in the dust. And it's not a *vivid* allusion to the snake's poisonous fangs, or to the story of Adam and Eve. A viper was believed in the sixteenth century to be the most malignant of all creatures, because it was said to kill its own mother at birth by eating its way out of her body.

A *vivandier* makes his living selling *victuals* to the army. If he's a Shetlander, he might supply *vivda*, which is meat dried in the air without being salted; most Scots would prefer *vivers*, the dialect name for general provisions and eatables. However you label it, food is *vital*; we need it to *survive*. And if you're half dead, *aquae vitae*, the water of life (what the Scots call whisky), will *revive* you.

In Ancient Greece, **kwi** hardened to a 'guei' sound; *su-gueiyes* meant living well. The goddess of health was *Hygeia*, whose name itself is *hygienic*. She is usually depicted as a young woman with a live snake in one hand and a goblet in the other – sometimes the snake is drinking from the cup. Whether it's a viper, and whether it's whisky, the classicists cannot say.

Perhaps ironically, life is not derived from *vivus* but from the Germanic root *liv*, which comes from the Indo-European word **lip** – to be sticky. To the early farmers, life was something to cling to, like glue. Fat is also sticky, which is why *lipoma* are fatty tumours and *liposuction* is a quick way to lose weight by vacuuming fat away. Perhaps that's why diets never work for long – etymologically speaking, fat is a fact of life.

L

Lab, to hang down

Lip, label, labourer, astrolabe

Lag, to straggle

Linger, delay, leg, slake

Li, shiny and wet

Slick, polite, glue, petrol

Lubh, to love

Love, libido, leave, believe

Luh, to shine

Lunar, lucid, lustre, luxury

Lab, to hang down

In the Stone Age, **lab** meant pendulous or dangling, like the *lobe* of an ear. Today, a *lab* is a place of scientific research and experiment. It's the same spelling, but the two words couldn't seem more different ... except that one leads directly to the other.

That early sense of something hanging down lingers in *dewlap*, the farmer's term for the *flap* of loose skin drooping at the throat of cattle. Animals *lap* water with their tongues hanging out. Flames that lick over a log are *lambent*.

In medieval times, to *lap* a baby was to swaddle it in folds of cloth, and we still talk of being in the *lap of luxury* – it suggests swathes of satin and silk. An object that partly lies on top of another is *overlapping* it. In early English, the skirts of a dress or coat, the hemmed part that hung low, was the *lap* or *lappet*; it could also be the hanging part of an apron, covering the upper legs – the part of the body we now call the *lap*.

In motor racing, the drivers *loop* round and round the track, doing *laps* – going over and over the same ground, as if over-lapping it.

We imagine that *lip-studs* are a recent fashion, but the Victorians had a word for them: *labret*. Reports of African women who distended their upper lips by inserting plates were sent back to England by the explorer Dr David Livingstone. He met the Makololo tribe of Malawi and asked a tribal chieftain why they did this. The chief replied: 'For beauty! They are the only beautiful things women have. Men have beards, women have none.'

A *label* is a piece of cloth or paper that hangs down, like the brown paper ticket tied to Paddington Bear's duffle coat when he arrived from Peru in England: it said, 'Please look after this bear.' A *labial*, on the other hand, is a sound made with the *lips*, like 'm' or 'p'. And a *laburnum* is a tree that is festooned in spring with hanging garlands of yellow flowers.

But by far the most important **lab** word is a Roman word that describes what hard work looks like – a man bent forwards under the burden of a sack or a hod of bricks across his shoulder. *Labor* means a heavy weight, and *laborare* means to do hard labour. The place of work is, in medieval Latin, a *laboratorium*.

It's been a *laborious* journey, but we got there: a *laboratory*, or *lab* for short, is a **lab** word.

Working together is *collaboration*, and any plan worked out in detail must be *elaborate*. *Lapse* is a related word: it comes from *lapsus*, a stumble, a falling down. That gives us *elapse* (to slip away), *relapse* (to slip back), *collapse* (to slip down) and *prolapse* (to slip forward). It is also the root of *labile*, meaning unstable.

Labradors are a breed of Newfoundland dog, from the north-east part of Canada called *Labrador*. According to the master etymologist Eric Partridge, the region was named in 1500 when the Portuguese explorers took a shipload of Inuit people prisoner and carried them back to Europe as *forced labour*. The frozen country they came from became known as *Terra del Laboratores*, the land of the slave workers.

The early French word *lamper* meant to *lap up* ale, and so *lampons* was a toast, meaning let us drink. English took the word *lampon* to be a coarse drinking song, the kind soldiers sing about the enemy or their own generals. Lampons were usually scurrilous and satirical – *lampoon* now means any kind of mockery and send-up.

Astrolabes were invented around 150 BC, probably by the Greek mathematician Hipparchus of Nicaea, who invented trigonometry. The earliest were tools to track the movement of the planets; as they became more sophisticated, astrolabes could be used to calculate the time at different latitudes, discover the direction of Mecca and compile astrological charts. A pointer or label hangs over the rim or the device, to indicate the exact reading.

Geoffrey Chaucer's essay *A Treatise on the Astrolabe*, written in the late 1300s, is regarded as the first scientific work in English.

The orloj or astronomical clock in Prague's Old Town Square features a fantastically ornate astrolabe, made in 1490. Every hour, the skeletal figure of Death turns an hourglass and tugs a rope, the signal for the chimes and a procession of the Apostles. The dials of the clock tell the date and reveal where the sun and moon are in the star signs. It was the clockmaker Jan Ruze's masterpiece – after it was finished, Prague's guildsmen and town councillors were so jealously proud of their mechanical marvel that they had Ruze blinded, to make sure he could never build another. Ruze took his revenge … he crept inside the clocktower with a hammer and smashed the workings. It was a hundred years before anyone could be found to repair it.

'*Dignus est operarius mercede sua,*' as the New Testament says – 'the *labourer* is worthy of his hire'.

Lag, to straggle

In northern England before the Second World War, children taking turns at games often picked who would go first, second and last with a playground chant: 'Fog, Seg, *Lag!*' It sounds Norse, but the root of the words is much older than that. **Lag** was the Stone Age word for the last one home, the straggler at the back.

Lag still has that meaning, to fall behind. It also means a convict, but in the nineteenth century the definition was more specific: a *lag* was a prisoner facing transportation to the colonies aboard a *lag ship*, which was the penalty for stealing. Five hundred years earlier, *lagging* was standard English for theft, though the word has been obsolete for so long that it does not even appear in the *OED*. The double meaning was originally ironic – if a sheep, for instance, didn't come home with the flock, and its theft could not be proven, the shepherd might say heavily that it was lagging.

It is likely that *leg* comes from **lag**, probably because a lame animal, lagging behind, would limp or drag its leg.

The word must also be closely related to the Old English *laet*, meaning slow, sluggish and tardy. That became *late* and *lately*. To be more late is *later*, and then *latest*. In medieval English, latest was pronounced *latst*, and turned into *last*.

The Latin *lassus* also seems linked – it means ready to collapse, exhausted and faint, and it gives us *lassitude*, a world-weary absence of enthusiasm. The Old French, *ah lassus*, meaning 'I am worn out', became *alas* in English.

Delay comes about from lagging: it is caused 'of lag' or, in French, *de* + *lag*. A *relay*, where the baton is passed by the hindmost runner to the next, shares the root.

Because straggling animals were prone to getting lost, if not stolen, they might be roped together. In Latin, *laxa* was a thong or a noose, and *laxare* was to loosen or *slacken* a bond. By the time it reached French a thousand years later, it was *laisser*, to allow – it gives us *lease*, a legal permit. To *release* an animal is to slip it off its *leash*.

Lax can also mean loose or *slack*; *laxity* is the opposite of moral and physical rigour, and *laches* is culpable negligence. A *laxative* loosens the bowels, though in the seventeenth century it could also ease emotional constipation and encourage conversation, as alcohol does – playwright Ben Jonson admired good talkers, 'Fellowes of practis'd, and most laxative tongues'. A drink or two helps us *relax*. To slacken off a thirst is to *slake* it.

Lasche in Old French survives in English as a dialect word – *lash* is soft and wet. Blend lash with luxuriant and you get *lush*, which used to mean verdant and is current slang for really good.

In Greek, the prefix *lago-* meant drooping. Rabbits and other *lagomorphs* have floppy ears.

When **lag** has a nasal twang, it becomes *lang*, which gives us *languish* and *languid*. The Old English *lange* is the source of *long*, with the sense that a laggard is a long way behind. *Andlang*, another word dating back to Saxon times, became *along*. Long becomes *lengthen*, following the same grammatical quirk that turns strong into strengthen.

A *lance* is a long weapon. A *lunge* is a long thrust. An *oblong* is an elongated square. To *linger* is to hang around, not leaving. To *indulge* is to tolerate or enjoy someone or something for a long while.

To *lounge* is to move without urgency, from the medieval French *longis*, a man of slow movements. A lounge used to mean a saunter or a stroll, but by the eighteenth century it was a room with *loungers* or easy chairs, where people could recline as they talked, especially in a clubhouse or hotel. As the middle classes grew, it became the elegant term for a sitting room at home.

The idea that lagging was a euphemism for cattle-rustling and other animal thefts came round again in medieval France. *Purloigner* meant to slow things down or *prolong* them – *pro + long* was to place at a distance. The sense developed, of course, that this was exactly what an *old lag* did for a living: he helped himself to somebody else's property and retired with it to a safe distance. And that's how we get *purloin*.

Li, shiny and wet

The shiny, wet dew on a dawn meadow is summed up in the syllable **li** – the Greek word for that morning phenomenon was *leimon*. Or perhaps it was the *slick*, *slippery* mud on the banks of a tidal river – the Latin word is *limus*. It might even have been the silvery trail of a snail, or *leimax* in Greek. But the most useful kind of **li** to Neolithic hunters was the sap that oozed from trees. It could be spread on twigs to snare thrushes and sparrows – *birdlime*.

In Old English, *liman* meant to stick and *geliman* was to stick together – which became *glue*. If you're *gluten* intolerant, that's where the problem started, etymologically. *Glutinous* means sticky, and *deglutination* is a messy word for unsticking things.

A floor covering patented in 1860 by Frederick Walton in Staines, Middlesex, made from canvas coated with *linseed* oil, was trade-named *Linoleum*, which got trimmed down to *lino*. That doesn't come from the Latin *linere*, to smear, but from the source of linseeds – flax, or *linum*. Flax also gives us *linen*.

Middle Eastern *oil* came from *olives* long before the *oil wells* were discovered: the Latin for an *olive tree* was *olea*, which gives us *oleaginous* or *oily*. *Petrol* is also a **li** word: it is *petra + oleum*, rock and oil.

Etymologists argue about the origin of *letters*. Some trace the word to the past tense of *linere*, which is *litus* – meaning smeared, or perhaps scrawled. If that's right, *literature*, *alliteration* and *illiteracy* are all literally **li** words. When the first Greek scribes began to scratch words on slate with a stylus, their mistakes could easily be *obliterated* with a trickle of water – they were *deleted*.

In northern Europe, an 's' was prefixed to lime, to make *slime*. It also became *sleek*, *slither*, *slink*, *slide* and *slice* – all words that describe different kinds of *slipping*.

The origin of *slight* is the early Dutch *slicht*, a level plain – the Netherlands were full of mud flats. It acquired a sense of being *slightly* inclined, and thus became anything that was nearly-but-not-quite.

The wettest **li** is *liquid*. In Latin there are three forms: *liqui* means to flow; *liquere* to be liquid or, by extension, clear; and *liquare* means to filter or melt. The first gives us *liquor* – or, if your preferred *libation* is a crème de menthe to a whisky on the rocks, *liqueur*. Flowing speech is *prolix* or verbose. The second gives us *liquidation* and *liquidity*, and the third *deliquesce*, meaning to dissolve into liquid, and also *dilute*.

By adding a gutteral sound to **li**, early Indo-European speakers made **ligh**, which meant then what it means today – to *lick*, or make wet with the tongue. A smooth-tongued figure of speech is *litotes*, which is a downbeat way of giving upbeat praise – using a double negative to state a positive: 'That isn't a bad idea, and you're not as stupid as you look!'

When good manners are polished to a high shine, they become *polite*. *Politeness* has nothing to do with politics or the police, obviously – they both stem from *polis*, the Latin for a city.

Think of the Victorian city and you're in *Limehouse*, the dockside streets of London's East End, where the Regent's Canal feeds into the Thames. It's in Limehouse that Lizzie Hexam and her father Gaffer go trawling the river for the bodies of drowned suicides, in Dickens's *Our Mutual Friend*, and that supervillain Fu Manchu had his hideout in an opium den in the novels by Sax Rohmer. It wasn't only the centre of the nineteenth-century drugs trade in Britain; the first cholera epidemic in London took hold here too, brought by sailors from Hamburg in the early 1830s. Eight hundred people died in the initial outbreak. The district takes its name from the oasts where *lime* for the building trade was dried during the fifteenth century and later.

David Lloyd George was Chancellor of the Exchequer in 1909 when he made a tub-thumping, rabble-rousing speech in Limehouse – and that kind of populist, crowd-pleasing oratory is still called *Limehousing*. Lloyd George, after all, was a very slick politician.

Lubh, to love

O ne of the songwriting hooks that made The Beatles so successful was their trick of using pronouns in titles: they made their songs sound personal. 'From Me to You', 'Please Please Me', 'I Wanna Hold Your Hand' … 'All our early songs always had this very personal thing,' Paul McCartney once said to a newspaper. And it wasn't just the early hits – the last song the band recorded was George Harrison's 'I Me Mine'.

But even more pervasive than pronouns is a word that hasn't changed in 8,000 years – *love*. The Beatles had US number ones with 'She Loves You', 'Love Me Do', 'Can't Buy Me Love' and 'All You Need Is Love', and McCartney had more with 'My Love' and 'Silly Love Songs'. In fact, in the past seventy years, from Benny Goodman's 'Taking a Chance on Love' to Rihanna's 'We Found Love' and beyond, there have been more than 120 American chart-toppers with 'love' in the title. It's the most powerful word in pop.

In medieval English a *loveday*, or *dies amoris* in Latin, was a counselling session, a meeting to find an amicable end to a quarrel. Margaret of Anjou, the wife of Henry VI, staved off civil war in 1458 by staging a mass loveday in London, when the sons of noblemen killed in the Battle of St Albans three years earlier walked arm in arm to St Paul's Cathedral in procession behind the king – a very public reconciliation.

A *love-apple* is a Tudor name for the tomato; in German the equivalent *Liebesapfel* is a toffee apple. *Lovelocks* were sported by courtiers in Elizabethan England – one curled tress, much longer than all the rest, draped over the shoulder. Shakespeare is supposed to have worn one. These days, *love locks* are a menace – instead of carving their initials on a tree, couples scrawl them on a padlock and hook it onto railings, especially on bridges, before throwing away the key. The Pont des Arts over the Seine is buckling under the weight of countless thousands of love locks, and in Rome police will fine young *lovers* on the spot for vandalism if they add to the glut of padlocks on the Ponte Milvio.

The Latin for desire is *libet*, which is not the root of liberty – that comes from **liv**, to grow. Libertine, though it now means a debauchee with depraved sexual desires, originally meant a freed slave: it stems from **liv** too. But *libidinist* is a **lubh** word, meaning a lecher. *Libido* is a word coined in 1912 by Carl Jung, to mean sexual energy: it's Latin for lust, and *libininous* has meant lustful and lewd since medieval times. Lust isn't a **lubh** word either: it stems from **las**, eager. And lecher comes from **ligh**, to lick, and literally means a licker – which makes lecherous old men sound even more horrible.

No, **lubh** isn't related to the coarser, more wanton words; its etymological descendents are far subtler. In Old English, *leof* meant dear or pleasing, and became *lief* – now an archaic word, though its meaning is still understood: 'I'd *lief as not* do that' is a pompous way of saying 'I would rather not'. Another little-used word is *livelong*, as in *the livelong day*: it has nothing to do with long life, and simply means very long. A *leofman* in Old English was a suitor: it became *leman*, or lover. The word is forgotten now, but it suggests that Hercule Poirot's devoted secretary *Miss Lemon* was not a sour old spinster but a would-be paramour.

Leaf in Old English meant permission, especially to depart or be absent – now we spell it *leave*. Being *absent without leave* is still a court-martial offence in the Forces; much safer to get an official *furlough*.

Logically, *relieve* ought to be spelled *releave*: it means allowing someone to leave, by taking their place.

The German for permission is *Verlaub*, which literally means through kindness. And the German *glauben* means *belief*, a word that in Middle English was spelled *bileafe* – it means by kindness or, more loosely transliterated, God willing. A thousand years ago, belief was not blind faith but a hope.

So when Doris Day had a hit in the mid-1950s with a jazz standard whose lyric was by Gus Kahn, she thought her ultimatum to her lover was a straight choice ... but it turns out to be three variations on **lubh**: '*Love* me or *leave* me / Or let me be lonely / You won't *believe* me, I love you only'!

Luh, to shine

Neolithic farmers had many words for *light*. There was **bhal**, the blazing brilliance of the sun; **arg**, the shimmering reflection of sunshine on metal; and **diw**, the dazzle of daylight. And then there was the *luminous* intensity of the full moon – **luh**.

Luh is an unearthly radiance. The brightness of the moon is exaggerated by the black of the night sky, and most **luh** words convey that sense of a light in the darkness. In Sanskrit, *loka* means the vast unseen depths of the universe, and *lokaloka* are the mountains at the end of the world.

Luna was the Roman name for the moon (in Greek it was *Selene* – *selenotropic* plants turn towards the moon, and *selenites* are the moon's mythical inhabitants). *Lunacy* was intermittent insanity, attributed to the *lunar* phases. A *lunette* was a horseshoe for the tip of the hooves, shaped like a crescent moon; it was also the semi-circular groove for the victim's neck in the block of a guillotine.

Lux is Latin for light, directly from the root word **luh**, and a *lucifer match* (a wooden taper tipped in combustible chemicals and invented around 1830) is literally a *light-bearer*: *lux* + *fer* (see **bher**). *Lucifer* was poet Geoffrey Chaucer's name for Venus, the 'morning star'; in ecclesiastical Latin, around the fifteenth century, it became a synonym for Satan. The rebel archangel was said to be the brightest light in the heavens before his fall from grace. It's probable that the Norse fiend and trickster *Loki* is so named because he was originally the god of fire. Other **luh** names, like *Lucy* and *Luke* and *Lucian*, don't have such diabolical connotations – the Roman goddess of childbirth was *Lucina*, because she brought children into the light.

Lucifugous means shunning the light, like a vampire. *Luciferous* is another word for *illuminating*.

To shine was *lucere* in Latin, the root of *lucid*, which means resplendently clear. Before the introduction of modern psychology, when *lunatic* was a catch-all for diverse mental illnesses, the term *lucid intervals* referred to periods of respite. To *elucidate* is to make a thing clear by directing a light onto it.

Lucent, a 500-year-old English word, means shining: a bright light shines right through a *translucent* surface. A *lucarne window* is a skylight. A *lucernal* microscope has a light glowing beneath the glass slides. Incidentally, glow-worm, in the Provençal dialect of Occitan spoken in southern France, is a *luzerno*.

Luculent means full of light – it is usually applied to writing, especially dazzling or brilliant passages. *Lucubration*, which literally means to work by artificial light, is long and laborious study – burning the midnight oil. A *lucubrator* is a nocturnal student.

All that *illustrates* how **luh** lights up the language. It's easy to see how it became *lustre*, which is the sheen of reflected light, and *lustrous*, which means burnished. *Lustring* or *lustrine* is a glossy silk fabric.

The word *illustrious* implies that the famous are beacons in the community – they are its *luminaries*, its leading lights. And **luh** also gives us *luxury*, the kind of world in which those luminaries live. *Luxus* in Latin meant shiny, probably in the same sense that we'd say flashy. The plural *luxaria* became *luxuriance*, and *luxurious*. Wallowing in *luxuries* is *luxuriety*, and a sybarite addicted to *luxuriation* is a *luxurist*. Licinius *Lucullus* was just such a man: a fabulous rich Roman, who was famous for the splendour of his banquets; his private bath-houses, meanwhile, were notorious for their orgies. A particularly rare black stone he favoured in his huge villa, which was raised on stilts above the Bay of Naples, is still called *Lucullean marble*. *Deluxe* was originally French, *de* + *luxe*, the height 'of luxury'.

In Greek, *leukos* meant bright, and then white. *Leukaemia* means white blood, because it causes an excess of white corpuscles. A *leukaethiop* was a quasi-scientific term invented in 1819 for an albino black African, a 'white Ethiope' – though 'albino' was shorter, easier to spell and had been coined at least forty years earlier. *Leucosis* is a disease where some parts of the body appear bleached, and *leucous* just means blondes ... though *Gentlemen Prefer Leucouses* is a rotten name for a movie.

M

Ma, mother
Married, mammoth, Amazon, metro

Mag, mighty
Magnificent, maximum, mayor, omega

Mal, dirty
Malign, malaria, melancholy, small

Mei, to smile
Smirk, besmirch, miracle, marvellous

Men, to think
Mental, memory, monster, comment

Mor, to grieve
Mourn, mortal, murder, mortgage

Min, little
Minus, mite, mistake, minstrel

Ma, mother

If this book arrived from *Amazon*, be grateful it was only the postman who brought it. A visit from the warrior women dubbed *Amazonides* by the Ancient Greeks was a terrifying business, whether it was plunder they wanted or something else. Three thousand years ago, this all-female tribe that farmed and hunted on the banks of the Thermodon, in modern-day Ukraine, went annually in search of men. Some they enslaved, but most they bedded and, quite often, killed. The morning after the night before could be a nasty business with an *Amazonian* girlfriend. When their babies were born, all the boys were strangled; the girls were taught to read, plough and fight, and when they reached puberty their right breasts were burned off, the better to hurl a javelin or fire a bow. That's why the Greeks called them *a-mazos*, meaning without a breast.

In 1542 AD, the conquistador Francisco de Orellana was exploring the rainforests of Brazil when he was attacked by a party of long-haired, bow-wielding natives ululating in high-pitched shrieks. He escaped, but by the time he returned to Spain, the tale had grown; Orellana's stories usually did, since a good yarn helped him secure investment for future expeditions. He told the Spanish emperor Charles V that the South American jungle was ruled by warrior women ... and that's why the river and the 5.5m square kilometres (2.1 square miles) of forest surrounding it are known as *Amazonia*. Nearly half a millennium later, a Seattle businessman launched an online shop from his garage, and because he wanted a brand name that began with an 'A' and sounded big, he called it Amazon.

Ma meant *mother* 8,000 years ago, because the sound evoked a baby's cry. Both the Romans and the Greeks called their mothers *mamma*; the English upper classes say *mama*, the French say *maman* and the Irish get back to basics with *ma*. An Indian wet nurse is an *amah*.

Prehistoric man regarded the sky as father of humankind and the earth as mother. The Tatars, a nomadic people who have lived north of the Black Sea for at least 1,500 years, call the earth *mama*. Sometimes they dug up skeletons or even whole corpses, preserved in peat or permafrost, of huge creatures that they called *mammonts* – 'the monsters that burrow in the earth'. French explorers misheard the word, and that's where *mammoths* came from.

The Ancient Greek for mother is *meter*, and the mother city Athens was their *metropolis*. A *metroscope* was a tool for listening to a child in the womb; a *metrotome* was a surgical tool used in Caesarian sections. Anything to do with the *metropole* was naturally *metropolitan*, including a city's underground railway or *Metro*.

In Latin, *mater* is mother, but not all mothers – only the kindly, nurturing, *maternal* types. All *mammals* suckle their young, but *motherhood* is more complicated for human females: first comes *matrimony*, next the *marital* bed and then the *maternity* dress, as a baby grows in the *matrix* or womb. A *married* woman with experience of childbirth is a *matron*. To *matriculate* usually means to have your name inserted in the rolls of your college or *alma mater*, but *matriculation* can also mean to adopt a child.

To the Greeks, *Mother Nature* was Demeter; at her annual festival it was the custom for her devotees to whip themselves with the bark of trees. The bark was symbolic of how the life force, anchored in the trunk of the tree, reached out every spring through the branches and twigs to its tips, and put out buds. The tree is the mother of its own leaves – the *mater* and the *material*. All life, according to the *materialist* viewpoint, is merely *matter*. Anything *immaterial*, of course, doesn't matter.

The Roman word for wood is *materia*. In Portuguese, the word is similar but slightly more nasal, which is why the thickly wooded archipelago of islands north of Tenerife, and the sweet strong wine that is casked there, are called *Madeira*.

Mother's ruin, in the nineteenth century, was gin, whereas *mother's milk* was brandy. *Mother's blessing* was laudanum, a mixture of brandy and tincture of opium. In the 1960s, *mother's little helper* was the tranquiliser Miltown, a dangerously addictive muscle relaxant, or perhaps the sedative Valium ... as well as the title of a top-ten hit in 1966 for the Rolling Stones.

Mag, mighty

What do Sultan Suleiman the *Magnificent, Maharaja* Ranjit Singh, the Pope and *Mahatma* Gandhi all have in common? The splendour of all their titles is rooted in a prehistoric syllable signifying greatness: **mag**.

Magnificent means doer of great things, a soubriquet the *mighty* Suleiman earned by conquering half of Europe and leading the Ottoman army to the gates of Vienna in 1529, when he was thirty-five years old. He married a concubine from his harem, a slave girl called Roxelana from Ukraine, and wrote passionate poetry to her: 'My woman of the beautiful hair, my love of the slanted brow, my love of eyes full of mischief, I'll sing your praises always.'

Maharaja means great king, and though Ranjit Singh was blind in one eye from smallpox, he conquered the Punjab, seized the Khyber Pass and defeated the Afghan army in the early 1800s. He owned the largest diamond in the world, the Koh-i-Noor or Mountain of Light; after Singh's death, when his Sikh Empire was broken up in 1849, the stone became part of Queen Victoria's crown jewels.

The Pope is *Pontifex Maximus*, which translates roughly as the great bridge-builder. The title goes back to the Roman republic, when it was the high priest's role to keep the peace between men and the gods; Augustus arrogated it when he became emperor, and though it is not one of the Pope's official titles, it has been adopted by the Vatican since Leo I in the fifth century. Pope Benedict XVI uses @pontifex as his Twitter handle, encouraging his 4 million followers to tweet the hashtag #askpontifex.

Mahatma means great soul in Sanskrit. The title was conferred on Mohandas Karamchand Gandhi by the Indian poet and Nobel laureate Rabindranath Tagore: 'The Great Soul in beggar's garb,' Tagore called him, because the guru of non-violent protest wore only a dhoti or cotton robe that he had woven himself. President Barack Obama has named Gandhi as his ideal dinner guest, possibly forgetting that the Mahatma, even when he wasn't fasting or hunger-striking, was a strict vegetarian.

In Rome, the aristocracy were *magnates*, a word that is unchanged in English. So is *magnum*, meaning large, though handguns and champagne weren't invented in Caesar's era. *Magnus* is Latin for great, though when it is paired with a feminine noun (such as *carta* or charter), it becomes *magna*. *Maior* means greater, which is why the largest of the Balearic Islands is *Majorca* and the most important man on the town council (in his own estimation, at least) is the *mayor*. His good lady wife might not be pleased to hear that *maiorissa*, or *mayoress*, originally meant chief of the female slaves. That title lacks a certain *majesty*.

Greatest of all is *maximum*. The most important sound bite in a Roman speech was the *maxima sententia*, which gives us *maxim*.

A Roman teacher was *magister*, which not only becomes *magistrate* but also *master* and *mister*, as well as *mistral* – the dominant wind.

In early German languages, the hard 'g' of **mag** became more gutteral and turned into *much*. The Scots word *muckle*, meaning a lot, shares the same root: it's the opposite of mickle, a little.

Magniloquence is lofty, pompous language. A *magnality* is a great and marvellous event, while *magic* is the wonders performed by *magi*, *archimages* and other sages of great wisdom.

In Greek, *megas* was great. In the Greek alphabet, the big 'O' was *omega* and the little 'o' was omicron. (That big 'O' was millenia before the *magisterial* Roy 'Big O' Orbison and his pop *masterpieces*, 'Crying' and 'Oh, Pretty Woman').

Countless macrocosms can be crammed into one *megacosm*. *Megalomania* is power-crazed insanity, which sounds very grand – that is, to use a word coined by Percy Bysshe Shelley in 1819, it is *megalophonous*. A *megascope* was a Victorian *magic lantern* that threw a *magnified* image onto a screen. The *megatherium* and the *megalosaur*, a sloth and a dinosaur, are both extinct, but you can still find *megapodes* in Australia; they are chicken-like birds that build mounds to nest upon.

In Old French, *magnus* became *magne*, meaning chief or most important; in Old English it was *maegen*, before the 'g' was softened, and then dropped out altogether, becoming *main*, the largest part. The main can be land or sea – the biggest islands of Shetland and the Orkneys are both called *Mainland*, and the coast of the Caribbean was the *Spanish Main*.

Mal, dirty

Moral complexities in the Stone Age could be summed up in three letters: **mal**. The early farmers understood that diseases sprang up where there was stagnant water and foul air, and death came to houses that lacked basic hygiene. Human and animal ordure spread death. Disease was bad, and thus it was bad to be filthy: sin and dirt were synonymous. The first moral laws were really rules on cleanliness.

From the start, the idea existed that dirt was spiritual as well as physical. Living in a midden could make people sick, but so could disobedience and dishonesty. **Mal** describes different kinds of evil in different European languages: in Lithuanian, *melas* is a lie; in Greek, *meleos* is vanity; in Latvian, *maldit* is to take the wrong path; and in Ancient Irish, *maldacht* is a curse – or in English, a *malediction* or *malison*.

In Old French, *meller* was a crude and critical word for copulation and similar dirty behaviour. It probably gives us *pell mell* – to go at it fast and hectic. *Meller* later became any physical altercation, or *melee*. Then it became *melange*, and also *mesler*, which in English turned into *meddling*.

To early farmers, runts and underfed animals were no good at market. *Es mal*, meaning it is bad, became *small* – the word was soon applied to anything of little worth. In Ancient Greece, sheep and goats were *melon*, because they were smaller than cattle.

The Latin *malus* is bad or wicked. Many early French words used *mal-* as a prefix, such as *maladie*, which was *mal + habere*, literally to have badness, and so sickness or a *malady*.

Maleficent means doing bad, and *maledicent* is speaking evil; *malengin* is deceit and spiteful machinations, and a *malversion* is corrupt government or *malpractice* in high places, which can lead to a *maletoit* or unjust tax.

Worse even than taxes is *malaria*, so called because it was believed to be caused by bad air. There was nothing *malign* about this: it was just a *mal-entendu*, a misunderstanding. *Malignity* can be a disease, especially a tumour, or a special loathing for another person, wishing harm upon them so fervently and persistently that the *malevolent* thoughts turn inwards and wreak havoc.

Maladroit means thoroughly awkward and clumsy; if you're only slightly clumsy, though, the word is *maladresse*, which is just tactlessness. To do something at the wrong moment is to be *malapropos*, which gave eighteenth-century playwright Richard Brinsley Sheridan the name for his most famous character, *Mrs Malaprop*, who was always muddling her words: '... promise to forget this fellow,' she ordered her love-lorn niece, Lydia Languish, 'to illiterate him, I say, quite from your memory.'

That's a *malapropism*; a *malapert*, on the other hand, is a presumptuous or saucy person, or just plain impudence. A nasty nature is *maltalent*. If you're having a bad day, that's *dismal*, which stems from *dies*, the Latin for day. Sea sickness is *mal de mer*. Soldiers and sailors who feigned *malaise* were *malingering*.

In Sanskrit, *malinas* was filthy and *mlanas* was black. The word was similar in Ancient Greece, where *melas* meant black, the colour of dirt. *Melancholy* is a dark mood, and a *melanoma* is a black cancer.

But not all *mel* words are medical. *Melanic* or *melanochroi* means having black hair and a dark complexion, and *melanocomous* is simply black-haired. One of the nicknames of the Greek demi-god Hercules was *Melampyges*, or Black-arse, because one night he was robbed in his sleep by a pair of *malicious* gnomes called the Cercopes. Hercules caught them, trussed them and hung them by the feet from the tips of his bow, which he slung across his shoulders. Bouncing along upside down, the Cercopes could see up the hero's loincloth, and spotted that his backside was covered in matted dark hair. They started mocking him, and the name Melampyges made him laugh so much that he had to put them down and let them go. His father Zeus was slightly less amused at their antics, and turned them into monkeys.

Mei, to smile

The *smile* is a universal gesture. Everyone recognises it, all over the world, even members of tribes in the Amazon rainforest or the Andaman Islands who have never made direct contact with the outside world. Explorers who encountered unknown peoples in Papua New Guinea in the 1950s discovered that smiles were immediately recognised.

(Laughter, on the other hand, meant something different to New Guinea tribesmen. A fatal sickness called *kuru*, whose symptoms included uncontrollable hysterical laughter, was decimating the tribes in the first half of the twentieth century. As Western influence spread and the practice of cannabalism died out, so did the virus: it was apparently spread by eating infected human brains.)

Smiling is not taught. It's a reflex that starts at around four weeks old. Anything that looks like a face will make a baby smile at first, even two dots on a card, but as the child develops, different sorts of smiles appear – and the widest is for faces it recognises, especially its mother's.

The Stone Age word for a smile is one of those syllables that forces the lips into the appropriate expression. It's natural to smile as you say **mei**. The initial 's' appeared in Sanskrit, where *smayate* means he is smiling, and in Celtic tongues, the Old High German word is *smielen*, as in the Louis Armstrong song … 'When you're *smielen*, the whole world smiels with you.'

In Old English, the word was *smearcian*, which became *smirken* by the Middle Ages and is now *smirk*. In Scots dialect, *smicker* means to smile at someone with a lecherous glint. The early English *smerian* was to laugh at something, and *bismerian* was the opposite, to treat it with derision and scorn – which gave us *besmirch*, originally implying contempt. The Tudor word *smirch* seems to have been coined after the original meaning of *besmirch* was forgotten: it suggested mud-slinging, a face and reputation soiled by muck.

Mirus meant something strange and wonderful in Latin, a sight to make you smile. *Mirari* was to be astonished by a bizarre sight – what you see in your *mirror*, for instance. It's the root of *miracle* and *miraculous*, which hint at the supernatural. Anything *mirific* will excite astonishment. There was a medieval word, *mirable*, which signified something that was unusual *without* being the work of angels. *Mirari* was also the basis of *admirari*, to *admire*, which literally means to wonder at. An admiral, however, ought to be an *amiral*: it's an Arabic word, like *emir*, and means leader. The 'd' crept in because the title was confused (perhaps deliberately, by the admirals themselves) with the Latin *admirabilis*, to gaze in awe.

A *mirage* is a strange sight, reflected into the hot air. And because *mirari* carried the idea of looking out for the unexpected, a watchtower in Spain was called a *mirador*. These days, it's the name of half the hotels on the Costa del Sol.

The Old French version of *mirabilis* was *merveille*, which became *marvel* in English. It's rather *marvellous* to think that the Stone Age word for a smile has become a brand name for a comic book and blockbuster movie franchise that has given entertainment to billions.

The prehistoric word for *laughter* was **klak**. It became *hlah* in northern Europe, which suggests that the earliest farmers tended to *cackle*, while the Celts let rip with a *belly laugh*. *Hlah* evolved into *hlaehlan* in Old English – we would spell it *ha ha*.

In Greek, **klak** is the root of *klatzo*, to make a high-pitched noise. Think of that next time you hear a *klaxon*.

In Latin, meanwhile, it was *clangere*, to make a great din or *clangour*. That gives us *clang* and *clank*, and also a family of pink woolly aliens that, if you were a child in the 1970s, you might remember: they lived on Blue String Pudding, and tended trees that grew musical notes for fruit. Created by TV animators Oliver Postgate and Peter Firmin, they were the *Clangers* ... whose strange whistling language would put a smile on anyone's face.

Men, to think

Nomads 20,000 years ago understood that it was the human ability to think that made them different from the animals that they hunted and herded. The prehistoric paintings at Lascaux in southern France of horses, aurochs and deer project *mental* images onto the cave walls: it is proof that we were conscious, and probably had been for hundreds of millennia.

But there are many ways to express what the brain does, and various cultures had different interpretations of **men**. In India, it was the soul; in Scandanavia, reflective thought; in northern Europe, love; and in Mediterranean countries, intellect. The word *mind* comes from the Latin *mens*: we still recite it in the phrase *mens sana in corpore sano*, a healthy mind in a healthy body. But in Sanskrit, *manas* is the soul and spirit as well as the mind, and in Old High German *minna* is love. The *meaning* of *menas* in Lithuanian is understanding, and in Old Norse *minni* is *remembrance* or *reminiscence*. The Ancient Greek for mind is *menos* – but there is a closely related word, for madness: *mania*.

Graphomania is the compulsion to write books, which might be to blame for what you're reading – unless that's *logomania*, an obsession with words. *Erotomania* is the stalker's delusion, the conviction of being loved by a complete stranger; *misomania* is a paranoid loathing for the world; *oniomania* is shopaholic's disease, the compulsion to buy things; *potomania* is the urge to get hopelessly drunk.

Tulipmania swept Holland in the 1630s, when the flower was so much in demand that a single tulip bulb was exchanged for 90kg (200lb) of wheat and 180kg (400lb) of rye, four oxen, eight pigs and twelve sheep, 480 litres (105 gallons) of wine, 600 litres (132 gallons) of beer, two tons of butter, 450kg (1,000lb) of cheese, a bed, a suit of clothes and a silver goblet – total value 2,500 gold florins, or around £200,000 today.

Mnestis was Greek for *memory*, which is easily *remembered* with *mnemonics* and forgotten again with *amnesia*. *Mnemosyne* was the mother of Zeus's children, the Nine Muses – because in the prehistoric world, none of the arts (epic poetry, love poetry, dance, music, hymns, history, tragedy, comedy and astronomy) was possible without memory. Her name in Rome was *Moneta*, and coins were *minted* at her temple – Moneta became *money*, and started the *monetary* system. Perhaps this explains why modern society has money on the brain: it all began with the mind.

The Roman goddess of wisdom was *Minerva*, who sprang in full armour from the brain of her father, Jupiter, after he ate her mother. She was a serious-minded and celibate young woman, who fought off an attempted rape by the blacksmith god Vulcan. Cleaning herself up after the assault, she wiped his *semen* off her leg with a scrap of wool and threw it to the earth, where it spawned a baby – a *monster* called Erichton, that was half child and half snake, and so hideous that women who saw it went mad and hurled themselves from the top of the Acropolis.

Semen is from **su**, to produce young, and **men** in the sense of the soul – containing not just the seed but the spirit of life. Monster was originally something foretold in a vision or *premonition*: *monstrare* is Latin for 'to *demonstrate*', and *monstrance* in English is proof. A monster could be a prodigy or a marvel – they weren't all *monstrosities*. If anyone tells you differently, *remonstrate* with them – show them this book.

Because *minne* was love in northern Europe, the French called their little darlings *mignons*. In the sixteenth century, at the court of Henry III, *Les Mignons* were a dandified and effeminate band of courtiers, 'the dainty ones'. The king lavished gifts on them, but the more pampered they were, the more jealous they became. In April 1578, six of them re-enacted a Roman battle, and things got heated: two of them were killed on the spot, two more died later (one suffered nineteen stab wounds) and another suffered serious head injuries.

In English, *minion* originally *meant* a sweetheart rather than a servile underling. If you feel a loved one expects too much work of you, *comment* on it (literally, bring it to mind) and show them it is wrong – *admonish* them.

Mor, to grieve

The Neolithic herdsmen of the steppes have left us their burial kurgans, and the Bronze Age Celts of Britain their barrows. We have their tombs, and at religious sites such as the Flag Fen causeway in Cambridgeshire, archaeologists have uncovered thousands of valuable objects sacrificed to the gods – metal bowls hammered flat, sword blades twisted into knots, even wooden boats scuttled and sunk. These objects have been ritually 'killed', perhaps to accompany the dead in the next world.

Death and funeral rites were central events for prehistoric communities. We know that much, but of course we have no recordings of the ceremonies, no pictures, not even any written accounts. Some of the most revealing evidence about these rituals can be decoded from the words associated with them and what they mean to us today – words such as **mor**, the Indo-European syllable for grief and sadness.

Mor is the root of *mourn*, and also of *moan*. That implies that grieving was a noisy business in the Stone Age. To make the assumption more compelling, a compound word exists for silent grief: the Latin *memor* is **men** + **mor**, which literally means mind grief. Our word is *memory*.

Because the Romans were not a bunch for moping around, *memorare* came to mean celebrating a life or an event, often in story. *Memoriae* were *memoirs*. A note to help us remember is a *memorandum* or *memo*; other related words are *commemorate* and *remembrance*.

Mors in Latin means death, and it's the root of *mortal* and *immortal*, as well as *morgue* – a place where unclaimed bodies are kept. Charles Dickens, who had a *morbid* streak a mile wide, liked to visit the *mortuary* in Paris to stare at corpses that had suffered violent death and were awaiting *post-mortem*: he called it, 'the attraction of repulsion'.

In London and Paris during Dickens's time, a common prostitute was a *mort*. The word probably derived from the Dutch *mot*, which simply means a woman … but it took a dark twist, because mort implies that a streetwalker's life might be cut short by disease or violence.

The word for violent death, of course, is *murder* – and the word for regretting a murder is *remorse*. In the time of medieval poet Geoffrey Chaucer, to *remord* yourself was to torment your mind with regrets.

For hundreds of years, *mortal* was the all-purpose intensifier, much as we use swear words now. To be *mortal cold* was to be very bloody cold indeed. The slang use probably stems from priests' talk of *mortal sin*, which unlike venal sins could see your soul damned to hell for all eternity – very bloody serious, in other words. In Victorian England, if you were so drunk you couldn't stand, you were not just mortal drunk but *mortallious*.

Alamort means dispirited: in French, *à la mort* is to the death. *Amort* comes from the same phrase, and means apparently lifeless. Monty Python's parrot was amort, as well as *moribund*.

The Ancient Greek *martur* was a witness. It became *martyr* in Latin and English, meaning someone whose death bore witness to their faith and piety. These days, a martyr is anyone who has borne any kind of suffering for a long time: you might be a martyr to your job, your children or gout. Encyclopedias of martyrs both Catholic and Protestant were popular in the seventeenth century – they were called *martyrologies*.

In Old French, *mortgage* literally means a dead pledge. The debtor must pay back the loan within a fixed time or lose his mortgaged property – either way, the debt will be dead and buried by a pre-agreed date. A similar word is *amortise*, which means to wipe out a debt and so render it dead.

In Latin, a pause for thought was *mora.* It came to mean any kind of delay. *Moration* means tarrying, though it is not much used now. A *moratorium* is what banks now call a 'payment holiday' when a debt is deferred for a fixed time.

A *remora* is a fish with a long sucker-shaped organ on its head. Rather than waste energy swimming, the remora attaches itself to bigger fish and whales, and allows itself to be towed along. Because remoras often clamped themselves to the undersides of ships, sailors named them after the Latin word for delay or hindrance.

Min, little

The Cornish word for little is *minow*. Cornish or Kernowek died out as a first language in the 1770s, and was declared extinct, though it is now enjoying a revival – and in 2010 was ruled to be not extinct after all by UNESCO. Cornish had never entirely died out, of course, and some of its words survived in English. *Minnow* is one of them, a tiny fish.

Cornwall's tin mines date back to the Bronze Age. The Indo-European root for mining is not known; probably there wasn't one, since the technology for deep digging was developed in the Celtic era. The Manx word for a mine is *meain*, and the Cornish is *moina*. Many miners were little men – it helps not to be 6 foot 6 inches when you're crouching in a subterranean cavern – but miner is not a **min** word. In any case, we spell miner with an 'e'. The Latin word for small is *minor* with an 'o'.

Minor is the opposite of major, which is why the Balearic Island of *Minorca* is smaller than its neighbour Majorca. According to this logic, a schoolteacher should outrank a clergyman, because in Latin one is a *magister* and the other is a *minister*. But minister derives from a slightly altered meaning for *minor*. In Rome, it became one who serves, such as a priest at Mass – an official, but a lowly one.

This notion of service explains why nurses are sometimes called *ministering angels*. It is also why politicians claim glibly to be serving the people: they all want to be *prime minister* ... even though the title equates to 'head butler'. The ones who really run the country, of course, are the civil servants: the *administrators*.

In Old French, a *ministral* was a servant. Any bright lad can clean a chamberpot, but French ones had an extra talent, more often than not, that promised a living wherever they went – they could sing. They were strolling players, or travelling *minstrels*. *Minstrel shows* in America a century ago featured white musicians in blackface, playing spirituals and Dixieland jazz, as well as performing burlesques and doing song-and-dance routines. Their popularity began after the US Civil War, and persisted until the 1970s: *The Black and White Minstrel Show* was a Saturday-night staple on BBC1 up to 1978.

In music, a *minim* is a long note, worth two crotchets – but everything is relative and its name means little because it's only half as long as a semibreve. Long, open notes are not suited to a *minikin* voice, which is constricted and shrill. *Minuets* are stately waltzes danced in *pas menus*, or short steps.

Mincing steps are little dainty ones – the way gentlemen assistants in department stores used to walk. (A venerable music-hall joke goes like this. Customer to man serving behind the perfume counter: 'Have you got any talcum powder?' Assistant: 'Certainly, sir, walk this way.' Customer: 'If I could walk that way, I wouldn't need the talcum powder!')

In Latin, *minus* is small, *minusculus* is very small and *minimus* is smallest of all. The earliest system of fractions was devised in Babylonia, now southern Iraq: the smallest fraction was one-sixtieth. So when the clockface was first divided up, it consisted of sixty tiny parts, or *minute* portions, called *minutes*. When the *minutes* are taken down in meetings, however, as a verbatim record, they have nothing to do with telling the time. *Minuta scriptura* means 'tiny writing'; the minutes are, quite literally, the small print or *minutiae*.

The prefix *mis-* comes from *minus* (Latin for small). Every *mistake*, every *misfortune*, all the *misbegotten misfits* and *misfeatured miscreants*, the *miserly* and the *miserable*, the *misinformed* and the *misquoted*, have the same negative starting position, their *minus point*.

On top of that are the words that stem from the Greek *misos*, or hate, which is really small-mindedness – *misogynists* loathe women, *misologists* despise debates, *misocapnists* can't stand tobacco smoke and *misanthropes* detest everybody.

Mimos in Greek is what we call *pantomime* – a grotesque parody of real life. The Latin word is *mimus*, and etymologist Joseph Shipley suggests that in Indo-European *mime* means reality made small. *Mimesis* is a figure of speech that *mimics* the language of another writer.

To make a thing smaller is *diminution*. To shrink it further is to *diminish* it, and further still is *minimising* and *miniaturising*, until it has been completely *comminuted* or pulverised.

The smallest coin in English currency used to be a *mite*, which was worth half a farthing or one-eighth of a penny in the Middle Ages. It was also a pitying word for an undernourished child. *Dust mites* are tiny insects, too small to be seen by the eye without a *microscope*.

To *mince* is to chop up food very small. It's a good way of disguising the less palatable parts of an animal, though a wise cook stirs plenty of chopped onion into *minced meat* to hide the taste. The *mincemeat* we eat in *mince pies* at Christmas always used to contain meat, especially venison, and beef suet. Don't try serving that recipe after the sausage rolls this year – we expect modern mincemeat to be dried fruit, chopped and soaked in brandy, although the suet is often still included.

N

Nek, to kill

Night, nocturnal, nectar, pernicious

Nem, to name

Numb, nomad, nimble, ignominy

Numbers

Universe, diploma, triangle, farthing

Nek, to kill

Because **neh** is no, **nekt** is no light, or *night*. The Sanskrit word for night is *nakta*, the Hittite is *nekuz*, the Greek is *nux* and the Latin is *nox*. But the hidden meaning within **nekt** is darker than *midnight*: to the Stone Age mind, night didn't just follow day, it murdered day.

Nek has survived as slang in English: *knackered* means worn out to the point of death, a *knacker's* yard is an abattoir and, in north-east England, to *knack* is to hurt badly – if you stub your toe it's painful, but if you break your foot it really *knacks*.

To the Romans, who knew a thing or two about it, *nex* was violent death. *Internecine* war is mutual destruction, when both sides are attempting the complete annihilation of the other. *Internecion* is a little-used word for a massacre, or *pernicies* in Latin: that became *pernicious* in English, meaning ruinous or fatal. The dictionary also lists *pernicion*, another little-used word for a massacre. Like the Inuit and their varied lexicon for snow, the Romans never tired of inventing words for mass slaughter.

Noxa in Latin meant harmful. It's the root of *noxious*, meaning unwholesome, and *obnoxious*, which is something worse – reprehensible, offensive and probably illegal. In the Rat Pack slang of Frank Sinatra and Dean Martin, to be disgustingly drunk was to be *obnoxicated* – *obnoxiously* + *intoxicated*.

Nocent means guilty or harmful. It's not much used, but its opposite is – *innocent*. *Innocence* isn't always *innocuous*: sometimes naivety looks like silliness, and so a *ninnocent* gives us *ninny*. A persistent ninny becomes a *nuisance*.

In Athens, a corpse was *nekros*. A city full of corpses is a *necropolis*, and a magician who can communicate with them is a *necromancer*. Carrion birds, zombies and fashionable chefs who collect and cook roadkill are *necrophagous*. The process of decomposition and post-mortem decay is *necrobiosis*, though there is also *necrosis*, which is much worse – that's when the flesh of a living creature starts to die and rot. If your doctor announced you were getting *necrose*, you'd be mortified … literally.

Nectar was the drink of the gods, because it conferred immortality; another word for it is ambrosia. Nowadays we think of nectar as honey – the origin of that is probably not its delicious sweetness but its antiseptic power, which wards off infection and death. Honey isn't just good for sore throats; medieval medics used it as a poultice for infected cuts. The sweetest fruit is the *nectarine*.

Nox, the Latin for night, became *nott* and then *natt* in Norse, and *neaht* in Old English. Most of our *night-* words are matter-of-fact, like *nightshirt* or *night-light*, rather than morbid and portentious. The only really dark one is *deadly nightshade*, a name for belladonna, which has black, poisonous berries. Otherwise, for every *nightwalker* or street prowler, there is a *night watchman*; for every *night-hag*, riding the skies on a broomstick to dispense *night terrors* to children, there is the sweet song of the *nightingale*, and a *nightcap* for the grown-ups … not just the name for a stripy, tassled hat, but a snifter of brandy before bed.

A *nocturne* is a dreamy piece of music, but if it loses the final 'e', a *nocturn* is part of the liturgy called matins that monks sing and recite before dawn. *Nocturnal* animals are active at night, such as *noctules*, which are the biggest of British bats. *Pernoctation* is spending the night in prayer.

In Roman creation myths, the goddess *Nyx* was the daughter of Chaos. She married her brother Hell, or Erebus, and bore two children – Aether and Hemera (light, and day). If she had stopped there, the world might have been all right, but she also gave birth to Doom, Pain, Sorrow, Deceit, Strife, Blame and Old Age. Not content with that brood, she had two sets of triplets: the Furies, and the Parcae, who were apparently old women from the moment they were born. One held a distaff, wound round with all the human lives that were yet to begin; one had a spindle, with which she wove the threads of life into individual destinies; and one had a pair of scissors, which snipped short each life. Nyx rode in a chariot drawn by owls and bats, and carried two more children under her arms – Sleep and Death.

Don't have *nightmares*.

Nem, to name

Nem is the root of *name*, *number* and *nomad*, and the connection between those three concepts reveals a great deal about human societies when language was first developing.

To name a person or an object implies ownership: things that belong to no one are not worth *naming*. A baby, for instance, had to be given a name to define its allegiance to a family, a tribe or nationality, and probably a religion. That remains true today, with the legal and ritual significance of baptism and the birth certificate.

Most possessions are too *numerous* to be named individually, but must still be alloted to an owner. Vehicles are registered, luxury goods are insured, children's clothes are name-tagged and so on. Tallying up our worldly goods is akin to naming them. Things don't really count until they've been counted.

Nomadic herdsmen driving their cattle, goats or camels from one feeding ground to the next, were defined by their flocks. They had to know the exact number of their animals, and often branded them too, stamping a symbolic name on them. The word *nomad* comes from the Greek *nomas*, which means to roam in search of pasture.

The Greek for name was *onoma*. *Onomatopoeic* things make their own names, like splash and zap and twang – the *-poeic* suffix means making, and comes from the same root as poet, a maker of words. An *onomasticon* is a dictionary of names, and *onomatology* is the study of names. An *onomancer* can tell your fortune from the letters in your name.

Anyone without a name is *anonymous*, and with a false name is *pseudonymous*. Two things with the same name are *synonymous*. *Antonomasia* is calling someone by an epithet instead of their name – the Iron Lady for Margaret Thatcher, the Boss for Bruce Springsteen or the Little Tramp for Charlie Chaplin.

Homonyms are words that sound alike but are spelled differently, such as discreet and discrete. *Heteronyms* are the opposite: they sound different, they mean different things but they are spelled the same – live and live, for instance, or lead and lead.

Nomen was name in Latin. A *nomenclature* is a vocabulary; you're holding a *nomenclator* – a book containing lists of words. The philosophy of *nominalism* denies the reality of objects as abstract concepts: only things that actually exist are worthy of the name. That's typical of philosophers, to reduce everything to the lowest common *denominator*.

When we describe things by giving them names, whether we're talking about scientific classification or merely the local landscape, that's *taxonomy*. Like all words ending in *-nomy*, it comes from the Greek *nomos*, which means both a district and a law. An *oikonomos* ran a household and managed its finances – that's the basis of *economics*. A *metronome* counts out time, and a *gastronome* lays down the law about food.

The French were particularly clever with names. A *nom de plume* was an author's disguise, and a *nom de guerre* was a soldier's. Both were protected from *ignominy*, or damage to their reputations. On the other hand, by revealing your real *surname* (in Old French, *sour* + *nom*, meaning onto the name), you might win *renom* – the repetition of your name by admirers, which gives us *renown* in English.

Numerare in Latin was to count. As well as *numeral*, it gives us *supernumerary*, which used to mean left over or surplus to numbers; these days, thanks to a touch of bureaucratic legerdemain, it means an employee who is not, strictly speaking, on the books but who can be called into action when required ... one of many *anomalies* in the modern office. *Nummary* is dealing in coins, because *numismatics* is the study of money.

The Greek *nemein* means to distribute. Never slow when it came to handouts, the medieval English turned that into *nimel*, to take – though they had to be *nimble* to get anything. That was shortened to the slang *nym*, a thief. His *nimbles* were his light fingers. If the city guards laid hold of him, he'd met his *Nemesis*: she was the goddess of vengeance who distributed men's fates. Like a dark angel, Nemesis had wings so that she could swoop down to mete out justice all the faster. One of her duties was to defend the memory of the dead from insults. Some accounts say that Nemesis, and not Leda, was the real mother of Helen of Troy ... but that was probably a *misnomer*.

The past tense of *nimel* is *nume*, which means taken. Take away all feeling and we're left *numb*. A *numb hand*, in Dickens's London, was a clumsy oaf. *Numskull* is such a stupid word that it has lost its own 'b'. What a dimwit ... a real *numby* ... not deserving of any other name.

Numbers

Early Indo-European speakers counted in tens, as we do. Their names for numbers have changed little as new languages evolved: look how similar the French *un deux troix* or the German *ein zwei drei* are to **oino dwoyh trih**. That suggests Neolithic man understood the concept of an abstract number system, in which ten could mean ten horses, or ten humans, or ten anything. It would be thousands of years, however, before Indian mathematicians started to write down the decimal system, and so took the credit for inventing it. When counting was first invented, very early in the Stone Age, man probably counted in fours, at least up to twelve – that's why eleven and twelve have their unique names, whereas thirteen, fourteen and so on are really three-and-ten, four-and-ten, etc. According to this theory, we counted on our fingers (not using our thumbs) up to eight, and then began again, which explains why **newn**, the word for *nine*, is also the word for *new* ... and why *novem*, the Latin nine, is so much like *novel*.

1 – oino

One is one and all *alone*, which is another way of saying *lonely*. If you have just one apple, you have *an* apple; the indefinite article in English was always 'an' until about 1200 AD, when it was shortened to *a* in front of words that began with a consonant. If you eat the apple, of course, you'll have *none* – you won't have *any*. And if the apple wasn't yours in the first place, you'll have to *atone* for your theft: atone is a contraction, meaning to reconcile or put things *at one*. You'll *only* do that the *once*. In Latin, one is *unus*, which gives us *unity*, the *universe*, *unisex* hairdressers and the *unicycle*.

2 – dwoyh

Two is *double*, though it's also written as *twain* – and twain ten is *twenty*. The Greeks made it *di*, which is why anything cut in two is *divided*; the Latin prefix changed 'd' to 'b', making *bi*, which gives us *bisected*. We can thank the Greeks for *diverse*, *different* and *diploma* (which originally meant a paper folded double; see **plak**). The Romans, on the other hand, gave us *bipeds*, *bigamy* and *binary* numbers. Computers measure information in *bits*, which is an elision of *binary digit*. The Latin for two retained the 'd', though: it was *duo*, as in *duplicate*, *duplicitous* and *dubious*, meaning in two minds.

3 – trih

Three is the *trinity*, the *triangle* and the *triple* word score. It becomes *thirteen* and *thirty*, and – as Frankie Howerd used to say – 'nay, *thrice* nay!' In Latin, **trih** became *ter*, as in *tercentenary*, which is the 300th anniversary, and *tercet*, or three lines of poetry with one rhyme. Roman falconers believed the *third* egg in a nest would always hatch a male chick, which is why *tercel* means a male hawk. The Norse word for a third part of any land, from a field to a country, was a *thriding*: Yorkshire, which was governed by the Danes 1,200 years ago, was divided into *North Thriding*, *East Thriding* and *South Thriding*. The words were run together, until the county consisted of three *ridings*, which has nothing to do with horses.

4 – kwetwor

At first **kwetwor** looks little like *four*, but it is a lot like *tetra* (the Greek four was *tettera*) and quite a lot like *quad* (the Latin four was *quattuor*). *Quarters* are *fourth* parts but also the lodgings of soldiers or the cabins of sailors; to be *given quarter* was a stay of execution, but *quartering* was hacking the arms and legs from a victim. A *tetrapolis* is a region containing four cities, each ruled by a *tetrarch*; a *tetraglot* speaks four languages; a *tetralogy* is a set of four plays, three tragic and the last a satire; a *tetrapod* is an animal with four feet (unlike a *tripod*, which is a camera stand). In Old English, anything divided into quarters consisted of *feorthungs*, which became *farthings*: in pre-decimal coinage, a farthing was a tiny coin, much smaller than the old penny – hence the *penny-farthing*, a bicycle with one huge front wheel and one miniature wheel behind.

5 – penke

It's hard to see the connection straight away between **penke** and *five*, even when the 'p' shifts to 'f'. But 'fenke' is very like *finger*, and of course there are five of them (counting the thumb) on each hand. It's obvious where the Romans got their *quinque*, written as V. In a *quincunx*, five objects are arranged in a square, four at the corners and one at the centre, like the spots on dice. *Quentin* was traditionally the name of a *fifth* son, and the *quin-quagesima* were the *fifty* days before Easter. The Greek five was *pente*, which gives us the five-sided US government building, the fiftieth day after Easter, the first five books of the Bible and a Roman slave galley with fifty oars – *Pentagon*, *Pentecost*, *Pentateuch* and *penteconter*.

6 – sweks

Noon, the *sixth* hour after sunrise, in Latin is the *sexta hora*, when Mediterranean folk sensibly choose to have a *siesta*. The Roman *sex* (we politely pronounce it as *six*) gives us *sextant*, an astronomical tool that can measure angles of up to 60 degrees; *semester*, which now means an academic term but originally referred to *sex menstris* or six months; and the *Sistine* Chapel, so called because it was Pope *Sixtus* IV who began building at the Vatican palace in 1473. Six in Greek was *hex*, and a *hexagram* is a six-pointed star – a favourite symbol of witches, who could use it to put a hex on victims. Insects, being six-footed, are categorised as *hexapods*.

7 – septm

September, unhelpfully, is the ninth month of the year; it used to be the *seventh*, until Augustus Caesar inserted a couple of extras … August, named after himself, and July, after his predecessor Julius. A river that splits and flows into *seven* branches is *septemfluous*; the Nile is a famous example, the River Lea on the Essex border a lesser one. The seven stars of the Plough in astronomy are the *septentrions*, because *septem triones* is Latin for the seven plough-oxen. The Greek *hepta* gives us *heptarch*, the seventh king. A *heptad* is a group of seven things, such as days in a week, and anything divided into seven parts is *heptamerous*. Logically, if you were 'heptamorous', you'd have sex once a week, but English isn't logical and the word doesn't exist.

8 – okto

Eight comes from the Old English *eahta*, which comes from the Old Saxon *ahto*, that is still some distance from the original **okto**. The Greeks and the Romans, on the other hand, didn't change it at all, which is why the *octopus* has eight legs, the *octangle* has eight sides, an *octastyle* building has eight columns and *octogamy* is having eight wives. An *octave* is a full musical scale of eight notes, but it is also an ecclesiastical word meaning an eight-day festival, and the name of a wine cask that holds an *eighth* of a pipe, which is 105 gallons (about 477 litres), or two hogsheads. Simple mathematics will tell you that this means there are four octaves to a hogshead. Yma Sumac, known as the Peruvian songbird, became famous in the 1950s for her four-octave vocal range; she claimed to be an Inca princess, and wore spectacular headdresses, though never an actual hogshead. In South America, there's a rat-like rodent called the *octodon*, because it has eight teeth.

9 – newn

If you're *dressed up to the nines*, you are in your finest clothes – perhaps a reference to an eighteenth-century proverb, that '*nine* tailors make a man'. *Nineteen* was the average age of US conscripts fighting in the Vietnam War, according to the intoned lyrics of a number-one hit by Paul Hardcastle in 1985. The Australian butcherbird, a sort of magpie, is known as the *nine-killer* because it catches insects and small lizards and impales them on thorns to impress its mate, often nine at a time. *Nona hora*, the church service traditionally held at 3pm or the *ninth* hour after dawn, was moved back to midday in the Dark Ages. Confusingly, 12 o'clock became *non* and then *noon*.

10 – dekmt

Decem is the Latin *ten*: hence *decimal, decade* and *decimate*, which was the Roman punishment of slaughtering every *tenth* soldier in a legion that had mutinied or shown cowardice. A *decuria* was ten men, and by the Middle Ages in England a *dicker* was ten fleeces or hides; *dickering* was bartering, perhaps trying to get an extra one thrown in for free. A *decima* was a tenth part, which is why anyone who looked like they could afford to give a starving man ten cents during the Depression of the 1930s was begged, 'Brother, can you spare a *dime*?' The Ten Commandments are sometimes referred to as the *Decalogue*, and the hundred tales written down by Boccaccio in the fourteenth century and supposedly told by ten people over ten days are the *Decameron*.

100 – kentm

Philologists, who study language, divide Indo-European tongues into two groups: the ones that have a soft 's' name for 100 such as *satem* in Sanskrit, and the hard 'k' languages that include Latin with *centem*. It's typical of philologists to pick a key word that makes a useless example because, although the Romans said 'kentem' with a hard 'k', it arrived in English as *centem* with a soft 's' in words like *century, percentage* and *centigrade*. The Greeks made matters worse by changing **kentm** to *hekaton* – that's why a *hectare* is 100 ares, an 'are' being 100 square metres. A *hectograph* was an early carbon-paper device, invented in 1869, which could print multiple copies, though the name was an advertising gimmick: it couldn't manage 100 at a time. A *hecatomb*, now meaning the sacrifice of many victims, was once the slaughter of 100 oxen to appease the gods.

P

Pa, to feed and protect
Father, patriot, repair, foster

Pe, to open
Petal, penny, fathom, spade

Pel, a hide
Pelt, pallor, full, film

Pend, to hang
Pendant, spend, ponder, pencil

Per, to travel
Far, fare, percentage, experience

Pi, to hate
Fiend, pain, fickle, fake

Plak, to plait
Pliant, simple, complex, flask

Pod, foot
Pedal, foot, pedigree, trapeze

Prei, first
Prize, praise, prime, private

Pu, to stink
Putrid, purge, puff, foul

Pa, to feed and protect

*P*apa appears to be one of the oldest words in the world. In Mandarin and Cantonese Chinese, the word for dad is *papa* or *baba*; in Arabic and Hebrew it is *aba*. There's a parallel in the Algonquian language, in which *papoose* means *baby* – and the Paleo-Americans, ancestors of today's Native Americans, first migrated across the Bering Straits from eastern Asia around 12,000 years ago.

It's quite likely that, because **ma** and **pa** are the first sounds of baby *babble*, the words did evolve naturally in these different language groups. But it is also possible that they are proto-words that have existed for tens of thousands, even hundreds of thousands of years, since our ancestors first began to develop language. Perhaps babies say **ma** and **pa** before any other words (why not 'Ooo'? Why not 'Yee'?) because those sounds, over many millennia, have become hard-wired into our brains – the words we know by instinct.

Pa is our protector, the *paternal* figure – a *father* or a *husband*. Because a 'p' sound shifted to an 'f' in northern Europe, the Germanic equivalent of *pater* in Latin is *vater*, which becomes father; a compound word hus-**pa** or house-**pa** becomes *husband*. In Latin, *pappus* was *grandfather*.

(A sci-fi aside: in Middle English, *derve* means to wound or hurt, while *vaeder* in Anglo-Saxon is a variant of father, and thus the name *Darth Vader* gives away the major plot twist of *Star Wars*.)

The father of a tribe is the *patriarch*, but the man who kills his male *parent* is a *parricide*, possibly to get his hands on his inheritance or *patrimony*. *Patriarchy* is government by the city fathers, though *patriarchal* can simply mean old and venerable. To love your fatherland is *patriotism*, and friends from that land are *compatriots*. In medieval English, to *repair* was to go back to where you came from – to return to your own country.

In early Persian, **pa** also means protector, which gives us *pasha*, *pashalik* and *satrap* – all rulers who lived in *palaces*. In Sanskrit, *patis* is master, but in Latin the word is *potis*: hence *potent*, *potentate*, *despot* and *plenipotentiary*. The *pope's* office is the *papacy*. A *pastor* was originally a shepherd, which is why country scenes and songs are still referred to as *pastorals* – now, a pastor's flock gathers in a church rather than a shearing shed. With the 'f' shift, pastor becomes *foster*, meaning to nourish, encourage or to cherish like your own child. A *foster-nurse* feeds another woman's baby or *fosterling*.

Patronage is money and support, from the strong to the weak. To be *patronising* is quite different – that's talking down, like an adult to a child. The former spelling of *pattern* was *patron*, meaning a model of excellence.

What is more surprising is that **pa** has so many connotations of food. The most obvious is *pap*, which is soft mush for weaning a child, but also a nipple, from the Latin *papilla* (that's why *papula* are pimples). Flour and water mixed together make *paste*, which can be dried as the basis of *pasta*. In Ancient Greek, *paste* was mushed barley. If you're feeling more ambitious in the kitchen, try a *pastry*, or a *pasty*, a beef *patty*, perhaps some *pâté*, or a *pain au chocolat*, or even a *parfait*, which is whipped cream, eggs and ice cream with fruit, served in a tall glass. All the ingredients should be in your *pantry*, though you might have to nip down to the *patisserie* with your bread basket or *pannier*. At any rate, it will be quite a *repast*, which literally means you are eating again.

If you're a smoker, you might want to enjoy a *panatella* after your meal: that's a thin cigar, so called because it looks like a miniature stick of French bread or *pain*.

Thanks to that 'p' to 'f' shift, **pa** is also the root of *fodder*, as well as *forage*. To sally out in search of *food* was to *foray*.

Fibre that is mashed and rolled, like food, becomes *paper* – *pulp* it again and you can use it for *papier-mâché*, which can be moulded into any shape. You might even make a useful box to keep your documents in: a *papeterie*. Write on the paper with *pastels*, which are crayons made of ground pigment and gum-water.

In Afrikaans, *papbroek*, literally meaning soft trousers, is slang for a coward.

You might think this is all *poppycock*, but that's a euphemism for *pappy cack*, or a pile of soft crap. Tell that to your papa next time he's talking shite.

Pe, to open

One of the factors that drove Indo-European languages across the planet was the way new words built on old, letter by letter. It wasn't so much a mother tongue, more a construction kit. **Pe** supplies an eloquent illustration.

Pe meant to *open* out. The act of speaking the syllable describes it: it starts with the lips compressed, and ends a moment later with the mouth open.

The perfect **pe** word is *petals*, the part of a flower that opens up. *Pan* is another, a wide-open pot. The Spanish rice dish cooked on broad pans is *paella*, and the shallow silver dish on which the bread is placed at the Eucharist is a *paten*. The Latin word for a cooking bowl is *patina*. The kneecaps, shaped like little dishes, are the *patellas*, and the name for suckers, for example on the feet of water beetles, is *patellulae*.

The Old English word for the top of a man's head is the *pate*

– slice it off, turn it over and you have a round-bottomed *plate*. The face was also called the *pan*, perhaps because the only time most people ever saw their own reflection was on the polished bottom of a *saucepan*; at any rate, that's why an expressionless gaze is said to be *deadpan*.

A *penny* is a coin shaped like a disc. A courtyard open to the elements is called a *patio*. To *patefy* is to make a disclosure or *patefaction*, and that's why a *patent*, which grants the rights for an invention to its originator, is an open explanation of what that invention is. *Patency* means being open or exposed to view – that's *patently* obvious.

Less obvious is the seaman's term for 6 feet (about 6.8 metres) of water, a *fathom*. It was originally the *span* of two arms opened wide, a Germanic word (hence the shift from 'p' to 'f'). In Old English, *faethm* was the arms stretched apart, and *faethmian* was an embrace, wrapping another person in your arms.

Pandere in Latin meant to open, and so *expand* is to spread out. But to make **pe** much more *expansive*, and to create a word for an essential agricultural activity, the early farmers added a building block to the word – an extra 's'. **Spe** meant to scatter.

A *spade* is a tool not only for digging but for *spreading* muck and scattering feed, like a flat pan on a stick. The smaller version is a *spoon*, and the smallest of all is a *spatula*, an instrument with a flat end (or, in Latin, the flat bone of the shoulder). Anything spoon-like or spatula-shaped is *spathaceous*, *spathiform*, *spathose* or *spathulate*, but because so few things resemble spoons and spatulas without actually being them, these adjectives are among the most underused words in English.

Spatium in Latin was a clear and open *space*. *Spatiari* meant to take a walk far and wide; by a process of association, to give your thoughts an airing is to *expatiate* upon them.

The Roman word for a broadsword was *spatha*, which became *espade* in Spanish: that's how the leaf-shaped symbol on a playing card came to be called a *spade*. In French, a slender *spatha* was an *epee*, and the shoulder/spatula became *epaule* – so the little flaps that buttoned down, denoting an offficer's rank, were *epaulettes*.

In English, a *spadroon* is a light sword for cutting and thrusting, sometimes called a *spado*. *Spado* is also a late-medieval term for a eunuch, a man whose genitalia have been cut; when a female animal has its ovaries cut out, it is *spayed*.

If things are spread out too far, they become *spare*. But the one thing that can never be spread too widely is hope: the Latin word for hope was *speratum*. We all hope for enough wealth to be comfortable, which we call *prosperity* – but if you haven't got it, never *despair* (*de* + *speratum* is a *desperate* absence of hope). To the earliest merchants, who hoped to *prosper*, the key to making money was to transport their goods across wide distances swiftly, which was the original meaning of *speed*.

A bird that has been plucked, split open and grilled is a *spatchcock*, a vividly descriptive word that has been borrowed by linguists – when a phrase is roughly ripped apart and extra words are stuffed into it crudely, the sentence is *spatchcocked*. To boldly go, to humbly suggest: every time an infinitive is split by an adverb, that is spatchcocking. And when a swear word is inserted into the middle of another word, the technical term is *tmesis* (see **tam**), but really it's just spatchcocked. In-bloody-credible!

Pel, a hide

A Native American chief once had three wives. Two of them he loved, and he sat each of them on a bison hide and surrounded them with gifts. But the third wife he adored most of all: he placed her on a rare hippopotamus hide that had come all the way from Africa and he heaped presents upon her, twice as many as he had given either of the other two wives. Because, as the Greek mathematician Pythagoras's celebrated theorem on right-angled triangles declares ... 'The squaw on the hippopotamus is equal to the sum of the squaws on the other two hides.'

Pythagoras lived around 550 BC; the custom of honouring people by seating them on animal skins loaded with tributes predates him, perhaps by thousands of years. A **pel** was a hide, a *pelt*; in medieval England, a *pell* was the furred lining of a cloak, and also a roll of parchment – probably because the first documents were written on calfskin, or *vellum*. The pells that recorded government expenditure in the fifteenth century were kept at the Exchequer, archived by the *Clerk of the Pells*. *Pellage* was a tax imposed on the import of skins. *Pelage* with one 'l' is any hair or wool, and *peltry* is all kinds of untreated skins.

A *pelisse* was originally a fur cloak, and then a mantle lined with fur; later, it became an ankle-length silk or *velvet* mantle, with armholes. A *pilch* was a leather or coarse woollen jacket or, in Samuel Pepys's time, a flannel triangle wrapped over a baby's nappy. The Latin for a cloak is *pallium*, which gives us *pall* and *pallis*, and the fog-like *pallor* that lies like a blanket over a sickly face.

There's a closely related Indo-European root word, **pleus**, which means to *pluck*: it gives us *plume*, *plumage* and *fleece*. And **pilo** was hair – as in carpet *pile*, and *depilation*, which is hair removal, and *horripilation*, which is the hair standing on end. But most words related to skin and hair stem from **pel** – *pellagra* is a disease in which the skin reddens, dries, cracks and then *peels* off; it was common among peasants in Lombardy, apparently. A *pellicle* is a thin membrane, so thin that it can be transparent or *pellucid*.

In Greek, a *pelte* is a shield made from hide stretched over a wooden frame, and the soldier who bears it is a *peltast*. The Latin for skin is *pellis*, and a milk bowl is *pella*, because early cups and dishes were made from animal hide. In Greek, *pelux* is a bowl, and *pelavi* in Sanskrit is a vase; a basin in Latin is *peluis*, which gives us *pelvis*, the bowl-shaped bone that supports our own hide.

Pel also meant *full*, the idea suggested by a hide heaped with possessions, a bag loaded to bursting point or a bowl brimming over. By extension, **pel** became many; the vowel was elided, and dozens of words beginning 'pl' stem from this: *plenty, plenteous, plural, plus, surplus, plethora, plenitude … plenary*, which is the sensation of complete *fullness; plenipotentiary*, an ambassador who wields the powers of a monarch; *plenilune*, which is simply a full moon; *replenish*, and plain *plenish*, meaning to cram a house full to the rafters; and *plenarty*, which means *fully* occupied. **Pel** is even the root of a pseudo-scientific theory of astrophysics: in the seventeenth century, *plenists* believed that the universe was chock-a-block with invisible matter that left no room for a vacuum.

The north European shift from 'p' to 'f' turned **pel** to *fill*. *Fulsome* originally meant abundant and *plentiful*, but Shakespeare used it (in *The Merchant of Venice*) to mean something darker and more sordid – brimming with greed and lust. By the eighteenth century, fulsome signified a character stuffed with everything rotten: excessive, coarse, gross, foul-smelling, obscene and morally loathsome. These days it is commonly misused by people who assume that if 'full' is good, then 'fulsome' must be better.

This misconception can be convenient. Our last **pel** word is *film*, which used to mean a translucent membrane until Hollywood got hold of it. So the next time you're expected to laud a film that you secretly hated, you can say, 'It deserves to be praised *fulsomely*.'

Pend, to hang

Viv Nicholson and her husband won £152,319 on the pools in 1961, with a stake of three shillings and sixpence. The prize was the biggest ever seen in Britain, worth around £3m today; the cost of their coupon was the equivalent of perhaps £4 now. She vowed to '*Spend*, spend, spend' – and promptly bought furs, diamonds and an American car.

There are twelve definitions in the *OED* for spend: they include to pay out, to make use of and to pass time. Viv, unfortunately, chose the tenth, meaning: to waste or squander, to throw away. She was bankrupt within four years.

That was not the original idea of spending at all. It's a **pend** word, in the sense that by hanging or *suspending* goods they can be weighed and so valued. The word suggests that the first settlers had learned that weight, not volume, is the safest measurement: a stack of fleeces or a loosely rolled bale might not be worth as much as they first appear. The eye deceives but the scales don't lie.

Pendere is Latin for 'to hang' and thus 'to weigh', especially applied to gold. *Expendere*, which we shortened to spend, meant to weigh out. It implies care, calculation and thought … all the qualities that Viv disdained.

Pendulus meant hanging. English spells it *pendulous* or *pendulant*, like a *pendant* or a *pendulum*. A *penduline* bird's nest hangs from a branch, like a hornet's nest. In Scotland, a small property on a larger estate such as the gamekeeper's cottage is a *pendicle*.

A *penthouse*, usually a suite with splendid views at the top of a building, should strictly speaking be a structure attached to one wall, like a birdhouse on a tree. The word derives from an Old French medical word, *apentis*, which translates as *appendage* – it is appropriate but probably accidental that Bob Guccione's pornographic magazine *Penthouse* should take its name from an ancient word for a man's dangly bits.

It wouldn't be the first time that joke was made: in fact, the Stone Age word for the *penis* was **pen**. It was probably an early bit of slang and a version of **pend** – unless, of course, their term for the male anatomy came first, and **pend** literally meant to hang down like a penis.

Because the penis goes within, *penes* in Latin meant inside. That gives us *penetrate* and *impenetrable*. Because a window also lets light into the interior of a building, the word in French – with an initial shift from 'p' to 'f' – is *fenestra*. *Defenestration* is chucking someone out of a window.

Perhaps because the Romans had a crude sense of humour, their word for a tail was also *penis*, and a paintbrush was a *penicillus*. If you want to underline that grubby little fact, you might want to use a *pencil*, not a *pen*. And to restore a little respectability to this section, please note that when Alexander Fleming discovered his cure-all fungus growing in a petri dish that had been left on the windowsill of a London hospital over the weekend, he examined it under his microscope and saw tail-like tufts on the ends of the spores. That's why he named it *penicillin*.

In Rome, each family prayed to its own household gods, tiny figures made of wax that represented the deities of heaven and hell, and the spirits of dead heroes. Later, a fashion arose for making replicas of dead friends and loved ones, and worshipping them, like celebrities. These gods were called the Panates, because they were kept in the most private room of the house (in the same way, the innermost sanctuary of a temple was the *penetralia*).

All that is something to *ponder*, which literally means to weigh. Anything *ponderous* is heavy, and if there's too much of it, you have a *preponderance*. The Latin *pensare* also meant to weigh – it's the root of *pension*. A *pensioner* was an old soldier or servant who *depended* on a former master for his income or *stipend*.

When things were weighed together, that was *compendere*, which is why a book stuffed full of all sorts of facts is a *compendium* – and why, if we don't have enough to make the weight, we must *compensate*. When those things were then weighed out and distributed, that was *dispendare*; we would say *dispensed*. When things were hanging over the edge of a drop, that was *impendere* or, as we'd say, *impending*; hanging under was *suspendere*, or in *suspense*. If things were hanging from the front, on the other hand, that was *propendere*, which is why anything that is unevenly balanced has a *propensity* to fall over. There was another Latin word for that: *pendicare*, or leaning. The opposite of leaning is *perpendicular*.

Pensare is also the source of *pensive*, and the French *pensee*, which means a thought that hangs in the mind. In Scots dialect, *pensy* is thoughtful. All flowers had meanings in Tudor times, and what flower stood for thoughtfulness? *Pansies*.

Per, to travel

Long ago and *far*, far away, Neolithic farmers came up with a word to signify travel. They had never needed one before, but now they had domesticated the horse and invented the wheel, a word was urgently required. Not only could they explore and raid on horseback but they could colonise distant lands, arriving on carts laden with building equipment to set up new villages. The word was **per**, and it is the source of more English words than perhaps any other Indo-European root.

Travel was full of *peril*, but it brought *experience*. With knowledge of new lands, men became *experts*. That could bring *perfection* – or *perdition*. When new towns were reached, travellers entered through a *portal*; when they came to the coast, they sailed on from *ports*, and hoped not to encounter *pirates*.

As the language reached northern Europe and 'p' sounds were softened, **per** became *far*. That has survived unchanged, and also had a letter added to become *fare* – which can mean both to journey and the price of a journey. The idea of distance implied that one place was ahead of another: to the *fore*, or *before*. In Old English, *for* suggested something gone too far, beyond recovery: hence *forsake*, *forfend*, *forget*, *forbid*, *forswear* and *forlorn*.

Joseph Shipley lists nine ways in which **per** became a *prefix*. It can mean before, alongside, around, on behalf of, beyond, opposite to, through, against and by – all of them requiring movement or travel. In Latin it became *prae*, which gives us *pre*, meaning earlier – *prearrange*, for instance, or *precede*. It is used as the opposite of the Latin *post*, though the Romans had another word for that: *ante*. We're much more likely to say *pre-Christian* and *prehistoric* than ante-Christian or ante-historic.

To *precipitate* is to plunge headlong, or throw someone head-first, from *prae* and *caput*, the Latin for head. A *precursor* is a *forerunner*, from *prae* and *currere*, meaning to run. And *apprehension* is catching something – remember **ap** was to put, plus the Latin *prehendere*, as in a monkey's *prehensile* tail.

Para is the version of **per** that means beside – *parallel*, for instance, where two lines never meet, and *parallax*, where they do. A *parable* is a metaphor wrapped up in a fable: it comes from the Ancient Greek *parabollein*, meaning to compare. *Paradise* was first used by the Greek military adventurer Xenophon to describe the idyllic parks of Persian noblemen: it refers to the wall around the garden, within which was a piece of heaven. It's a *paradox* that *parados* also means a wall or embankment, to fortify a troop position on a battlefield.

Peri means about or around, as in *periphrasis*, a verbose figure of speech also called circumlocution. *Periplus* has other names too: circumnavigation, or globetrotting. But *periplus*, the Greek for a voyage around, is a much better word – it can mean a journey around the world, or the story of that journey, such as Michael Palin's television travelogues.

Pro can signify before: for instance, *prorogue* means literally to before-ask and so to postpone. Another legal term, *proxy* is a condensed version of *procuracy*, a document giving one person the power to act for another. But *pro* more usually signals that something is favoured – we are *proactive*, or simply 'very pro'. When we're *progressive*, we are literally taking strides forward – *pro + gradus*, the Latin for a step. The exception is *progressive rock*, generally called *prog*, which is music that goes in every direction but forwards.

Preter means above and beyond – anything too extreme to be natural is *preternatural*, and anyone with supernormal powers is *preterhuman*. Debris carried on the tide is *preterlabent*, irrelevant detail left out of a story is *pretermitted* and any human soul not lucky enough to be *preordained* for heaven has unfortunately suffered *preterition*.

In Latin, *per* means through, as in *per se* – through itself. The motto of the Royal Air Force uses this sense too: *Per ardua ad astra*, 'Through difficulties to the stars'. We say *per day* or *per week* without thinking that we are jumbling English and Latin. And with *percentage* ('all the way through to 100') and *perforce* ('through violence'), we have swallowed it up into a wholly English word.

Pi, to hate

Like **fri**, which was originally **pri**, **fi** began as **pi**. It seems to have carried a sense of quarrelling to the bone, and of wishing death upon the enemy, because there was a weaker hatred signified by **pien**, an extension of **pi**.

Pien meant hating someone almost-but-not-quite to death. It's the root of *fiend*, which at first meant any enemy but came to personify the arch-enemy of mankind, or any of Satan's devilish minions. But it can also mean someone who torments himself to the edge of death: a *dope fiend* or a *tobacco fiend*. Because of the slang habit of words to reverse their meaning, for the past century or so an *absolute fiend* might be someone who is infernally talented or clever, especially at some arcane study such as maths – but always with an overtone of self-destruction.

To injure without killing was to inflict *pain*. In Ancient Greek, that word became *poine*, which also meant a *penalty*. Penalty in Latin is *poena*, a word that still forms part of the legal jargon *subpoena* – a summons to appear or face the penalty. The Roman verb for *punish* was *poenire*, which became *punire*: it gives us *penal*, *penance*, *penitent* and *impunity*.

A neglected animal will *pine* – that seems a melancholy word today, implying sadness more than suffering, but in medieval English it meant sheer torment. To be sorry for inflicting pain is to *repent*, or *repine*.

To endure pain demands *patience*. The Latin for suffering is *passum*, which gives us *passive* and *compassion*, and also *passion* – the word's original meaning was the agony suffered by Christ on the cross. Spanish missionaries used the little blue *passion flower* (genus *Passiflora*) to illustrate the wounds inflicted on Christ's body: its pointed leaves represented the lance thrust into His side, its long tendrils were the whips of the jailers, the ten petals were the ten disciples who did not betray Him, its halo of filaments was the crown of thorns and the three stigmas were the nails (two through the wrists, one through the ankles). None of this appealed to the Japanese, who call the plant a clock flower.

Passionate came to mean irascible and ardent, and sexually charged. These days, a job applicant is required to be passionate, in the sense of mildly enthusiastic rather than madly amorous, but in the Elizabethan era passion was depth of feeling, especially sorrow. A *passional* was a book cataloguing the gory martyrdoms of the saints. Anything *passible* is capable of feeling pain or simply being susceptible to emotion – not to be confused with passable, only just acceptable, which won't invoke passion if your date-planning is not up to scratch.

In Neolithic times, the idea of **pien** or pain came to mean almost dead, and then just almost or nearly. That sense survives in *penultimate*, which is all but the last (the *penult* is the last day but one of the month); *peninsula*, which is almost an island, like Gibraltar; and *penumbra*, which is on the cusp of darkness.

In Germanic languages, 'p' changed to 'f', and so **fi** means to detest and despise a *foe*, and wish *fie* upon them. It is the source of *feuds* and the origin of all *fickleness*. It is even the beginning of that old-fashioned expression of contempt, *phooey*!

It might also be the basis of *fake*. That's a bit of thieves' slang, 200 years old: a fake was any kind of swindle in Napoleonic times. It wasn't until the end of the nineteenth century that it came to denote worthless merchandise. By then, fake had been used to cover every trick of villainy: to *fake a cly* was picking a pocket, *faking a screeve* was to write a begging letter, to *fake a pin* was the prisoner's dodge of injuring a leg to get out of forced labour and to *fake your slangs* was to strike off prison chains. The word's criminal past goes all the way back to the seventeenth century, when a *feager of loges* was a beggar who showed forged papers to earn a handout. Most dictionaries, including the *OED*, trace the derivation to an Old German word, *vegen*, meaning to polish or to thrash; bumfeague was Shakespearean slang for a spanking. But it's wrong to assume *vegen* is the antecedent of fake.

It's fitting that fake has a forged etymology; its real antecedents are in *faih*, which means deception in the language of the Goths 2,000 years ago. *Faih* stems directly from **fi** – nothing *false* about that.

Plak, to plait

Language is as useful as archaeology at uncovering the origins of civilisation. We believe, for instance, that early Stone Age man invented weaving almost 30,000 years ago: all paleolithic textiles have long since rotted away, but at a dig at Dolní Věstonice in Moravia, now part of the Czech Republic, in 1924, the faint imprint of woven cloth was discovered in mud deposits from 27,000 BC. That excavation is most famous for the Venus figurine, a clay-fired statuette of a female goddess.

Fragments of a linen burial shroud were found in Turkey, at the Anatolian city of Çatalhöyük, dating back to 7,000 BC. But the most compelling evidence that the earliest settlers could weave cloth is this: they had a word for it.

The verb **plak** means to fold or twist together: to *plait*. It gives us *pleat*, and *pliable*, and *supple*, and *pliant*. There's the wonderfully poetic *pleach*: it means to entwine. *Pleached* boughs are interlaced, like twisted wicker; to bend trees over and intertwine their branches to make an arch is called *plashing*. The queen of the underworld Persephone wore her 'poppied hair … Sad-tressed and pleached low down about her brows', according to the poet Algernon Swinburne.

To *ply* comes from the Middle English *plien*, meaning to mould like wax, and so to work at something – to ply your trade. The Latin *applicare* means to join two things together, which is why we *apply* ourselves to our work; first, of course, we have to fill in an *application* form to the *employer* as *suppliants* and wait for a *reply*. With the right qualifications, we might be able to *supply* a *diploma* or two. As we *display* and *deploy* our talents – literally, unfolding ourselves – we can be *explicit* (setting everything outside the folds: *ex-plicit*) or merely *imply* our abilities (keeping them hidden under the folds). But it's *complex*: we could be *exploited*, *implicated* as *accomplices* or somehow *complicit* in some *perplexing* business – the Latin *perplexus*, from **per** and **plak**, means tangled all the way through. It's enough to make you suspect a *duplicitous plot*.

As the *complications multiply*, they *triple* and *quadruple*; for instance, I might mention that *diplo*, meaning folded in two, is a scientific prefix, as in *diplocardiac* (a divided heart) or *diplodocus* (a 30 meter/100 foot dinosaur with *double*-beamed bones in its tail). Another monster, the *plectognathic* fish, has twisted jaws with its teeth fused into a beak.

In Greek rhetoric, *ploce* is to weave repetitions through a speech. Martin Luther King repeated the phrase 'I have a dream' nine times during his speech at the March for Jobs and Freedom, to a quarter of a million people at the Lincoln Memorial in Washington in August 1963.

One *replication* is *simple*; two is *double*, or *duple* – from the Latin *duo* + **plak**. A Spanish *doubloon* was a coin originally worth two *pistoles*, which themselves were worth two *escudos*, the basic gold coin. A doubloon weighs .218 troy ounces, the standard gold measurement, and at 2014 prices around £800 per troy ounce; that ought to make one doubloon worth about £160 today. But the price can be higher: in Raymond Chandler's novel *The High Window*, detective Philip Marlowe is hired to find a coin called the Brasher Doubloon, whose every owner has been murdered. That plot isn't exactly original – for instance, the boy's own tale *Biggles Flies West* by Captain W. E. Johns also centres on a cursed doubloon.

The shift from 'p' to 'f' turns **plak** to *flax*, which can be woven into linen: the blue flowers produce pods containing linseeds which, like the stalks, are yellow or *flaxen*. A *flax-wench* or a *flax-wife* was a woman who harvested the plant; *flaxbrakes*, *flaxcombs* and *flaxhackles* pounded, separated and straightened the stalks.

Anything bendable will *flex* – even light *reflects*. Mobile faces are *flexile*; muscles that move joints are called *flexors*, because they produce *flexion*. Our voices are capable of *inflection*, though we ourselves might be *inflexible*. An argument that has the power to bend or influence our minds is *flexanimous*.

Flex is also a cable that bends without snapping – though it can be cut with *pliers*.

A *flask* was originally the plaited cradle for a wine bottle, the kind you still see hanging up in pizza restaurants that haven't redone the decor since the 1970s. A bottle of wine gone off was a *fiasco*.

Simples!

Pod, foot

While giving a speech at the Royal Institution in Albemarle Street, London, in 1863, an eminent professor of linguistics named Friedrich Max Müller raised an appreciative laugh from his audience by quoting Voltaire. The great French philosopher, he announced, had defined etymology as *'une science où les voyelles ne sont rien et les consonnes fort peu de chose'* – 'a science in which the vowels count for nothing and the consonants for very little.'

Voltaire, like Oscar Wilde and Dorothy Parker, never said half the clever things attributed to him, and that epigram does not appear anywhere in his writing. But the remark wouldn't have seemed so witty if Max Müller had claimed it as his own.

There was truth in it, though. **Pod** is the source of *pad, pedal, pied-à-terre, podium* and *repudiation* – all the vowels are there. And as Jacob Grimm explained in 1822, when root words arrived in northern Europe during the Celtic era, the consonants changed according to uniform rules: 'g' became 'h', 'd' became 't' and 'p' became 'f'. Because early Indo-European was not written down, nobody could protest about shifting pronunciation, and spelling simply didn't exist. In the Bronze Age, there was no such thing as a *pedant*.

That consonantal drift turned **pod** into *foot*. Chairs, stairs, hills and beds all have *feet*. The average length of a human foot is the basis of imperial measurements of length, 12 inches (30 centimetres). The width of a foot is not the basis of anything, though in biblical times it was a unit of measurement too: in Deuteronomy, God warns Moses that he will not give the

Israelites any land in the Seir mountains, near the Dead Sea – 'no, not so much as a *foot breadth*.'

In the mines of Devon and Cornwell during the eighteenth century, raw tin ore, called black tin, was measured in *feet* too, with 60lb (27.2kg) of unsmelted ore being equivalent to a foot.

Highwaymen at that time who couldn't afford a horse were called *footpads* because they *padded* along the roads, wearing out shoe leather and holding up stagecoaches.

The richly brocaded cloth that is draped over the knights' horses at a medieval tournament is called a *foot-cloth*. It hangs down to the animal's *fetlocks*, or the clumps of hair fringing its hooves. *Fetterlocks* are chains that hobble a horse by its ankles; *fetters* are leg shackles for human beings.

To *fetch* a thing was originally to go on foot and get it. If it was dark, you took a *fetch-candle*.

In Greek, the **pod** stem formed *podion*, a base, which became *podium* in Latin and *puie* in Old French. In English, that's spelled *pew*, which originally meant the preacher's stall in church. A *parapet* is a podium that sticks out from a house.

Podalgia is pain in the foot, or gout. A *podobranch* is a gill on the leg of a crustacean: there are crabs that can breathe through their feet, apparently. That's different to being *podostomatous*, which is having a mouth that serves as a foot – some fish walk around on their mouths, handy for hoovering up the seabed. *Hippopodostomalgia* really ought to mean galloping *foot-in-mouth* disease, but don't try using it at Scrabble: it's not a real word.

Ped is foot in Latin, which explains *pedicures, pedestals, pedometers* and *pedestrians*. A *peddler* or *pedlar* tramped around the district, *peddling* his wares, unless he had a bicycle, in which case he'd be … you've guessed already.

To be *pedantic*, of course, is travelling slowly and with thoroughness, on foot. To *expediate* yourself from a difficult situation means to free your feet. An *impediment* stops you from walking easily. To *repudiate* a charge is to kick it back at your accusers. When the revolutionaries of *Animal Farm* painted their slogan on a barn, 'Four legs good, two legs bad', they were talking about *quadrupeds* and *bipeds*.

The animals in George Orwell's political fable wouldn't have liked the medieval French nobility, who were terrible snobs. These aristocrats became obsessively interested in drawing up their family trees, and they needed a word, a little bit of jargon, to explain lines of descent. It was noted that where a lord had three sons, their names were written below his, and connected by three converging lines. Those lines, said one wag, looked like the toes of a lanky bird that was forever looking down its beak, a crane – or in French, *le grus*. So the lines were *ped de grus* … which became *pedigree*.

Other notable facts: the *antipodes* are literally opposite our feet. *Piedmont* is an Italian region at the foot of the Alps, *pedes montium*. *Pyjamas* were invented in Persia, where their name literally meant leg garments. And that daring young man on the flying *trapeze* wouldn't have flown through the air half as easily in Ancient Greece, where *tra + pezion* was a small table with four feet.

Prei, first

There are no *prizes* for second place. The word is a synonym for coming first. To be first, you must come before or *prior* to everyone else: that's a *priority*. To the victor, of course, go not only the spoils but also the *praise*.

The tradition of the *prizefight*, where the winner takes the *prize money*, goes back to the Roman amphitheatres. By Tudor times, the word meant any *plunder* seized in war.

But prize also came to mean a specific sum. It might be money won in a bet, or paid to a working man in wages or handed over in exchange for goods – in every case, an exact value had to be agreed. This was the *price*. The Latin word was *pretium*, and often a negotiator was required to broker the deal: he was the *interpretium*, or *interpreter*. It was his job to *apprise* the value without *misprising* it, and then to share his *appraisal* before the goods started to *depreciate*.

The Latin for *pricey* is *pretiosus*, which became *precios* in Old French, and now gives us both *precious* and *precosity*.

A *princock* in Elizabethan times was a conceited dandy. Until the last century, *prinking* was getting dressed to impress. The Dutch for show and finery is *pronk* – when an antelope leaps and bucks in a mating dance, the Afrikaans word is *pronking*.

Prei is also the root of *prime*, the foremost or first. When a fish *primes*, it is leaping. Humans, gorillas and other great apes are called *primates* because we regard ourselves as the highest order of mammals. The first humans existed in *primeval* times and were very *primitive*. If it is ever proved that dolphins really are more cultured and advanced than we are, then technically they would be the primates. And there's no reason why we shouldn't be 'dolphins' – the word simply comes from *delphus*, the Greek for womb.

A *prime number* can be divided only by 1 and itself; the lowest are 1, 2, 3, 5 and 7, and the highest has not yet been discovered – primes might stretch to infinity. In 1742, the German mathematician Christian Goldbach theorised that all even numbers greater than 2 are the sum of two primes: it's called the Goldbach Conjecture, which sounds like the title of a Dan Brown novel but isn't. Yet.

In Middle English, *prim* meant delicate or fine. It retains that sense in the phrase *prim and proper*. In Georgian times, a prim was slang for a virginal girl, which might explain why the word has a maiden-aunt feel today. The *principal* singer in an opera is the first lady or *prima donna*.

Primarius was a Roman military term, meaning of the first

rank, and gives us *primary* and *primacy*. It is also the source of *premier*, which is replacing *prime minister*. The most capable leader is the one of 'first ability', or *pri* + *ceps* (from **prei** + **kap**) – *princeps* gives us *prince*, *principle* and the *Principia Mathematica*, an attempt by Alfred North Whitehead and Betrand Russell to sum up all the underlying laws of numbers.

In medieval Latin, a *primator* was a stevedore or docker, a labourer loading the cargo ships. *Primage* was a fee paid to the ship's crew to ensure that the goods were safely stowed: in Scots, the word was *primegilt*. Loading the first cannons, and later muskets, with ball and gunpowder was also a task that demanded careful handling, and became known as *priming* the weapon.

Priscian was a Roman grammarian, from Caesaria in modern-day Algeria, who lived around 1,500 years ago. He wrote the standard Latin *primer* used by medieval monks: a schoolboy error in grammar was known as 'breaking Priscian's head'. Thanks to his scholarship, generations of novices knew that *priuus* not only meant owned by one person but was pronounced *privus*, and was the root of all *privilege*.

Keeping yourself to yourself was the ultimate example of *priuus*, and was called *privacy*. *Privatus* in medieval Latin meant withdrawn from public life, perhaps because of great loss or sadness: *privare* meant to bereave. A *private life* was originally one of grief and sadness, not illicit affairs.

If it was a luxury to be *overprivileged*, the opposite was *privation* and *deprivation*. The solution for some was to *deprive* the wealthy of their burden of riches, by becoming a *privateer*. The word has nothing to do with piracy – a *private man of war* was originally a marauding ship, and its commanders were private gentlemen rather than naval officers ... though they did hold 'letters of marque' from the Crown, making them licensed robbers. Some people feel the same about *private banks* today.

Pu, to stink

The first swear word of childhood dates back to the infancy of language. *Poo* combines a grimace (narrowing the nose against a stench) with an exhalation (blowing the smell away). The mouth *pouts* and *puffs* the word out: poo!

To stink in Latin is *putere*, and to be unsoiled is *purus* – paradoxically, *putrid* and *pure* are both **pu** words. *Putid* (without the 'r') is a Tudor word, forgotten now, meaning worthless, horrid and disgusting. *Putrefaction* is decay and decomposition: it's a rotten word, like *putridity*, *putresecence* and *putrilage*. So is *suppurate*, which means oozing *pus*. Before antibiotics, *purulent* infections were often spread by venereal infections, and the vast majority of prostitutes suffered from them – hence the Spanish word *puta*, an *impure* woman.

The solution to so much *impurity* is *purging*. A *purgative* is a cathartic that cleanses the body; *purgatory* is the preparation for heaven, so Catholics believe, that cleanses the soul. To take all the rude words out of a book is to *expurgate* it.

A *purgery* is the refining room in a sugar cane processing factory where the sugar is bleached. When soup is passed through a sieve and all the pulp is strained out, what's left is *purée*. *Potpourri* literally means rotten pot: it used to be a stew of rancid meat and bad vegetables, with lots of spices and petals to disguise the flavour. Then a bright spark chucked away the meat and veg, and was left with a pleasantly *pungent* perfume.

In politics, a *purge* drives out the dissidents and the rebels – *Pride's Purge* sounds like a quack remedy for constipation, but in fact it was the Roundhead coup in 1648, exiling royalists from Parliament before the order to execute Charles I by the *Puritan* leader, Oliver Cromwell.

Poo is the word we say when we're disgusted, so to say it twice is doubly dismissive: to *pooh-pooh* someone is to wave them away. *Poop* is *pooey* – these days, as a euphemism, it is mostly American, but it used to be universal slang for the buttocks. It is also naval terminology for the rear end of a ship: the *poop deck* is the raised platform above the cabin at the stern of a galleon, where the captain and the helmsman stand.

With the shift from 'p' to 'f' in northern Europe, **pu** became *foul*. *Foul ground* and a *foul coast* were dangers to shipping, where the seabed was jagged with submerged rocks, and a ship could be *fouled* or wrecked, especially in *foul weather*.

When Britain's wool industry was at its peak after the Norman Conquest, there were no chemical baths to clean the fleeces. After the wool was carded and woven into cloth, the only cheap way to *purify* it was to soak it in tubs of urine and trample it for hours. Both animal and human waste was collected – for many peasants, the night-pail was a useful source of income. It was used to clean or *full* the cloth. *Fulling* is probably a **pu** word, because of the stench, but a *fuller* came to mean someone who stamped his feet for a living: that's why a trip and a kick in football is a *foul*.

A *foumart* is the Middle English name for the *polecat* (*Putorius foetidus*), a relative of the skunk. A *fulmar* is a disgusting gull that regurgitates a reeking oil from its stomach, to scare away predators. It doesn't smell *filthy* to the fulmar, of course; in fact, the chicks love it, and it is high in protein. But it has also been the death of the bird in the Scottish isles, where it was hunted to extinction in some places by crofters who burned the oil in lamps.

Where French was spoken in Cajun communities in Louisiana, the word for a whore – *putain* – migrated into English as *poon-tang*, about 100 years ago. It was still common slang after the Second World War: when John F. Kennedy became the US president in 1960, he confided in a friend, 'I guess my *poon* days are over.' A glance at any JFK biography will reveal that they weren't.

R

Re, back

Reverse, retro, rear, rescue

Reg, to lead in a straight line

Regular, ruler, right, erect

Ru, to cry out

Roar, rumour, rustic, room

Rud, red

Ruddy, rude, ribbon, robot

Re, back

Re is not a simple prefix; quite the *reverse*. At first it was just the opposite of **bhron**, meaning front, a root word that unexpectedly led nowhere – it gives us *frontier, frontage, affront, confront, effrontery* and not much else. But **re** is the start of more than 1,200 words in the *OED*, from *reabsorb* to *rezone*.

Originally, **re** meant back as opposed to front. Then the early Romans, 2,500 years ago, started to discover that going back was a lot more complex and subtle than going forward, and that **re** contained a multiplicity of meanings.

There was the idea of physically going backwards, as in *retreat, retire* and *recede*. There was the idea of negating a previous action, such as *revoking, removing* or *reversing*. There was the concept of putting things back as they were, to *restore, refresh* or *return*. And there was the idea of doing something again and again, as in *repeating, reiterating* and *refining*. Finally, there was a subtler inflection still – the idea that by doing things over and over, they were intensified: *resent, remark, reiterate*.

Reload, remake, reconsider, reuse (to choose four at random from the 1,200) – most of these words *require* little explanation. Some do – require stems from **re** + *quarere*, to ask. It's more than merely a *request*; it's verging on a demand … just as a request is more formal and underlined than a simple question.

And some **re** words are downright puzzling. Everyone wants to be *remembered* – but it's much less help then you might hope after you've been dismembered. *Remember* is **re** + *memor*, the Latin for mindful: it brings things back to the memory. But dismember is *dis* + *membrum*, meaning to separate the members.

Many lovely things are *redolent*, meaning they emit a pleasant odour, a sweet fragrance – one that often evokes memories. But nothing is dolent. It's not even a word. That's because redolent is from *olare*, Latin for to smell, and *red*, which is the form of **re** that Romans used before a vowel. That's why *redintegrate*, in Latin, and not reintegrate, means to *restore* to a perfect state. The addition of a consonant to separate one vowel from another is a favourite trick of Romance languages; English prefers the hyphen. Fowler rules that words beginning in **re** need a hyphen only if the next letter is an 'e': *re-examine, re-enact, re-establish* and so on.

Retro is all the rage: the 1940s hairstyle *revival* and the *renaissance* of vivid lipstick has *reinvented* the look of screen goddesses Veronica Lake and Lauren Bacall. *Retro* is Latin for backwards, which means that *ad retro* is tautologous: it says the same thing twice. *Ad* means towards … towards backwards makes no sense, yet the phrase worked its way into French, as *arriere*, which translates as back. *Arriere* gives us *arrears*, which is money owed – back rent, for instance, and not money back.

Shortened even more, it becomes *rear*. That can be the hindquarters of anything: even buildings have rears. It's a convenient euphemism, of course, for what the French call *la derrière*.

Sometimes, it is spelt *rere*. A *rere-brace* was a plate of armour protecting the back of the arm from the shoulder to the elbow – a vulnerable spot for a wound, because of the brachial artery. A *rere-supper* was the medieval word for a sumptuous meal on top of a late dinner, a glutton's indulgence that Sir Walter Scott described as 'an enormity'. The screen of wood or stone at the back of the choir in a church is the *reredos*; the word sometimes applies to the brick back of a fireplace too. And in a monastery, a *rere-dorter* was a privy out the back.

When you move house, you hire a *removals* van. But you might as well call it a *rescue* vehicle, because the two words basically mean the same thing. Rescue comes from the Old French verb *rescourre*, from **re** + *escorre*, which means to move. We think of rescues today as daring affairs that require helicopters and stun grenades, but the original sense of a rescue was simply to pull something back, out of danger.

I could fill the *remainder* of this book with *reflections*, *refutations*, *reduplications* and *regurgitations*, but that would be the *reprehensible rescription* of a *reprobate*.

Reg, to lead in a straight line

The secret of leadership can be summed up in a syllable, an all-purpose piece of business wisdom 8,000 years old. Since the dawn of farming, the ploughman had to steer a straight furrow. The flock needed a shepherd who knew the way to the next pasture, and who guided them by the shortest safe route. The tribe needed a decisive chief, one who did not vacillate. It's all summed up in a three-letter concept: **reg**.

The closest word that English has is *right*. Right is decent and good, but above all *direct*. It means *correct*, and immediate – go the *right way* and you'll get there *right away*, *right now*. An *upright* citizen is a *downright* good fellow: note that the *righteous* always travel in straight, *regular* lines – there's no such thing as being 'sideright' or 'sloperight'; the habits of good ploughing have never died out in language.

Regere in Latin originally meant to guide; since the Romans didn't go in much for guidance, it soon meant to command. That's why we have *regulations* and *regions* – rules, as well as areas for ruling. A *regime* is a system of government, and so is a *regimen*: once bureaucracy takes hold you have *regulators*, *register* offices and *registration* number plates.

Like the Old Celtic *rig*, and the Hindi *raja*, in Rome *rex* meant king. Kings *reign* ... but if that is impossible, because they are too young or too infirm for *regal* duties, a *regent* steps in. The last *Prince Regent* of England was George III's son, the Prince of Wales, who assumed the *regalia* (literally, *royal* powers and *sovereign* privileges) in 1811 when his father's mental health collapsed. This avoided an *interregnum* – a period without a king.

Rex implied greatness, and unchallenged majesty – not merely king, but king of kings, the *maharaja* or great king. A lesser monarch was *regulus* or, if she was female, *regula*. *Regula* also meant a straight measuring rod, and by elision (that is, people becoming too lazy to sound the 'g'), regula became *ruler*. There's nothing *irregular* about that.

Another missing 'g' turned **reg** into *roi* in medieval France. Going to the right was *ad roi*, which explains why *droit* is now French for right and *adroit* is a synonym for dexterous (while *maladroit* is clumsy). In England, *roi* became *royalty*, but in Spanish it was *real*, as in *Real Madrid*. The destruction of the Armada in 1588 ended the Spaniards' hopes of conquering the English kingdom, or *realm*. The path around Hyde Park where the gentry paraded their carriages and horses, and where riders still canter today, was the *route de roi*, which meant King's Way. Londoners who didn't speak French and were not impressed by the miles of dung encircling the park changed it to Rotten Row.

Rectus in Latin is straight, or *erect*. The *rectum* is the lower intestine, leading straight out. A *rector* is a spiritual guide and, as all lovers of nineteenth-century fiction know, he lives in a *rectory*. A shape with four straight sides is a *rectangle*, and if it has five, that will have to be *rectified*; that is, straightened out.

In Tudor England, to play *rex* was to act as master, usually as a game. The 'e' was pronounced long, as 'reex', and until the eighteenth century playing *reaks* meant japes or pranks.

The hidden meanings of words lurk at a subconscious level, especially in names. Fans of the medieval TV fantasy *Game of Thrones* will know that one of many usurpers who declares himself 'King in the North' is enslaved and tortured by his enemy. When his spirit and sanity are broken, he is given a new name: *Reek*. His torturer tells him it is because he stinks; he *reeks*. But this mocking name for a man who played at being king is deeply resonant, even if the viewer is not consciously aware of the reason – for he has been playing 'reex'.

Ru, to cry out

*R*udra was the god of storms, a four-headed destroyer who fired bolts of lightning from his bow. To his Ancient Vedic worshippers, he was 'fierce like a wild beast' and could spread disease with his breath or blow clean air over the land as he chose. Of all the thirty-three major deities in this 3,500-year-old Indian religion, sometimes called Bhramanism, Rudra was the one its worshippers most feared.

His name was inspired by the moaning noise of the wind; a sound echoed in different ways by the lowing of cattle, the howling of wolves and the cawing of *rooks*. The first Stone Age settlers had a word for it: **ru**. It was the sound of nature.

The closest word in English is *roar*, but **ru** was so much more than that. It was the *raucous rumpus* of the farmyard, the *rumble* of the ground as a herd of cattle moved and the bellow of the ox in *rut*. In medieval French, *ruit* meant sexual *roaring*, either animal or human, and that's where we get *riot* from: during the Hundred Years War, the French evidently were not such urbane and sophisticated lovers as they claim to be today.

The Dutch *ruiter*, 500 years ago, was a word for a mercenary, especially a German cavalryman, the kind that killed, razed, raped and plundered as they tore through the Lowlands. The Germans spelled it *reuter*, though by the time that the pioneering journalist Paul *Reuter* set up a news agency from the London Stock Exchange in the 1850s, the *reuters* had settled down a bit. In Shakespeare's day a *rutterkin* was a bully, a 'swaggering gallant' who made a lot of noise.

The Latin word for the throat was *rumen*, and so to chew the cud – when a cow brings predigested grass up its gullet into its mouth – was *ruminare*, which thoughtfully gives us *ruminate*.

The wind does not always roar; sometimes it whispers, and that is where the concept of *rumours* comes from – words borne on the wind. The original Anglo-Saxon sense of *rune* was a murmur or whisper, and so a mystery. Later it became the word for a secret conference, and then for the arcane lore of written letters: a mystery known only to a few initiates. *Runes* were not merely an alphabet but a set of magical signs, spells carved into stone.

Because **ru** was an animal cry, the fields where the cattle grazed were **rus**, and that word survived unscathed into Latin, to mean the countryside. In English it became *rustic*, which started off as the opposite of urban. Then it became a term of contempt for the uneducated, superstitious peasantry, and by the Elizabethan era it signified yokels, buffoons and moonrakers – the kind of bumpkins and *roisterers* who would spend a drunken night trying to fish the moon's reflection out of a village pond. In the eighteenth century, rustic carpentry and masonry was rough-hewn with sturdy joints, and since that didn't tend to tumble down or fall apart, houses and furniture made in the rustic style gradually became popular … especially with *ruralists*, the townies who wanted to escape to a *rural* life, for the weekends at least.

Room was originally not an enclosed indoor area but a place outside with sufficient space to graze animals. It's a clear area, in the sense of *making room*, or giving yourself some *elbow room*. A room became an indoor compartment only when it had a *roof* above it. A *roomful* is as many as the space will hold, and in Chaucer's time *roomsome* meant ample or capacious. The word *roomage*, or internal capacity, survives in American English; there's an echo of it in *rummage*, which once meant to arrange cargo in a ship's hold and now means to ferret through crowded or untidy storage. Next time you have a good rummage around, remember that, by definition, you should be making the room more tidy.

Rud, red

The first painters used ochre, an iron-rich earth that was mixed with saliva and animal fat before it was applied to cave walls. Some of the most ancient, depicting men, horses and bison, at the Chauvet caves in southern France, are over 30,000 years old. Ochre can vary from yellow to brown, but it is predominantly red – the most important colour in the Stone Age world.

Red is the colour of life and death, of blood, meat and the rising sun. *Ruddy* faces are signs of a *rude* constitution, because they attest to good circulation.

Rude usually means coarse, or ill-mannered. In the sixteenth century, a *rudesby* was an insolent, brawling troublemaker, whereas a *rudas* was a foul-mouthed drunken old woman. To be *rumbustious* is to be boisterous and boozed up – it's a punning mix of *robustious* and rum. Rude can also mean *robustly* healthy, but its original meaning was half-finished, because it comes from the Latin *rudis*, meaning raw – like red meat. *Robustus* in Latin was strength, sometimes in the sense of being hard as oakwood: the oak was *roboreus*, because of the hardness of its timber. To *corroborate* a story means to stiffen and strengthen it, literally to 'confirm' it. A *roborant* is a strengthening, invigorating medicine or tonic.

In Russian, *rabota* means hard work; in Old Slavic, it signi-fied slavery. *Robot* in Greek, and *robota* in Ukrainian, is forced labour. It's the word that Czech playwright Karel Čapek was playing with when he invented *robots* for his 1921 play *RUR*. Čapek's storyline, about sentient metal humanoids that tire of being servants and decide to rule the world instead, has been part of the *rubric* (that is, the laws) of science fiction for a century. In Rome, the laws were the rubric, because they were written in red ochre. In today's civil service, rubric is red writing, highlighting a heading or passage.

A *red letter* is an important piece of news; a scarlet letter, on the other hand, was the brand that Hester Prynne, the heroine of Nathaniel Hawthorne's novel, was forced to wear on her dress – a bright red 'A' for adultery. Red is the colour of shame, because it's the colour of blushing – the involuntary flush of blood to the face. The fear of blushing is *erythrophobia*, from *erythros*, the Greek for red.

Rubeus is the Latin word for crimson red, and so *rubescence* is another term for blushing. The French took *rubeus* and turned it into *rouge*, a fine powder made from dried safflower petals that *rubified* the cheeks and lips. To *raddle* your face was to paint it red. It's a common mistake to think that being *raddled* is to be worn out by excess and self-indulgence; it simply means to be badly and brazenly made up, like an elderly woman of low repute.

Rubella is German measles, which causes a bright red rash, and *rubeola* are the red pimples in measles and smallpox. A *rubefacient* is an ointment that causes a rash when you *rub* it in – again, rub goes back to the idea of red meat, because vigorous rubbing will chafe the flesh till it is raw.

Rubor is any kind of *redness*, and *rubification* is heating a sub-stance till it glows red. Oxidation can also turn some metals red, with *rust*. *Russus* is another Latin word for red – the *rosy, russet* shade. *Rutilus* is yet another, a golden red, and *rufus* is one more, a more ginger colour. William II, the son of William the

Conqueror, was nicknamed *William Rufus* because of his red face. Squat and strong, with a pot belly, he never married and took little trouble to hide his homosexuality. He had a *rudimentary* sense of humour – his idea of a joke was emptying a chamberpot over his brother from a balcony. The incident sparked three years of civil war.

A *rosarium* in Latin was a *rose garden*, called a *rosery* in English. This flowery title was taken for Tudor prayer books, especially the *Rosary of Our Lady*, which contained a set of devotions or repeated prayers. To help the pious keep count, 165 beads strung on a thread is a *rosary*, and 55 beads make a *lesser rosary*.

Roseate means *ruby-red*, whereas a *rosette* is a knotted bunch of *ribbons* like a *rose*. We know ribbons were once always red, because the Old Germanic word is *ruban*.

Ruddle is an ochre, used by farmers for marking their sheep and by house-proud Victorians for polishing out the scuffmarks on their stone doorsteps. A *rowan* tree has red berries – rowan seems a long way from **rud**, but in Norse it was *raun*, and before that *rugn* – its name might literally mean red one.

The root word **rud** has survived unchanged into English as the name for a deep-bodied freshwater fish with red fins and tail – the *rudd*.

S

Sa, to sow
Seed, secular, sapphire, Saturday

Sat, to be full
Sad, satisfy, satirist, insult

Sed, to sit
Settee, sedan, cathedral, resident

Spek, to see
Spectacles, specific, inspector, bishop

Sta, to stand
Stable, stammer, solstice, ecstasy

Streg, to squeeze
Strain, string, strangle, prestige

Swear Words
Punch, skittle, oracle, fizzle

Sa, to sow

'We plough the fields and *scatter* the good *seed* on the land', begins the children's hymn. There's good seed and bad seed, and the word has ambiguous connotations: seeds are the source of all new life, but they also represent overripe maturity and decay. Anything *gone to seed* is beyond its best, but worse still is *seedy*, which means grubby and base.

In biblical language, a man's seed are his children, the product of his *semen*. One good place for studying the Bible is a *seminary*, which in the Roman Catholic church is a college for trainee priests, though the word originally meant a *seedbed* where young plants were nurtured. To *sow* seeds is to *disseminate* them; it's more precise to take a *seed drill* and *insert* them in the soil. The original meaning of *season* was sowing time. *Sative* plants are cultivated, not wild.

One possible derivation of a *cycle*, the length of time it takes for the world to come round to the same point, is that, instead of being a kind of circle, it comes from the Latin *saeclum*, a generation – from one sowing to the next. In French, a *siècle* is usually a century, and *fin de siècle* implies decadence and rebirth at the end of an era.

In the Gothic language, spoken from the Atlantic to the Crimea during the Dark Ages, *mana-seeth* was the seed of man, or mankind. *Secular* life is everything beyond the strictly spiritual: secular art, for instance, is not religious. A *secularist* believes that morality has nothing to do with the worship of God, and church-going is irrelevant in a good life. The Spanish Inquisition was the *secular arm* of the Catholic church in the sixteenth century, and kept the clergy at arm's length from the nastiness of torture as it rooted out heretics.

The oldest of the Roman deities, *Saturn*, who was originally the god of the harvest, might also derive his name from **sa** – for early farmers, harvest brought the promise that what was sown would bear fruit and everyone could eat their fill. His festival was held not in autumn but at midwinter, the *saturnalia*. Even the city's slaves were allowed to celebrate, and the festivities became a week of unbridled licence and depravity. Perhaps that is why the god's reputation gradually became darker and more sinister, until *saturnine* came to mean gloomy and malign. Satan, the name of God's arch-enemy, is almost the same, and oddly unrelated – it comes from the Hebrew *satan*, which means an adversary. Hebrew is not even an Indo-European language, so the similarities between Saturn and Satan are all coincidence.

Medieval alchemists identified lead with Saturn. That was no recommendation, since the alchemist's vocation was to get rid of lead by transmuting it into gold. *Saturnism* is now the pathologist's name for lead poisoning.

In Saxon England, one day a week was sacred to the god, *Saeternesdaeg* or *Saturday*. His name in Sanskrit was *sanis*, and his holy blue stone was the *sanipriya*, which the Greeks called *sappheiros* and we call a *sapphire*. Artificial sapphires can be created by heating aluminium oxide to more than 2,000 degrees centigrade, but if you want to make your own jewellery there are easier ways … such as inserting a flake of grit into an oyster and waiting a couple of years for a *seed pearl* to form.

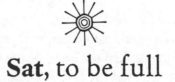

Sat, to be full

Rock music is full of *sad* stories. Mick Jagger tells us that he tried and he tried but, you see, he was on a losing streak: 'I can't get no *satisfaction*'. Freddie Mercury, on the other hand, had paid his dues, time after time, and done his sentence (but committed no crime). He had achieved *satispassion* – atonement for his sins through a sufficiency, a *saturation* of suffering.

To be *sated* is to be glutted, filled to excess. It's an exhausting business, being *satiated* with pleasure, and the early English verb to *sade* means to become worn out and tired. In Chaucer's time, *sadness* was weariness, but also *satiety*: sad meant full of woe.

Sade has nothing to do with sadism, a perverse lust for cruelty that can never be *satisfied*: it is named after the Napoleonic Count Jean Baptiste François Joseph de Sade, whose depraved rantings condemned him to spend more than thirty years in prisons and lunatic asylums.

The Latin word *satis*, meaning enough, also forms a compound word with *facere*, to do. *Satisfacere* means what it says: to do enough. Don't, and you will leave people *unsatisfied* … or, what is worse, *dissatisfied*. The former means they want more; the latter means they are not happy.

The phrase *ad satis* means to the point of being enough, and in Old French became *assez*. *Aver assez*, in medieval law, was to have enough wealth to cover your debts, and so *assets* came to signify property that could be turned into cash.

A dish of mixed meats or fruits in Ancient Rome was *satura lanx*, a *satisfying balance*. Shortened to *saturi*, it was applied to the writing of caustic wits such as Horace and Juvenal, who wrote *satires*. At first, the emphasis was on the mix and the medley, but soon it gave way to derision and lampoon, and *satirists* were celebrated for the ferocity of their *satirical* attacks.

The Greeks had a word that meant insatiable sexual desire in a man: *saturiasis*. It described the lecherous demons that lived in the forests and worshipped the god of debauchery, Dionysus – the *satyrs*. The Romans called them fauns: they had the legs and hooves of goats, and their bodies were covered in hair. When orangutans were first discovered by Europeans in Indonesia, in the Middle Ages, they were called *simia satyri* – monkey satyrs.

Doctors still use the term *satyriasis* for a state of priapism or constant male overexcitement. But the word is not related to *salacious*, which comes from the Indo-European root **sal**, to leap or jump. Jump is modern slang for sexual intercourse, and the wordplay is at least 8,000 years old, because **sal** could refer to a stallion covering a mare. But there's nothing saucy about a *salmon*: it's just a fish that *sallies* forth up river and leaps waterfalls.

The Latin *exsultare* translates as to leap out or jump up and down vigorously, in *exultation*. The opposite was *insultare*, to leap in upon someone and attack them, either physically or verbally with *insults*. An *assailant* is an attacker who leaps out at victims, and commits an *assault*. In Latin, *saltare* was to leap repeatedly, and thus to dance, which tells you something about the Roman style of dancing – they were probably all doing the *salsa*. A *saltarello* is a Spanish or Italian dance, full of leaps and bounds.

To *saltate* is to dance and jump, and generally to be *saltant*. Frogs are *saltatory*, and move in hops and skips, whereas jumping spiders are *saltigrade*. A *saltimbanco* is a charlatan and a bounder.

Because *resultare* was to leap back, *resultatio* was an echo, a sound that came leaping back at you – and in consequence we got the word *result*. *Desilire* meant to leap down; *desultory* means unmethodical and leaping about from one thing to another. A *desultor* is a circus bareback rider, leaping from horse to horse, and perhaps performing *somersaults*.

Sed, to sit

The socialite Nancy Mitford tweaked a million middle-class inferiority complexes in 1955 with an essay called 'The English Aristocracy', which pointed out that our vocabulary reveals our social class. Upper class or 'U' people, Nancy said, use straightforward language, while the aspiring lower-middles or 'non-U' classes prefer to employ euphemisms and affected 'faux' words. False teeth and glasses are 'U', dentures and spectacles are 'non-U'. If you're posh, you say napkin, pudding and lavatory; if you're common, you say serviette, sweet and toilet.

Nancy's highly-tuned sense of snobbery failed her in one case, however. Consider the main piece of furniture in the sitting room (or lounge, if you lack class): the 'U' term was sofa, while the 'non-U' called it a *settee*. But sofa is the highfalutin, show-offish word, from the Arabic *suffah* meaning cushion. Settee is Indo-European – it just means the thing we *sit* on. Clearly, Nancy's rules were not *set* in stone.

The Old English for a *seat* is *setl*, which gives us *settle*, meaning to *set yourself down*. *Saddle* is closely related; it comes from *sadl*. In medieval French, a seat was a *sie* – a bishop in his high seat oversees his domain, which is why it is called a *see*. When soldiers sit and wait for a city to fall, that's a *siege*.

In Ancient Greek, a seat is *hedra* – the 's' of **sed** has shifted to an 'h'. *Kata* is Greek for down, so *cathedral* is literally a *sit-you-down* – in practice, a high-backed seat with two arms, or a throne. That's why *chaire* in French is a pulpit, and although it seems unrecognisable as a descendant of **sed**, that's how we got our *chair*.

In English cathedrals, the clergy occupy the *sedilia* (three chairs crowned with canopies and pinnacles) because to sit in Latin is *sedere*. Disporting yourself calmly, without leaping around, is *sedate* behaviour – if you simply can't sit still, perhaps you need a *sedative*. The yeast that settles at the bottom of a bottle of beer, or the mud on the bed of a river, is the *sediment*. Before cars took over, wealthy folk who didn't want the trouble of a horse and carriage could hire a *sedan chair* and be carried in comfort; the four-door family cars known in Britain as saloons were christened *sedans* in the States.

To give up is to sit down in the face of the enemy, or *cede*. Agreeing to their demands is *acceding* and *conceding*. If you've been compelled by force to *cease*, *concessions* will be *necessary* or you might end up *deceased*.

The higher the chair, the greater the authority in ancient courts, so if you sit above a colleague, you *supersede* them. The one who sits highest of all is the *president*. A writ of *supersedeas* halts legal proceedings, until the *presiding* judge *intercedes* and points to some *precedent* that restarts the *process*. A very *sedentary* business, the law: that's why the *sessions* are often known as *assizes*. Both words derive from the Latin *adsidere*, meaning to sit at a table – it's also the root of *assiduous* and *assiduity*.

To sit habitually in one place is *obsidere*, which we might call a little *obsessive*. *Obsidion* was Latin for a *siege*, so a Roman general who rescued a besieged city would be honoured with a wreath of grass called the *corona obsidionalis*. He might also earn a triumphal *procession*: the word implies that the victor is either seated on a horse or carried on a throne.

Dissidere in Latin is to sit *outside*, as a *dissident*. *Insidere* is to sit *inside*, of course, but there's a concept hidden within the word: it becomes *insidiae*, which means an ambush. *Insidious* means deceitful, treacherous and cunning – all the traits needed to *set a trap*.

Subsidere is to sit under, or in reserve. Government loans are *subsidies*: they prevent many businesses from *subsiding*. On the other hand, to sit back and perhaps do nothing is *residere*. That gives us *residence* and *residential*, and also *residue*. The people of the lowest classes, far below even the commonest 'non-U's, are the *residuum* – a term coined by the Quaker MP and radical campaigner John Bright. He fought for universal suffrage, the right for every man to vote, but even he believed it should not be given to the criminal classes or the *residents* of the workhouse … the disreputable poor. Many of whom, no doubt, were our *ancestors* – ultimately, the people who were sitting here before us.

Spek, to see

The Roman historian Pliny the Elder claimed that Emperor Nero used a large emerald to help him watch gladiator battles at the circus, holding it up to his eye like a lens. Nero was presumably short-sighted, since this appears to be the first known use of a prism to correct a *spectator's* eyesight. Never mind designer Ray-Bans – precious stones the size of pigeon eggs must qualify as the most expensive *spectacles* ever.

Specere in Latin means to see, and *speculum* is a mirror. A *specula* is a watchtower, a place for *spying* out the land. Lookouts on long watches have a lot of time alone with their thoughts, and so *speculate* initially meant to reflect and contemplate, before it acquired its commercial sense of investment and risk-taking.

Because *specio* in Latin means 'I look at', scientists adopted the word to help them categorise their discoveries. Life was divided into *species*, by *specialists*. Most creatures belong to a definite, *specific* type, but some only look like they do, which makes them rather *specious* or dubious. These are *special* cases, which can be *specified* at a later date, according to *specifications*.

Species took on two more meanings in Latin. *In specie* meant in kind, as opposed to in cash, though in the seventeenth century it came to mean payment in gold or silver. These days *specie* means coinage in general. But in Roman times, it referred to merchandise: traders could avoid taxes by exchanging goods, without cash changing hands. Aromatic herbs from the East such as saffron and cinnamon always held their value, and so were a popular source of *in specie* funds. In medieval French, *espicer* came to mean trading in these goods, which the English called *spices*.

Spek is the core of all sorts of 'looking' words. If people look up to you, that's *respect*. If they look askance, that means they *suspect* you. If you look down on them, that is technically *despect*, an obsolete word for contempt. We don't say, 'I feel despect for that man', but we do say, 'I *despise* him'. *Despite* used to mean the same thing – utter scorn and disdain. The word was shortened to *spite*. John Milton liked the word *despiteful* to describe Satan, when he felt he was overusing *despicable*, but we just say *spiteful*. *Despite* is now a shorter way of saying *in spite of*.

Because *spectare* in Latin means to gaze at, we have *expectations* – *ex* + *spec*, things we are looking out for. If we are gazing inwards, that is *inspection*. The term *inspector* was coined around 1600, for an official who examined weights and measures. The first British *police inspector* was James Buchanan, appointed in 1779 in Glasgow – the perfect hero for a historical detective thriller, if ever there was one. One of the earliest inspectors to appear in literature was Javert in Victor Hugo's *Les Misérables*, published in 1862. There have been brilliant inspectors like Morse and Rebus, and *conspicuous* disasters such as Clouseau.

Like policemen, *spies* must be on the lookout. In Old High German, *spehon* means to examine closely. *Espier* in Old French is *spying* or, as the security services prefer to call it, *espionage*.

The best spies are *perspicacious*, because to look right through an object was *perspicere*. In painting, the art of making it appear that the viewer could reach into the picture is *perspective*. The things ahead of us are *prospective*, and those behind us *retrospective*.

Spek switched its letters around in Greek to *skep*. The *sceptics* in philosophy were doubters, the ones who could see right through everything. Most *sceptical* of all was Pyrrho, who mistrusted all his senses. He refused to believe what his eyes told him, and his friends had to follow him to make sure that he didn't deny the existence of a cliff edge and walk off it.

A watcher was *scopos*, which gives *scope* as an ending for numerous words. A *horoscope* is compiled by watching the stars, usually with a *telescope*. An *episcopant* is a *bishop*, who watches over the *episcopacy*: he would be a 'biskop', but the 'k' slowly softened to an 'h' – it was *bisceop* in Old English, and *bischop* in medieval times.

Some readers may still be transfixed by the *spectre* of Nero at the Circus Maximus, staring through a gemstone prism that probably acted as a *kaleidoscope* and split the *spectacle* into a *spectrum*.

It's a pity he didn't think to use fossilised amber, which was cheaper than emerald and just as *transpicuous*. The old word for amber was *aspic* – it means to see through or, simply, clear.

Sta, to stand

A t first sight, **sta** is the most obvious of roots. It has barely changed its sound in 8,000 years, and that makes a *statement* about how early man saw himself: to be human meant *standing* upright. It was all about our two-legged *stature*.

There are many obvious derivatives in English: *stable, understand, statue, stamp, stance, stalwart*. Food left standing goes *stale*, and water becomes *stagnant*. Animals *stand* at night in a *stall*; the Latin was *stallum*, which gives us *stallion*. To come to a *standstill* is also to stall, to prevent a thing is to *forestall* it and to put a thing in place is to *install* it.

But **sta** is much more pervasive than that. Hundreds of words *stem* from it, and many are far from obvious at first. The Old English *staell* meant a spot for a man to stand in his lord's hall, perhaps with the aid of a ceremonial *staff* – his *station*, which reflected his *status*. It came to mean his place at the great table, where he sat on his *stool*. But *staell* also transformed into another word, thanks to a process called thinning, where a long vowel becomes shortened. The 'ae' sound became a clipped 'i', and staell turned into *still*, which means standing motionless.

To get stuck on a word is to *stammer*, or to *stumble* over it. In Old Germanic, *stum* meant dumb, and we still talk about keeping *schtum* when we want to *stay* quiet.

In Latin, *statarius* means upright and immobile, like a sentry outside Buckingham Palace. A *stationarius* was a *stall-holder* in the marketplace, who kept to a fixed spot: produce sellers with their barrows of vegetables might come and go with the seasons, but the bookseller was always there, whatever the weather – he was the *stationary* (unmoving) *stationer* (publisher) who sold *stationery* (papers).

Circumstare meant to stand around. As every fan of detective thrillers knows, the facts surrounding a case are *circumstantial*. That's a *constant* – which, in Latin, means to stand firm. To stand together, on the other hand, is *constituere*, which is why a body of voters are a *constituency* and the laws of the land are its *constitution*. The opposite is *destitution*, which is the result when all your friends stand away from you – they become *distant*.

When something stands in your way, it is an *obstacle*. You can still reach your *destination* if you are *obstinate*: it is your *destiny*. These last three, with 'stin' at their core, seem a long way removed from **sta**, but Eric Partridge, who had a nose for these things, believed that the Roman word *stinare* was a nasal version of the basic *stare*, meaning to stand. Obviously, those famous Roman noses affected their pronunciation.

Obstare meant to stand against. It became *oster* in Old French, with the sense of running people off their land. In English, the word is now *oust*.

To stand back was *restare*, which gives us *rest* as well as *restitution*. To stand forward, on the other hand, was very different – it implied a woman in the street pushing herself forward (*pro stare*) to sell her body, a *prostitute*.

To stand under was *substare*, which explains *substantial*, a solid foundation; to place under was *substituere*, which explains *substitution*; to place over was *superstare*, which doesn't exactly explain *superstition* – until you remember that for the Romans, inexplicable rites and sacrifices to the gods possessed a paradoxical force in a nation that was basically cynical about religion. *Superstitia* were the preditions of oracles and soothsayers that went above and beyond the rational.

In the later Roman Empire, a *vassus* was a servant. It was a word borrowed from Celtic: in the northern tribes, *vastis* was a house, and the original concept was probably that the dwelling stood in one place, instead of moving around like a nomad's tent. *Vastis* shares that meaning with our *homestead*.

Vassus, the servant, meant a man whose duty was to stand by and await orders. It became *vassal* in Norman French, a peasant who swears allegiance to a landowner in return for his protection, but it also became *valet* – a young nobleman in attendance at court. In twentieth-century England, a valet, as Jeeves sometimes reminded his employer Bertie Wooster, was a gentleman's personal gentleman, and not a butler. Jeeves would have been less pleased to know that the word also turned into the French *varlet*, a scoundrel.

When the sun stands still, that's the *solstice* – *sol* + *stare*. When events are imminent, they stand up close – *in* + *stare*, which gives us *instant*. But when they stand beyond us, they are *ex* + *stare*, or *extant* ... and if that blows your mind and sends your consciousness to stand outside your own body, you can count yourself very lucky ... that's *ecstasy*.

Streg, to squeeze

Note to readers of an anxious disposition: some of the ideas here are gory, brutish and quite *distressing* ...
Mr Spock started the trend in *Star Trek*, with the Vulcan

nerve pinch, a martial-arts technique that rendered a victim unconscious with one tweak to the base of the neck. He also patented the Vulcan death grip, with the heel of the hand to the base of the nose, inducing an instant coma. Action heroes such as Jason Bourne and Jack Bauer took it a stage further with the 'military neck break' – a quick twist of the head that was silently lethal. But what no leading man ever does is to wrap his fingers around a minion's neck and slowly squeeze the life out of him. Only a villainous seven-foot henchman would ever do that. For one thing, it requires callousness, even sadism. And for another, *strangling* demands great *strength*.

Death by *strangulation* was a form of ritual killing in prehistoric times. The mummified corpse of an Iron Age man was found in peat bogs on the Jutland Peninsula in Denmark in 1946: at first it was assumed he was a recent murder victim, because his corpse was so well preserved. In fact, he had been dead for 2,400 years – *strangled* by a thin length of *string*.

The rope around the neck was not generally used for killing, however. The Greek *strangale* means a halter, of the kind still used in Mediterranean countries to lead donkeys. For early farmers, a noose was probably an effective method for subduing and taming wild horses, or even dogs – in much the same way that the gauchos of the Wild West used the lasso to round up steers.

The basic implication of **streg** is that something is pressing hard against flesh. In Rome, where the citizens loved baths but had not invented soap, a bone scraper like a window-cleaner's squeegee was used to sluice sweat away: it was called a *strigil*.

The Latin word *stringere* means to draw tight. In English, *stringent* rules are rigorously binding, and *astringent* cleansers make the pores close up – much better than dragging a *strigil* over your face. The opposite of *stringere* was *distringere*, to draw things apart and separate them. That's where the concept of *districts* comes from. But being pulled to pieces is an upsetting experience, and *distringere* is also the basis of *distress*.

In Old French, *stringere* became *estraindre*, or *streynan* in medieval English, meaning to draw something tight, such as a bowstring. That's why an athlete *strains* every fibre – until he pulls a muscle, which is also called a *strain*.

When a prisoner was bound in ancient times, he was *restrained* (from *restringere*, or bound back) and placed under *constraints* (from *constringere*, or bound together). He might also be blindfolded: in Latin, that is *praestringere oculos*, which literally means to bind the eyes beforehand. That came to refer to blinding, by having the eyes gouged out or burned away with red-hot coals, and this in turn gave rise to a ghoulishly comic word – *praestigiousus*. It meant blindingly brilliant, like the sun or, indeed, a red-hot coal. That's where we get *prestigious* and *prestige* from.

Sleight of hand can also dazzle the eye, if the conjuror is clever enough. A magician's tricks were called *prestigiae*, which gives us *prestidigitation. Hey presto!*

Early Indo-European had a related word, **snar**, which translates as to pull tight. Its meaning has barely changed with snare. In northern Europe it lost the 's' and became *narwa* in Old High German, which means a scar – where a wound was pulled tight with needle and thread. That's the origin of *narrow*. The Old German *narke* is related, meaning numbness – the way a limb loses its feeling when it is tightly bound with a tourniquet. *Narke* became *narcotic*, a medieval word meaning any substance that induces sleep or unconsciousness. *Narcosis* is a state of drugged insensibility, which is much better than a tourniquet if someone is about to sew up a gaping wound.

Snar became *neuron* in Greek, which originally meant a tendon but that is now a cell in the brain that transmits information along a string of other cells. The plural of neuron is *neura*, which is why people of a *nervous* disposition are said to be *neurotic*. Which, after all that bloodshed, you would be entitled to be.

Swear Words

When Dr Samuel Johnson was at the height of his celebrity in London, after he published his pioneering *Dictionary of the English Language* in 1755, he called on two genteel ladies – Mrs Brooke, the wife of a Lincolnshire clergyman, and her sister Mrs Digby. The sisters congratulated him on declining to include any 'naughty' words in the book. 'What! My dears!' exclaimed the doctor. 'Then you have been looking for them ...'

They hadn't been looking hard enough, in fact: fart and piss are both in there. Johnson defines one as 'to break wind behind' and the other as 'to make water'.

All the 'naughty' words that we think of as Anglo-Saxon are actually far older – people have been using the same expletives for thousands of years. To save readers the trouble that Mrs Brooke and Mrs Digby had – of searching out the rude words individually – they are collected here together.

puk – fuck

With the Celtic shift from 'p' to 'f', **puk** became *fuck*, and it probably meant exactly what it does today. Two sorts of words have evolved from it. The first are to do with piercing (an obvious sexual connotation) such as *puncture* and *point*. The others have to do with *punching* – because a fist clenched from the elbow is a universal sexual gesture.

Pungere is the Roman word for to *prick*. The original sense of *pungent* was *sharp-pointed*, though only botanists employ that meaning now. It can mean *poignant* and distressing, but its commonest meaning is as an adjective for penetrating tastes and odours – the ones that make the back of your throat *prickle*.

A *punctum* is a dot, a *puncture wound* – it might be caused by a *puncheon*, which is a needle-sharp bodkin or awl for drilling holes … a cross between a dagger and a *hole punch*. When material is drawn tight around a hole, it *puckers*.

Punctuation pierces a sentence. To be *punctual* is to arrive on the dot. To *pounce* is to swoop and seize prey in claws or talons.

The Italian *puntiglio* means 'a fine point', and in English it became *punctilio*, a trifling detail or an error so minor that only a *punctilious* pedant would point it out. A play on words produced *pundigrion*, a made-up name for a word with two or three meanings. Pundigrion sounds pompous and mock-learned, the kind of tongue-in-cheek coinage that would appeal to lovers of word games. In Restoration times, there was a fashion for shortening words to the first syllable, and pundigrion became *pun*. Such low humour didn't amuse everyone: the critic John Dennis said scornfully in 1722, 'He that would pun would pick a pocket'. That didn't stop the author Thomas Sheridan from publishing a pamphlet listing thirty-four rules for *punning*, the *Ars Punica*. Rule no. 32 was, 'Never to speak well of another *Punster*'.

If your conscience is *pricked*, that's *compunction*. To delete a word is *expunging* it: originally this was done with a needle, pricking holes in the parchment until the text became illegible.

Dots marked on cards were the easiest way of keeping score at cards, which is why we score *points*. In Spanish, a point was *punto* – so taking a chance to win the game is having a *punt*.

The fist in Latin is *pugnus*, and to fight with bare knuckles is *pugnare*. That gives us *pugilist* and *pugnacious*, and of course *punch*.

To *expugn* or 'vanquish by force of arms' comes from the Latin *expugnare*, which meant to fight your way out. The opposite is *impugnare*, to fight your way in, and it gives us *impugn* (which generally means to assault an enemy's reputation, with angry words and even slander). *Repugnare* is to fight back, and in English, *repugn* means to resist strongly. *Repugnance* is a visceral, instinctive disgust.

In Greek, a *pygme* was a measurement, the distance from fist to elbow – the tiny tribesmen of central Africa were said by the earliest explorers to be no taller than that, and were therefore dubbed *Pygmies*.

skei – shit

There's no clear English equivalent of **skei**. It means to hurl something away or spit it out, like *shying* a stone, putting the *shot* or dropping a parcel down a *shute*. Or taking a *shit*, of course.

In the Middle Ages, the Old English 'sk' sound was softened to a 'sh', so *sceotan* became *shoot*. That word really implies speed: 'The *shuttle shot* forward faster than a *gunshot*.' When we *get shot* of something, it's gone for good. We *shut* the door, and *shoot* the bolt home.

In German, *scheissen* is to defecate. During the gold rush of the 1850s, Australian miners borrowed the word, and a *shicer* became a term for an unproductive dig that yielded no gold, nothing better that a *shit–hole*. *Shice* soon meant worthless money and *shicery* was fraud, practised by *shysters*. Following the same pattern, to *skive* came to mean doing no work, because a *skiver* was a useless idler.

In ten-pin bowling, the pegs are sometimes called *skittles*, but in Old English, the *skytel* was the missile itself. That's why we try to *skittle* the pins over. To the Vikings, a *skutill* was a harpoon. Also in Old Norse, *skytta* meant to shoot about: the word is the same in English, but we spell it *skitter*. A lively horse is *skittish*. *Skite* is still a dialect word for *horseshit*, and so for boasting. And the *skitters* is a slang name, like the trots, for diarrhoea. They are all *scatological* words.

So is *scat*, for that matter – as well as improvised jazz singing, it's the hunter's word for animal droppings. For an early farmer, whether he's spreading muck or sowing seeds, the process is much the same: he *scatters* it. And with the 'sk' to 'sh' shift, scatter becomes *shatter*, which makes sense when you think how fragments of crockery scatter everywhere when a plate shatters.

gn – cunt

Gn, to beget, has its own entry already, but as well as reproductive words such as *genitals* and *gynaecology*, it supplies us with a more basic one: *cunt*. In Latin it was *cunnus*; this can still be seen scrawled in 2,000-year-old graffiti at Pompeii. In polite Roman society, it was a word to be carefully avoided. 'We don't say *cum nobis* [with us], but rather *nobiscum*,' warned the essayist Cicero. 'If we said it the other way, the letters would run together in a rather obscene way.'

Etymologists can't explain how **gn** gained a 't' at the end, but in northern Europe it became *kunte*. The medieval English word for a rabbit, though, was *cunny*, which was probably a sexual pun: *kunte* and *cunnus* were both synonyms for the sex act, which is the raison d'être of the average rabbit. But there are rabbits in the Bible: the Book of Leviticus includes it in the list of animals that are not fit to eat. The preacher couldn't very well stand up in church and say 'cunny' – people would snigger. So the pronunciation was altered, to *coney* with a long 'o'. *Coney Island* in New York, where the funfairs are, was named *Conyne Eylandt* by the first Dutch settlers because it was overrun with rabbits.

Lexicographer Eric Partridge reckoned that the word cunt stemmed from **keu**, to conceal (because the female genitals are less visible than the male), or from **ku**, to swell (because **ku** was also a word for cow, and cows are female). Neither of these suggestions seems very convincing.

The earliest recorded use of the word is from a London street map dating to the reign of King Henry III, around 1230, where an alley amid the stews or brothels of Southwark was called Gropecuntelane. During the Puritan era in the seventeenth century, the word was declared legally obscene: a publisher who printed it could be prosecuted and fined or even imprisoned. Samuel Johnson ignored it, while Francis Grose's 1811 *Dictionary of the Vulgar Tongue* listed it as '*c**tt* … a nasty name for a nasty thing'. It was not until 1960, when Penguin Books faced an obscenity trial for publishing *Lady Chatterley's Lover*, that it became acceptable again to print the word. It was first said on British television by former Sex Pistols frontman John Lydon, during a live broadcast of the reality TV show *I'm a Celebrity … Get Me Out of Here!* in 2004.

In Sanskrit, *cushi* meant a ditch, which appears to be a vulgar double meaning. The sexual sense must have persisted, because in Hindu *cushi* means pleasure – and it made its way into Anglo-Indian slang, meaning easy or comfortable. A soldier who 'got it *cushy*' had a minor wound that took him out of the front line, perhaps to be sent home – what First World War troops called 'a Blighty one'. Just like cunny, cushy acquired an unexplained 't' at the end: in *Only Fools and Horses*, Del Boy (played by David Jason) always pronounced it *cushty*.

ors – arse

Ors is the Indo-European word for mouth. *Oral, oracle* and *oratory* all stem from it. But not every sound we make comes from the voice box – some noises come from the other end, our fundamental *orifice* … otherwise known as the *arse*. In Saxon England, it was pronounced *ears*, and *earsling* was a common term of abuse – it meant a dried tag of dirt hanging from a sheep's tail, and Saxons said it the way we might say idiot. The Anglo-Saxon for buttocks was *earsendo*, or *arse-end*, while the anus was *earsoerl*, or *arsehole*. *Ears* wasn't always regarded as a vulgar word: when Abbot Aelfric of Eynsham, known as Aelfric the Grammarian, compiled a glossary of Latin terms, around 1000 AD, he translated *tergosus* as *earsode*, meaning *broad-arsed*.

There has always been a connection between the arse and stupidity, probably predating that word *earsling* by thousands of years. In Tudor times, doing things the wrong way round was getting them *arsy-versy*. These days, we say *arse backwards*. The Romans meant something very different by *ars*: it was the creative arts, as in '*Ars longa, vita brevis*' – 'Life is short but art endures'. In Napoleonic times, *ars musica* was jocular slang for a fart … both the heavenly gift of music, and a blast on the bum trumpet.

tit – tit

The earliest meaning of **tit** still survives in English today. Some farmers still talk about getting newborn piglets or puppies *on the tit*, as in *teat* or nipple. It was probably an onomatopoeic word, imitating the sound of a baby suckling. For that matter, so was **pap**. Both are words for the whole breast now, though *tit* is more common, in every sense.

Because the teat is the small, functional part of something much bigger, *tit* became a word for anything small; in Napoleonic times, for example, it was a foal or a pony. The smallest family of garden birds are the *tits* – *blue tits*, *great tits*, *coal tits* and so on. In Old Welsh, any small bird is a *titlingr*. The Icelandic *tittr* is a *titmouse*, a bird of the chickadee family. A *titter*, on the other hand, is the littlest of laughs, not loud enough even to be a giggle. And small talk is *tittle-tattle*.

Titchy means little. The slang word became popular thanks to Harry Relph, a midget star of the music hall around the time of the First World War. He earned his stage name, Little Tich, not only because of his size but because his parents used to tease him as a boy that he was the spitting image of Victorian England's most notorious missing person … Sir Roger Tichborne, a wealthy baronet and London landowner who disappeared at sea en route to Jamaica. Little Tich's best-known act was the Big Boot Dance, performed on tiptoe in clodhoppers that were almost as long as he was tall. Film of his act, shot in 1900 at the Paris Exposition, still exists.

Titanic means the opposite of titchy, because it comes from

a completely different proto-language. Tito was the sun god to long-vanished tribes in the Middle East, who probably spoke a forerunner of Arabic. The Ancient Greeks adopted the name for their primeval gods, the Titans, a giant race who were overthrown by Zeus and the immortals. Titanism is a revolt against the established order of the universe.

In Latin, a nipple is *titta*, and *titillate* is to tickle. *Titillation* can be sensual stimulation, or just an itch or tingle. *Titivation*, on the other hand, is to make small adjustments and improvements to your dress, like straightening your hat or applying lipstick. Now there's a handy *titbit*.

piss – piss

Piss, the sound of a man urinating, is still *piss*, though if you're *pissed* in Britain you're drunk, while in the States you're angry. In Australia, a *pisso* is an alcoholic, and in France, a *pissoir* is a public toilet. In New York in the 1920s during hot weather, expensive restaurants placed blocks of ice in their urinals, to prevent the smell from drifting over towards the diners; to *piss on ice* became slang for living the high life.

pard – fart

If any word proves that Stone Age man had a bawdy sense of humour, **pard** is that word. It's impossible to think of its meaning and say it without laughing. By comparison, *fart* is a nasal noise, almost prissy. But fart has been the English slang for flatulence since Anglo-Saxon times at least, when the word was *feortan*. In Sanskrit, it is completely unchanged from the Indo-European root: *pard* is to break wind backwards. The shift from 'p' to 'f' also explains *fizzle*, which describes (and sounds like) a miniature fart.

The twee English apology, 'I beg your *pardon*', stems from the Latin *perdonare*, which literally means to forgive: *per*/for + *don*/

give. But since the Romans had a dirty sense of humour, the word has a double meaning: in Ancient Greek, *epardon* means 'I broke wind'. Next time you say pardon, remember that you're not only begging forgiveness … you are also admitting, 'I just *farted*'.

The *partridge* gets its name from the way its wings clatter and whirr like a thunderous fart when it takes flight. But it wasn't an Englishman who made that unsavoury connection: it was the French who first called it a *perdrix*.

The French also dreamed up a weapon of war based on the fart, which in France is *le pet*. Shaped like a bell, the *petard* was charged with gunpowder and wheeled up to a barred door. When the cannon was fired, the blast would blow the gate off its hinges. It was a dangerous machine, more likely to injure its own artillerymen than the enemy; in *Hamlet*, the Prince talks about the risk of having 'the engineer hoist with his own petard'. Shakespeare rarely makes a mistake with a word, but in fact the engineers had worked out long before that they didn't need to be anywhere near the gun when the fuse was lit. That was the job of a common soldier called a *petardeer*.

T

Tam, to cut

Atom, anatomy, tonsure, entomology

Teks, to make cloth

Text, textile, technical, tissue

Ten, to stretch

Tent, thin, tender, attention

Ters, dry

Terrain, torrid, toast, Mediterranean

Tor, to twist

Torque, torture, throw, tortoise

Tu, to swell

Tube, total, thumb, trifle

Tup, to strike

Type, typical, tambourine, stupid

Tam, to cut

The first stone tool was just a rock with a sharp edge – a rudimentary knife. The oldest flint blade, made not by *Homo sapiens* but by an earlier hominid, is 1.4m years old, discovered in a Spanish cave named the *Sima del Elefante* – Elephant Chasm cave. Humans have been cutting things since we first worked out how to wield stones.

Tam was one of the most basic Neolithic words. It appears to have had a dual meaning: to cut, and to choke – that is, to cut off the airway. When a large animal is slaughtered in a primitive society, its throat is cut; a small one gets its neck wrung. The word in either case is **tam**, and by extension **tam** meant to cut in any sense.

In Ancient Greek the word became *tom*, a syllable that was surgically inserted into all sorts of medical words. The human body, when flayed and dissected, was the *anatomy*.

The singer Tom Waits, a man who sounds as though his mouthwash is blended from charcoal-filtered whisky and hydrochloric acid, appeared on a US talk show in 1977 and defended his fondness for alcohol. 'I would rather have a bottle in front of me than a frontal *lobotomy*,' he said. Later, he admitted he had seen the one-liner scrawled on a toilet wall.

A lobotomy is a gruesomely simple bit of brain surgery, where a scalpel is inserted under the forehead, above the eyeball and under the rim of the skull, to sever the frontal lobes. Lobes are 'roundish, projecting parts' in the brain (from the Indo-European root **lab**, to hang down) – so this twentieth-century fad in psychosurgery takes its name from two Stone Age mono-syllables. **Lab, Tam**: it's like banging two rocks together.

In the gangster slang of America's underworld at the start of the twentieth century, a bang over the head was a 'haircut' ... as in, 'Give da guy a haircut, Huey!' That didn't mean Huey was a barber or that he was literally going to *tonsure* the unfortunate wretch – that is, cut his hair.

Lobotomies are now regarded as the *epitome* of drastic brain surgery. The Greek prefix *epi-* originally meant upon and is used at the front of English words to mean upon, over and above or utmost. So epitome literally means the highest, ultimate cut: the director's cut, if you like.

Apotome, in Greek, meant to cut off. Now it's a mathematical term defining the line that cuts a square in half from corner to corner. To *dichotomise* is to cut something in two, which is why a logical *dichotomy* divides everything into mutually exclusive groups: all objects are either red or not red, for example. This proposition can be disproved every time you drive up to traffic lights and they change to red and amber – 'The lights were not red, officer ... that is, not exactly.'

Using logic, the Greeks worked out that the smallest speck of matter possible would be the one that could never be cut in half – the *atom*. It was 4,000 years or so before Ernest Rutherford demonstrated that the Greeks were wrong and so discovered *atomic* energy. A huge amount of scientific study was done in the intervening millennia, most of it published in books so long that they had to be cut up into *tomes* or volumes.

To assess the content of ore in a rock, a miner must cut into it, which gives us *esteem* and *estimate*. Both words derive from the Latine *aestimare*, to fix or calculate a price: *aes* is brass. So the 'brass cut' (*aes* + *tom*) is the cross-section that reveals the value of the seam in a mine.

In grammar, the term *tmesis* means cutting a word into a longer word – 'Abso-bleedin-lutely,' as the autodidactic rag-and-bone man Harold Steptoe liked to say. And in biology, all insects have bodies divided or cut into segments: they are *entomic*, and the prefix *entomo-* means pertaining to insects. *Entomology* is the study of insects, an *entomolite* is a fossil insect and an *entomotomist* is someone who cuts insects up – two toms in one word.

But the tom-tom has nothing to do with **tam**. It's an onomatopoeic name – hit the drum and it goes 'Tom! Tom!' Never cut a tom-tom, of course: you'll ruin it.

Teks, to make cloth

Teks is another word for cloth-making, probably by combining layers of furs and skins that did not have to be woven. These thicker, warmer clothes were needed as the Stone Age tribes migrated north to colder climes. They had discovered *textiles*. We already knew they could plait branches to make wattle walls and fences (see **plak**) – but **teks** implies a different *technique*. A new *technology* had been invented.

In medieval English, *texture* referred to the different kinds of weave – close-woven, rough or ribbed, fine, twilled or so on.

In Ancient Greece, a skill or craft was *techne*; these days, they are taught in *technical* colleges and *polytechnics*. A carpenter was a *tekton*, and in English a *tectiform* surface forms a roof or a lid. The gargantuan roof tiles that cover the Earth's surface, causing tsunamis and earthquakes when they rub or clash, are *tectonic* plates.

Anything overlapping is *tegular*. Romans covered themselves with *togas* and their roofs with *tegulae*, which became *tigules* in Old English and are now called *tiles*. Togas, by the way, are the reason that *togs* has been slang for clothes since the fourteenth century, and we talk now of getting *togged up* when we dress for an occasion. If you didn't have anything decent to wear in late Victorian England, you were *tog-bound*, and needed to pay a visit to the *tog-fencer* or tailor. The thickness of our duvet bed-covers is still measured in *togs*.

A *tegument* is any kind of covering; *integument* is organic – skin, rind, husk or shell. In zoology, animals with shells are *testacea*, such as the *testudo*, which is Latin for tortoise. The membranes covering the wings of beetles are *tegmena* or *tegulae*. The covering of the brain is the head, or in French *tête*. To cover something in front is to *protect* it, and therefore to uncover it is to *detect*. All it takes to establish a link between Stone Age cloth and Inspector Columbo's rumpled raincoat is a little *detective* work.

Text is words, but there is a deeper sense: it is the original wording, against which copies and translations may be measured. In particular, it is scripture, which is why a vicar still says, before a sermon, 'I take as my text …'

In Elizabethan times, *to text* was to write in *text-hand*, a large, non-cursive script, or in block capitals – often used for manuscripts, to make reading easier.

A *pretext*, meaning an excuse or a reason that masks the real motive, literally means something woven up front. *Context*, on the other hand, connects different passages of writing, weaving them together to create thematic wholeness. A *contexture* is a mass of things knitted together, such as this book.

The Latin *texere* for weaving became *tissere* in Old French, which is why we talk of a *tissue* of lies, and blow our noses on soft-ply *tissue paper*.

Technically speaking, Julius Caesar's last words were misunderstood by Shakespeare. As his oldest friend plunged the knife in, the emperor did not say, '*Et tu*, Brute?' meaning 'And you, Brutus?' Instead, he spoke Greek, and said, '*Kai su, teknon.*'

Teknon in Greek means a child … so *kai su, teknon* literally translates as: and you, child? In the slang of Rome's backstreets 2,000 years ago, it had a coarser meaning: 'Fuck you, kid!'

Ten, to stretch

The most important invention in human history was not the wheel or the fur tunic. It was the mobile home – a pyramid of flexible poles with animal skins stretched over them to form a shelter. We'd call it a *tent*. The Scythians lived in them around 600 BC, according to Herodotus, the Greek historian, who recorded the earliest description of tents (or, as the Scythians called them, yurts). The invention must date back many millennia before that, though. They enabled whole communities to follow their herds or migration trails, to shift between pastures, and to colonise new lands. With enough tents, a tribe could establish a pop-up town overnight. It was enough to make the surrounding nations feel rather *tense* – that is, it stretched their nerves.

The root word **ten** appears from Scotland to India. In Gaelic, *tana* meant flimsy, like skin stretched to breaking point. In Hindustani music, a *tana* is a rapid group of notes that expand or stretch out the central melody. In Old English, **ten** became *thynne*, which we spell *thin*.

There can be no tents without *tent pegs*, and so *tenere* in Latin means to hold firm. Anything that can be held is *tenable*, and to do so doggedly is *tenacity*. Plants and octopuses hang on *tenaciously* with their *tentacles*.

If you're paying rent in a *tenement*, you hold the right to live there – you're a *tenant*. Because we hold that to be true, it's a *tenet* of law.

Ten was *thinned* down to *tin* at the core of numerous Latin verbs, including *abstinere*, *obstinere*, *retinere* and *sustinere*. We spell the English derivatives with an 'ain' – the only exception, fittingly enough, is *obstinate*. *Abstain*, for instance, means to hold off. *Retain* is to hold back and *sustain* is to hold out. There's also *contain*, *detain*, *maintain*, *pertain* and *entertain* – the last one means literally to hold together, which will make sense to any *entertainer* who has struggled to keep the audience from turning on him.

But most derivations in English stem from the Latin *tendere*, to stretch. Meanings have a *tendency* to stretch too, and in Old French, *tendre* is to *extend* an offer – perhaps with the sense of stretching out a hand to shake on the deal. In English we still *tender* an offer, and pay for it in *legal tender*. *Tender* usually has a different meaning: raw or sensitive, like skin that has been stretched fine under *tension*.

A *tendril* is a young shoot that stretches out, and a *tendon* is a flexible muscle. Meat is hung on *tenterhooks*, to *tenderise* it. If some of those connections seem *tenuous*, that just means it's a bit of a stretch.

To thin out, and so to mitigate, is *extenuate*. *Extenuating circumstances* are a defendant's excuses, which might reduce the criminal charges and so *attentuate* the punishment – that is, make it less substantial.

In the late Roman military world, a *praetentura* was an advance *ententment*, a frontier garrison under canvas. Anything that reaches too far forward is a *pretence*. An illegitimate royal son who would be king is a *pretender*; a pompous oaf who garnishes his conversation with Italian phrases is *pretentious*.

Stretching your mind towards the subject in hand is called paying *attention*. There's a big difference between seeming *attentive* and looking *intense*: *intendere* means to stretch inwards, like someone dwelling obsessively on their own thoughts, *intent* only on themselves. As that self-absorption grows deeper, it *intensifies*.

If you're brooding on a home DIY project, and your *intention* is to build an *ostentatious extension*, you're an etymological mess.

The opposite of *extendere* was *detendere*, to unstretch. A prisoner in a tiny cell, unable even to stretch out his legs when he sleeps, is in *detention*. To stretch your mind or your muscles in an argument was *contendere*, which gives us *contend* and *contentious*. *Distending* your body is stretching it out of shape.

Portendere is to stretch into the future. A *portent* is an omen; *portentous* means threatening, though in the sixteenth century it was popular slang for extraordinary – just like we use awesome today.

In medieval French, an *entendre* was an intention or a purpose. A remark with two meanings, especially if one of them is suggestive, is a *double entendre*. The radio comedian Kenneth Horne, who presided over *Round the Horne*, a 1960s radio show crammed with such outrageously saucy jokes that concerns were raised in the House of Commons, liked to say, 'Whenever I see a double entendre in the script, I whip it out.'

The *entente cordiale*, or friendly purpose, was an alliance signed between Britain and France in 1904. Ten years later, Kaiser Wilhelm, who was not only ruler of Germany but Queen Victoria's eldest grandson, gambled that the UK would not risk war to save their allies the French if German troops invaded. He was wrong, and the First World War ensued. The Kaiser wanted European domination, but he would have been wiser to resist the prospect stretched out before him … the *temptation*.

Ters, dry

To a hippy New Ager, Mother Earth is our all-nourishing world, source of life and plenty. To many Iron Age societies, she was very different – the mother-in-law from hell intent on making your whole life a misery. The Romans called her

Terra, and she was the wife of the oldest of all the gods, Uranus; their children included the Titans, the Cyclops, the ocean and the giants, and their first grandchildren were the Sun and the Moon. Among her illegitimate children – Terra claimed the air itself had made her pregnant – were Grief, Mourning, Vengeance and Oblivion. The Romans were not a nation of optimists.

Because **ters** is dry, dry land is *terra*, and a step of flat land is a *terrace*. All around it lies the *terrain*. Beyond that is distant *territory*; land and seas together are *terraquaceous*. Aliens from other worlds are *extraterrestrial*. *Terra firma* means solid ground, and *terracotta* is cooked earth, or clay that has been baked hard. An orphan who grows up without knowing his parents is *terrae filius*, 'a son of the earth': the name was adopted by the official satirists at Oxford University in the seventeenth century, whose job was to mock and insult the professors on public speech days. One *terrae filius* called Henry Gerrard went too far in an hour-long 'roast' in 1669 – not only did he accuse the vice-chancellor of sleeping with the professor of divinity but he announced that all the town councillors' wives had the clap. Even in Restoration England, that was liable to cause offence, and Gerrard was expelled.

The *Mediterranean* is, literally, the sea at the middle of the Earth. *Subterranean* means underground, and *terra incognita* is unknown land. A level space in a garden is the *parterre*; it's also the pit of a theatre in front of the stage, and the name of the roughest elements of the audience who would stand there – the tickets were cheapest, and the *parterre* themselves liked being close enough to hurl abuse and rotten fruit.

The chief ingredient in curry powder is *turmeric*, sometimes called *tarmaret* or *tormarith* in early cookery books. The name stems from the Latin *terra merita*, meaning the good of the land. *Terra* is the root of other foodie words, including *terrine*, a French meat, fish or vegetable mixture cooked in a *terrine*.

A *terre-à-terre* is a horse that takes short, prancing steps, so that its hooves barely seem to leave the ground. A dog that digs rabbits and other prey out of their burrows is a *terrier*. A *terre-plein* is a bank heaped with earth, usually a rampart to defend a fort. It was also the name of a bottom-of-the-range Hudson automobile in the Great Depression. One of the twenty-nine tracks recorded by the seminal blues guitarist Robert Johnson was called *Terraplane Blues*: he's complaining that his *Terraplane* won't start because his girlfriend has been letting another man drive it. A few months later, Johnson was poisoned (with strychnine in whisky) by the jealous husband of a married lover. He died in 1938, the first member of rock's '27 club'.

In Ancient Greece, a *tarsus* was a flat board for drying figs. The word came to mean the flat of the foot, and then the ankle. That's why we so often read that footballers have fractured a *metatarsal* – these are the bones between the ankle and toe.

Ters is the basis of *thirst*, via the Old English *thyrstan*, and *torrid*, because the Latin *torrere* means to burn up. A *torrent*, now the word for a rush of water, was originally a red-hot flow of lava during a volcanic eruption. *Tostare* means to grill, which is why grilled bread is *toast*. In medieval times, people dipped toast in wine, much as we dunk digestives in tea, so the custom of saluting comrades with alcohol is called *drinking a toast*. The opposite of **ters** is **wed**, or wet, which is also the basis of water … but not wine.

In the Po valley, mounds of rich black earth were prized by local farmers as fertiliser because the soil was so rich in ammonia. ???? the only black stone they knew was marlstone or mudstone, they called it *terramarl*, which became *terramare*. Archaeologists discovered bone knives and metal bowls in the valley, and realised that the deposits had formed the foundations of Bronze Age settlements 3,500 years ago – these people grew wheat, beans, flax and grapes, as well as breeding cattle. They couldn't write, but they must have spoken Indo-European; they are typical of the settlers who spread their farming methods and their language across Europe.

Tor, to twist

Torque measures the force that turns a shaft. It's the essence of engineering, and the most important application of energy in history. Torque powered the Industrial Revolution, it drove the age of the automobile and it supplied electricity to every home in the developed world: steam engines, combustion engines and turbines all exist to generate torque.

The fact that the word has travelled 7,000 years or more unchanged suggests that even in prehistoric times we knew that energy was intensified when it turned a shaft. Pounding wheat into flour with stones, for instance, was laborious, back-breaking work. It was easier to twist the stones against each other instead of banging one on top of the other. Better still, use a handle to turn one of the rocks – a millstone. Millstones dating back 10,000 years have been discovered by archaeologists; they were certainly known in biblical times, around 800 BC. Hebrew slave women in Babylon, according to the Book of Isaiah, ground the flour for their decadent masters and then had to wade back to their quarters across the waterlogged terrain with their skirts hitched up: 'Take the millstones, and grind meal: uncover thy locks, make bare the leg, uncover the thigh, pass over the rivers.' The Babylonians could have built slave huts next to the mills, but where was the fun in that? The wet walk home was just one of the ways they invented to *torture* and *torment* their captives.

Tormenting originally meant twisting – and *torturing* comes from *tortus*, the past tense of the Latin verb *torquere*, meaning to twist. It's the other application of torque, to *contort* and *distort*. *Extortion* is literally wringing money out of a victim

– *ex-torquere*. A sharp response that hurls the argument back at an opponent is a *retort*, and so is a glass vessel with a long neck that bends downwards. If you're bending over backwards – twisting yourself – to be helpful, that's *retortion*; if you've got eyes in the back of your head, they're *retortive*. The herb *tormentil* is good for the pain of toothache, while wry neck, a rheumatic condition that pulls the head back so that the sufferer seems to be looking over his shoulder, is called *torticollis* by pathologists. A nose that turns up is *retroussé*.

This is a *tortuous* chapter, full of twists and turns. In heraldry, any S-bend shape with a double curve, such as a snake or a dolphin, is said to be *torqued*.

Torsion is the act of twisting a rod into a spiral – except in pathology, when it refers to a wringing pain in the bowels, sometimes called *tormina*. A *tourniquet* is a simple surgical device for cutting off the flow of blood, sometimes just a bandage twisted into a tight noose. It was also a synonym for a turnstile, but that usage died out 300 years ago. No one uses flaming *torches* these days either, but in ancient times they were *tortile* lengths of burning linen twisted around a stick: tortile, like *tortive*, means coiled or winding. In prehistoric Britain during the Bronze Age, about 4,500 years ago, until Saxon times 3,000 years later, chieftains wore collars and bracelets of twisted metal, called *torcs*. A man's wealth in the Dark Ages could be gauged by the number of torcs on his arms; they also served as portable currency: pieces could be clipped or broken off, or whole rings could be handed over as payment. *Torquate* animals have ring-like markings.

In Sanskrit, a spindle for twisting cotton was a *tarku*. The Anglo-Saxon *thrawen* means twisted, and gives us *thread*; it also gives us *throw*, in the earliest sense of *throwing* a pot, or shaping clay on a spinning wheel.

A *tort*, in law, is a wrongful or negligent act that demands compensation. *Tortious* means injurious or hurtful, or pertaining to a tort. A *tortoise*, on the other hand, is a dawdling, dilatory animal that never wronged anyone; it gets its name from its twisted forelegs that seem shaped for anything but walking (some authorities disagree, and say tortoise comes from the late Latin *tartuca*, which means animal from the blazing regions of Tartarus, i.e. Africa). *Tortrices* are moths; the singular is *tortrix*. Their larvae feed in rolled-up leaves, which is how they got their name – the green oak tortrix or *Tortrix viridana* is a tiny creature that looks like the snapped-off tip of a long leaf, but it breeds so fast and eats so voraciously that it can strip whole trees to the bare branches.

Anyone tied up is *trussed*. Any bundle of clothes was a *trousseau*, though more specifically now that is the collection of clothes a bride brings to her new home when she marries. Before she weds she is a sweetheart, though not in the sarcastic sense of Dickensian times, when sweetheart was shortened to *tart* and meant a girl who tended not to wait till she was married to enjoy the carnal side of life. Tart was a pun, of course, because it also meant a cheap, sweet treat … one that got its name because each little pie was made from a twist of pastry. To the French it was a *tourte*, in Italian a *tartera* and in Spanish *torta*, which is why the flat, round cake made from baked maize is called a *tortilla*: it means little tart.

Tu, to swell

*T*ube is one of the most versatile words in English. It's the television, because of the *cathode ray tube* that fired images onto the old fluorescent screens, and the telephone, which used to be called the *speaking-tube*. It's the *Tube*, London's underground railway, and it's a cigarette, the *cancer-tube*. Beer-drinkers in Australia get *tubed*, failure means going *down the tubes* and in surfer slang *tubular* means perfect, like the curved space inside a breaking wave.

Those widely different metaphors all share a shape: the TV component, the train tunnel, the lager can – they are all rounded. To the earliest Indo-European speakers, **tu** meant to swell up and **tub** meant rounded. *Tubby* is an insult that has been around for 8,000 years without changing – it still means plump, like *Tubby the Tuba*. These days everyone wants a flat *tummy*, but there's no such thing: a *tum* has to be *tumid* or *protuberant*. If you have a really fat *tum-tum*, you're liable to be labelled a *tub* of lard: in this sense, a tub is a round bowl or bucket, like a *bathtub*. It's also a derisive word for a ship – 'Rub-a-dub-dub / Three men in a tub'.

The plumpest part of the hand is the *thumb*. In Old Norse, the part of the glove that covered the thumb was the *thumall*, from which we get *thimble*. The thumb is the strongest but also the clumsiest digit, and something *well-thumbed* has been roughly used. But without the thumb, our hands would be nearly useless: for the victim in a torture chamber, the psychological horror of losing a thumb was almost as bad as the pain of the *thumbscrews* or *thumbikins*.

Vegetables that swell up in the ground, such as potatoes, are *tubers*. *Tubicles* are swellings, and *tuberculosis* was thought to be swollen abscesses on the lungs. *Thrombus* is a swelling of a different kind, and *tumours* are different again: all can lead to the *tomb*, which was originally a *tumulus* or rounded *tummock* over a grave. Something starting to swell is *tumescent*; the process of *tumefaction* continues.

The Latin for a swelling of people or a crowd is *turba*, and by extension *turbidus* meant confusion, muddle – a *disturbance* or a *tumult*. Rough seas are *turbulent*, and muddy, clouded waters are *turbid*, but you won't find turbot swimming there. Their name derives from their spiny tails: in early English they were known as 'thorn-butts'. A *turbit*, with an 'i', is a stout, barrel-chested pigeon.

A spinning object seems almost to swell in the air, because of centrifugal force. That's why in Latin *turbo* means something rotating, such as a *turbine*, or a *turbo-charged* engine.

The Turkish word *turban* comes from the Persian *dulband*: it is almost certainly Indo-European in origin, and a turban certainly looks like a swollen head. *Tulip* is another word that arrived in Europe from Turkey, and one that implies swelling – both the bulb and the flower are *turgescent*, even a bit *turnip*-like. But Turk doesn't share the **tu** root, because Turkish is not Indo-European but a Ural-Altaic language, closer to Mongolian and Korean.

The insect that we used to call a *turk*, on the other hand, or in Breton a *teurc*, does swell up as it gorges itself: these days it is better known as a *tick*.

In some Mediterranean languages there was a shift from 'b' to 'f', and tubers became *tufers* and so *truffles*. Pompous men, full of grandiloquent, *turgid* phrases, are swollen with their own importance, and in medieval French to mock at grandeur was *trufer*. That's how, in English, anything overblown but insignificant became a *trifle*. And if there's one pudding that puts on airs and graces, it's the *jelly trifle*.

Eat too much trifle and you'll get *tun-bellied* – a *tun* was a cask or barrel in medieval times. Full, it weighed a *ton*.

On the subject of food and drink, a *tureen* is a rounded soup bowl with a shallow base, and if you're having soup there's nothing nicer (though it's hardly good table manners) to mop it up with a hunk of bread and *butter*. Butter might seem a stretch from **tu**, but because of the way that milk grows fat and hard as it is churned, any kind of cheese in Greek was *turos*. A cow was *bous*, so dairy cheese was *bouturon* – hence butter.

When you're full, you are swollen to the limit, which in Latin is *totus* and in English is *totally* stuffed. When all the musicians in an orchestra play together, the passage is marked in Italian, *tutti* … as Little Richard sang, '*Tutti frutti, au-rutti*!'

Tup, to strike

It's strange that **puk** should become both the foulest and the best-known word in English, the expletive that is recognised all over the world, and that **tup** is coy, archaic and mildly amusing. They both have the same meaning – punches or hammer blows implying copulation. But while **puk** became the universal 'fuck', **tup** applies only to sheep: the ram *tups* the ewe. Around the time of the English Civil War, in the 1640s, a *tup* could be a ladies' man, a virile fellow, but that use is long obsolete.

In Ancient Greek, *tupos* is the impression or dent left by a blow. That's the original meaning of *type* – a series of imprinted images, every one identical because they have been hammered out by the same tool. Any object that exemplifies one type or class is *typical*, and it *typifies* it – these meanings go back to Shakespeare's time. Type as letters in a printing press is a much later sense, from around the time of the American War of Independence, in the 1780s. And the *typewriter* wasn't invented for another hundred years after that.

Stereotypes started out as moulded blocks of type, invented in the Napoleonic era to save printing time. Within a few years, the term was used in the way that we would say cliché today – for a phrase dulled by repetition. These days, when we say stereotype, it means what type used to mean.

Tympans, tambours, timbrels and *tambourines* are all instruments that are sounded by striking. A *timpani* is a huge copper kettledrum, played by a *timpanist*, whereas a *tympanum* is the eardrum. *Timbre* describes the sound of a bell when it is struck.

Typomania is the obsessive need to see your name in print. A *typolite* is a fossil, apparently embossed in stone. *Typtology* was the investigation of rapping noises at Victorian seances, supposedly made by spirits drumming on the tables.

The *Daguerreotype*, named after its inventor Louis Daguerre, was the earliest form of photography, presented to the world in 1839: after breaking a thermometer, Louis discovered that mercury fumes could be used to develop an image on a coated silver plate. His first picture, of plaster casts and a bottle in front of a curtain, was taken in his studio.

Studio is a **tup** word because Latin added a 's' and made *stupere*, which means to knock insensible or *stupefy* – putting the victim into a *stupor*. If the blow never wore off, they'd be left *stupid*. That's why anything so amazing that it strikes you dumb is *stupendous*. Repeated blows to the head will cause a *contusion*.

Stultus in Latin meant foolish, so *stultiloquence* is talking nonsense. If you listen to too much political twaddle or television babble, your brain goes numb, which is *stultification*.

The Greek for a *tree stump* was *stupos*, perhaps because it could be used as an anvil for hammering metal. The Old English word was *stubb*, which is why a burned-out cigarette is a *stub*.

Sergeant Stubby was a Boston bull terrier who was rescued as a stray and taken to France with the US 102nd Infantry in 1918. Gassed, wounded by shrapnel and injured by a German hand grenade, Sergeant Stubby never abandoned the troops in the trenches, and was decorated for bravery. The only dog ever to win promotion through combat, he even caught a spy – seizing him by the trouser leg and not letting go. He was a *stubborn* little fighter.

Stamp can mean a forcible downward blow with the foot. According to the dictionary, it is also 'an instrument for making marks', which takes us back to the first meaning of type. Because correspondence used to be sealed in wax that was marked with an impression, it was natural that when in 1765 letters were first marked to show that delivery taxes had been paid, this was called the stamp. The earliest adhesive *postage stamp* in Britain was the Penny Black in 1840. It was quickly discovered that black was a daft colour for a stamp, because it couldn't easily be cancelled: the postmark didn't show up. Penny Reds replaced them within weeks, and today a Penny Black is worth up to £15,000.

The Old English *astieped* means laid low, or bereaved – in the sense that the death of a loved one comes as a blow. A *steopbearn* was an orphan, a bereaved baby. That's how Cinderella, whose mother died when she was small and whose father remarried, came to have a wicked *stepmother* and two ugly *stepsisters*.

U

Us, sunrise

East, aura, virgin, sterling

Us, sunrise

Fire was vital to Neolithic farmers, and there were numerous words for everything that fire meant – words for the flames, the blaze, the glow, the heat, the tinder, the embers, the ashes. To breathe on a flame, for instance, was **idh**. Almost the only word we get from **idh** is *ether*, the element that ancient cosmologists believed filled outer space and which Victorian scientists supposed to be the odourless, invisible, undetectable medium that transmitted light. We still talk about radio signals being in the ether, but it's a useless concept – unlike **idh**, which implies sensitivity and skill in nurturing a flame, and not blowing it out in a huff and a puff.

Us was a closely related concept, the word for starting a fire and building it up. Because the sun comes up like a fire rising on the horizon, **us** could also mean the sunrise. Then it came to indicate the direction of the dawn, the *East*.

In Ancient Greek, the sunrise was *auwus* – and, since Neolithic Hellenes had trouble, just like Roy Hodgson and Jonathan Ross, with their 'w's and their 'r's, *auwus* became *aurus*. The English word for dawn's gold-and-rose light derives from this: *aurora*.

Aurora was the Roman goddess of the dawn; she married Astraeus, a giant who had waged war on Jupiter, and their children became the winds and the stars. She is depicted in classical art as a veiled mother figure, drawn in a chariot by white horses, but unlike her daughter, Virgo, she was highly sexed, and a dangerous woman to cross.

When one of her lovers insisted on returning to his young wife, she changed his face, to prove to him that the girl he loved would happily slip into bed with a stranger. And when her toy boy Tithonus, son of the king of Troy, begged to be made immortal, she granted his wish but refused to give him eternal youth, beauty or vigour. By the time he was a couple of hundred years old, Tithonus had grown too feeble to move, speak or eat. All he could do was plead for death in a continuous croak. So Aurora turned him into a cicada, a noisy, buzzing insect like a grasshopper. Be careful what you wish for: some goddesses have a vicious sense of humour.

The Latin word for gold was *aurum*, which leads to *aurous* (containing gold), *aureate* (gold-coloured), *aureity* (the properties of gold), *aurify* (turn into gold), *aureole* (a golden halo), *auricomous* (golden-haired) and *aurifex* (a worker in gold). The old medical word for jaundice is *aurigo*. And because Aurora rode in a chariot, an *auriga* is a charioteer.

The Greek name for their dawn goddess was *Eos*. Their astronomers realised that, as the winter months wore out, Eos arose closer and closer to due east until, at the equinox on 20 March, first light arrived exactly on the compass point. That day signals the beginning of spring; so the Germanic dawn goddess was *Eastre*, and the festival in her honour became *Easter*.

The Romans also used the Greek goddess's name to mean Spring itself: Eos became *Eor*. And that's the root of *virgin*, from *Virgo*, Aurora's chaste daughter.

But the Romans weren't finished with fire-starting. They took the root **us** and named the goddess of fire *Uesta*. The Romans pronounced 'u' as 'v', rather like Victorian Cockneys, and so Uesta was *Vesta*.

After Aeneas brought the sacred fire from Troy in *The Aeniad*, six Vestal *virgins* tended the flame. The girls were chosen by lot, between the ages of six and ten, from free families (never slaves) and for thirty years they would serve the goddess in her sanctuary in the Roman forum. Their chastity was enforced by the death penalty – priestesses who had lovers were buried alive, in a chamber below the *Campus Sceleratus* (Evil Field) with food and water for a few days, to suffocate or slowly starve.

Two millennia later, **us** turned into pounds, shillings and pence. That's because the medieval English term for men who hailed from the East was *Easterling* ... and in the money markets of thirteenth-century London, the Easterlings were masters of the universe. They ran monopolies in wood, wheat, fur and flax; their naval strength was so powerful that they wiped out all pirates in the Baltic; and they practically ran Scandinavia. They were Viking financiers, and the Easterling money was the only money that mattered in London ... hence, *sterling*.

Wa, empty

Vacuum, avoid, waste, avalanche

Wagh, to transport

Wagon, weight, waylay, voyager

Wak, to cry out

Vocal, voucher, vaccine, advocate

War, to guard

Warden, wardrobe, warren, beware

Wid, to see truly

History, interview, wise, dimwit

Wa, empty

What an eloquent noise **wa** is. It's impossible to say it without sounding peevish and fed up. **Wa** is irritability, disappointment, complaint and chastisement all in one bitter syllable. An empty bottle, an empty purse, an empty stomach: **wa**!

In Latin, which spelled **wa** as *ua*, *uacare*, *uanus* and *uastus* define three different kinds of emptiness. Remember that the Romans pronounced 'u' as 'v' and you'll see how *uacare* is to be *vacant*. It gives us *vacate*, *vacuum* and *vacuous*, which can mean empty of matter or *devoid* of ideas. *Vacuity* is one degree emptier, the complete *vacancy* of mind. A *vacuole* is an empty space, and a *vacation* is an absence of leave or holiday – a *vac*, in university slang. To empty either building or bowels is an *evacuation*: the Old French word was *voit*, which has become both *void* and *vomit*.

To make yourself scarce is to *avoid* or *evade*. Accountants know there's a big difference: tax *avoidance* is the legal use of rules and loopholes, but tax *evasion* is plain unlawful.

Uanus means hollow, which is the essence of *vanity* – all show on the outside, empty on the inside. Boasting, arrogant speech is *vaunting*. You hear it from *vain* people. *Vainglory* is unwarranted pride in your own accomplishments. The Book of Ecclesiastes says gloomily that everything in life is empty show – 'Vanity of *vanities*; all is vanity.' Or, as depressive investigator Rustie Cohle put it in 2014, in the TV crime series *True Detective*, we are 'programmed with total assurance that we are each somebody, when in fact everybody's nobody.' This cheerful thought has been echoing for centuries: John Bunyan in *The Pilgrim's Progress* applied the name *Vanity Fair* to the world, and William Makepeace Thackeray borrowed it for the title of his nineteenth-century society satire. In 1983, the publisher Condé Nast, with an absolute absence of irony, launched a fashion magazine called *Vanity Fair* – it shows no sign that it will *vanish* yet. To put that another way, it is not *evanescent*.

Uastus means *vastness*, a desolate *waste*, some place that has been *devastated*. *Vastation* is widespread destruction, and *vastitude* is the immensity of space. Glendower is vaunting when he brags, in Shakespeare's *Henry IV, Part 1*: 'I can call spirits from the *vasty* deep.'

Idle people who fritter time and money are *wasters* – if they do it with deliberate, malicious intent they are *wastrels*, a crossbreed of wasters and scoundrels. In eighteenth-century England, *vastly* became a fashionable bit of ironic slang – people used it instead of very, the way they might use totally today. That is like vastly interesting, innit?

The moon, when it empties away, is on the *wane*, and it sheds a *wan* light. In Old Gothic and Norse, *wan* or *wans* meant to lack, or to be *wanting*. Originally, to *want* a thing was simply to be without it; before long, it meant to desire it, because absence makes the heart grow avaricious. A *wanton* woman wasn't always sex-crazed – she was just badly brought up or in Anglo-Saxon *wan-towen*, lacking education.

A dip or hollow in the land is a *vale* or a *valley*, from the Latin *uallem*. The Old French for downward was *aval*, meaning to the valley: it gives us *avalanche*.

Because **wa** is empty, **hwa** is to breathe out and empty the lungs. You can't say it without doing it … *hwaaaa*. With a hard Latin 'v', a sigh becomes *vapour*. Anything that creates *vapour* is *vaporific*; anything that can be *vaporised* is *vaporose* or *vaporable*. Anything weak as mist is *vapid*, or insipid. In Latin, *uappa* was stale wine, where most of the alcohol had evaporated. A *vapourer* talks incessantly, usually the most gassy nonsense. To be *vapourish* is to be prone to depression – in Georgian times an *attack of the vapours* was a dismissive term for low spirits and sudden nervous indisposition, usually affecting women. If you were genuinely poorly – that is, you were male and you had a sniffle – the best cure was to put your head over a *vapour bath* or bowl of boiling water infused with herbs, and inhale. Your symptoms would *evaporate*.

Wagh, to transport

Ox-drawn *wagons* became common across Europe around 5,000 years ago, rolling in *convoys* down valleys and across grasslands as nomadic communities and their herds grew bigger. **Wagh** is transporting people and possessions on wheels, instead of carrying them on foot. Several root words to do with travel start with 'w' sounds: **uen** means to come and gives us went; **wolw** means to roll and gives us Volvo (which is Latin for 'I roll').

Wagon was pronounced *wagan* in Saxon times. In medieval English, it lost the central consonant and became *wain* – that's why Constable's painting of a farm cart fording a river is called *The Hay Wain* and not *The Hay Wagon*. By the same process, the Saxon *weg* became the modern *way*. In pre-Norman England, a *wayfarer* was a *wegferender*, and *wegelagan* was laying in wait to *waylay* him. You can work out *aweg* and *allewegs* for yourself. What you might not guess is that *wegan*, in Old English, became *weight* – the burden carried by the wagon. If the cargo isn't tied down well, it will roll from side to side on the *wagonbed*, and that's the source of *wagging*, as well as *waggling*. The other problem, if your possessions aren't safely secured, is that some joker will steal them – he's a *wag-halter*, or what we would call a *waggish* fellow.

Anyone who has tried to read the Anglo-Saxon epic *Beowulf* and managed more than a few lines will know that the North Sea was called by poets the *Whale Way* or *whael weg*. That doesn't mean trains ran on it; whale way is a kenning, a metaphor that avoids repeating a prosaic name. Blood is battle sweat, a warrior is the feeder of ravens and a ship is a sea steed. Most of those expressions have been forgotten, but we still think of the ocean as a 'way' – for this reason, its surface consists of *waves*.

With the invention of the wagon came cart tracks, with ruts for the wheels. The Indo-European term for this technological innovation was **waghya**, meaning road. In Latin, it became *via*, pronounced 'weea'. A road that was well maintained was *viabilis*, or *viable*, and a road that was carried on pillars across a valley was a *viaduct*. To travel with companions was *conviare*, or *convivial*, but to leave the track was *deviare*, or *deviation*. Verdi's opera about a woman led down the wrong path is *La Traviata*.

To set off on a journey was *inviare*, but the rich and busy soon realised that it was too time-consuming to make the trip themselves – so they sent *envoys* in their place. If the envoy was going to collect a payment, he would take what the French called *une lettre d'envoi*, and what we call an *invoice*. The journey wasn't always easy: often the envoy would encounter something in the way, which in Latin would be *obvius* – since he could see it from a distance, it was *obvious*. If his *conveyance* could not find a way through, then the road was *impervius*, which we spell *impervious* … so he would have to turn round and go back on the road by which he came, the *prae via* – the *previous* way.

If all this toing and froing seems inconsequential, consider that a crossroads where three paths met was called a *trivium* by the Romans. Since all roads lead to Rome, it didn't much matter which you chose: the decision was *trivial*.

Vehere means to transport in Latin: another **wagh** word. *Vehicle* is the immediate derivative but there are others, more unexpected. Carrying compliments back to the great and good is *revehere*, and that's why modern celebrity culture doesn't just admire the Z-listers – it *reveres* them.

The past tense of *conuehere*, to bring together, is *convectus* – it's the origin of *convection*, as well as *convex*, but more interesting is plain *vex*. The point is that when people are brought together, they get on each other's nerves. In fact, everyone *vexes* everyone else: a typical family Christmas.

Evehere, to carry out, goes through the same grammatical process: the past tense is *evectus*, which gives us *eviction*. And *invehere*, to carry into, became *inveigh*, which is an attack with words ... so the past tense *invectus* gives us *invective*, savage words for a verbal assault. That's why *evehere* is also the root of *vehement*.

In Old French, **wagh** became *veage*, which changed into *voyage*. The first spaceship to voyage outside the solar system took artefacts that scientists hoped would give extraterrestrial intelligences a sense of human civilisation. One was a gold-plated audio disc, including music by Mozart and Bulgarian folk singer Valya Balkanska, and Chuck Berry's 'Johnny B. Goode'. The joke at NASA is that alien-watchers at the CIA's ultra-secret Area 51 compound have already had a response from beyond the stars: it said, 'Send more Chuck Berry!'

The name of that spaceship is *Voyager II*.

Wak, to cry out

If **hwa** is to empty the lungs, **wak** is to empty them noisily, with a loud *voice*. The Latin for voice is *vox*; the Sanskrit is *vak*. *Vox populi* is the voice of the people – or, in the old-fashioned newspaper feature called a *vox pop*, it's half a dozen passers-by collared on the street to answer a topical question. A more authoritative answer might come from *vox Dei*, the voice of God. The rock god Paul Hewson, singer with U2, originally took the stage name *Bono Vox*, though he lost his Vox along the way. Machines have voices too: *Vox* is an electric amplifier manufacturer, set up in Kent during the 1950s by a keyboard-maker called Thomas Jennings – Vox became the sound of British pop after its amps were adopted by The Shadows and then The Beatles.

Vocalis is a Latin word that reveals how much value the early Romans placed on the importance of language. It means blessed with the gift of speech, with the implication that to possess a voice is to be illuminated by a spark of the divine.

From *vocalis* we derive *vocal*, and *vocalist*. A *vocalic* word is one that consists mainly of *vowels*, such as eerie, ooze or ooidal, which means egg-shaped. *Vocalism* is the exercise of the voice, especially for singing.

The Ancient Greek word for a *vow* or prayer was *eukhe*. In Latin it was *votum*, which gives us *devotion*, *devout* and *votive*.

The Latin for to call is *vocare*, which is why a *vocation* is a calling from God. To *revoke* a decision is to call it back; to call an image to mind is to *evoke* it. An assembly called together is a *convocation*; prayers to summon spirits are an *invocation*. The lawyer who speaks on behalf of clients is an *advocate*. To *vouch* for someone was originally to bear witness for them when summoned by a court, and a *voucher* was a document of proof or a written guarantee. To *vouchsafe* a favour is to grant it, though the word implies a condescending and pompous manner.

A steward, bailiff or any minor official who performs a public calling is a *vogt*. The writer *A. E. van Vogt* had a vocation for science fiction; in the 1940s and 1950s he turned out 3,000 words of febrile prose, six days a week, hammering away at a heavy typewriter – physically gruelling as well as mentally exhausting. Most of his stories don't make complete sense, because when you're writing that fast it's easy to lose the narrative thread, but the best (such as *The Weapon Shops of Isher*) are astonishingly imaginative.

The noisiest animals to be domesticated when man first started farming were cattle, so yet another Indo-European word for a cow was a **wak**. That's why the Spanish word for a cowboy is *vaquerro*, and that's where the American English word for a rodeo rider comes from – a *buckaroo*. A *vaccary* was a medieval word for a dairy farm.

In the 1790s, the Gloucester doctor Edward Jenner noticed that the milkmaids who worked on dairy farms never seemed to get smallpox. Most contracted *vaccinia* or cowpox, but though this disease did leave the skin pockmarked it was not fatal, as smallpox often was. Jenner surmised that a dose of cowpox could prevent the more serious disease, and so he experimented with giving deliberate doses of cowpox … and discovered the *vaccine*.

War, to guard

*W*eard is the Old English word for a watchman, standing *guard* against murderers and thieves. Some were personal *bodyguards*, protecting the *wary* feudal lord and his family; others were *wardens*, like the beefeaters at the Tower of London, whose function is to *safeguard* the Crown Jewels. The Saxon word for property is *ead*, so a *steward* on guard against theft was an *eadweard*. That's how the name *Edward* was born.

During the reign of *Edward VII*, a fashion arose for 'stovepipe' trousers, tapering to the ankle. Forty years later, young toughs started wearing the style again, with cutaway frock coats. The newspapers needed a nickname for these lads with their bicycle chains and flick knives, and *New Edwardians* didn't quite seem threatening enough. At first they were the Cosh

Boys, but then, because *Ted* is short for Edward, a *Daily Express* subeditor coined the phrase *Teddy Boys* for a headline in 1953.

Every visitor to London is in danger of buying a fluffy toy dressed in a *horseguard's* tunic and bearskin, but teddy bears are not natural *guardsmen*: they are named not after *King Edward* but US President Theodore 'Teddy' Roosevelt. On a bear-hunting trip in Mississippi in 1921, after he failed to bag a single animal, his friends captured a wild black bear and tied it to a willow tree as an easy target. Roosevelt refused: it was unsporting, he said. For the rest of his life, Roosevelt had a reputation as an animal-lover – entirely *unwarranted*.

Ward and guard, warden and *guardian* have nearly identical meanings, though the 'w' words arrived in England via the Germanic languages and the 'gu' words from France. *Garder* in French means to keep, and a *garderobe* is a walk-in *wardrobe*, a room where clothes are kept. In castles, it became the armoury, a place to store weapons – but then, in castles, a *gardyloo* was a hole in the outer wall for dumping human waste, with a *warning* cry of '*Gare de l'eau*', or 'Watch out for the water!'

Many cultures have folk tales of *guardian angels*. In Scotland these were called *wraiths*, and they were visible only at moments of impending disaster, urging us to *beware*. Our less superstitious era doesn't believe in ghosts, but we have the utmost faith in *guarantees* and *warrantees*, which are bits of paper to protect our rights. When we claim on them, we expect our just *reward*.

Weird is not a **war** word; it probably stems from *weordan*, an Old English verb meaning to become. But **war** does give us *weir*, in the sense of a flood defence across a river. Damming a stream makes it easier to catch fish – a trick prehistoric man probably learned by watching beavers. In Saxon England, a landowner caller Ecgi built a weir to create a fishing pond, north-west of London: *Ecgi's Weir* was recorded by charter in 975 AD but had gone a century later when the Domesday Book was compiled. It is remembered, though, or at least the road that led there is – the *Edgware Road*.

In Norman French, a *warenier* was a game reserve for the local aristocracy to enjoy hunting and fishing. In medieval English it became a *wareyne*, and now it's called a *warren*. The only animals you'll find there these days are rabbits.

The most obvious **war** word is *war*. Etymologists can't trace this derivation back further than the Viking era: in Old Norse, it was *werre*, while in Old High German, *werra* means quarrelling and confusion. It seems possible, though, that to Neolithic man a war – not cattle raids or skirmishes, but a series of battles – could be forced only by a need to defend the whole tribe. The oldest images of war have been found on pictograms excavated at Kish, 50 miles south of Baghdad, in what was the ancient kingdom of Mesopotamia. They date back more than 5,000 years, but war must be much older than that – the first fortifications at Jericho, the world's oldest city, were built 7,000 years ago – walls 3 meters (10 feet) thick, twice as high as a man. The engineers, unfortunately, had not reckoned against attack by angels and trumpets … as the spiritual hymn goes, "Go blow them ram horns," Joshua cried … when the walls came tumbling down.'

Like ward, the word war arrived in English from two directions: with a 'w' from northern Europe, and with a 'gu' from France and Spain, where it is spelled *guerre* or *guerra*. *Guerrilla*, literally, means *little war*, though in the modern world it means an urban *warrior*.

Wid, to see truly

To anyone who loves *history* and *storybooks*, **wid** is perhaps the strangest and most satisfying root word of all. *Wisdom* and *ideas* flow from it – it's the source of every *interview* and all the *visual arts*. **Wid** is a mystical word to *idolise*.

For Neolithic man, **wid** meant more than just seeing – it was the knowledge that came from interpreting and understanding what lay before our eyes. **Wid** was *visionary*. **Wid** was *wise*.

In Germanic languages, it was *wit* – much more than a sense of humour and a sharp tongue, wit was reasoning and conscious thought. We needed our *wits* about us: they were our five senses, the *bodily wits*. That's why, when we're baffled, we say, 'I'm at my *wits' end.*'

To *wit* a thing was to know it. Someone who knew what they had seen was a *witness*. The past tense of wit was *wot:* the archaic *God wot* means God knows, as in the Victorian poet T. E. Brown's exclamation, 'A garden is a lovesome thing, God wot!' The mad king George III had a verbal tic, asking '*wot wot?*' every time he spoke. That became a fashion among the dandies and drones, and 150 years later P. G. Wodehouse's aristocratic *dimwit* Bertie Wooster was still protesting feebly, 'I say, *what?*' or greeting friends with a cheery '*What-ho!*'

A *witan*, in Old English, was a wise man, and in Anglo-Saxon times the parliament was the *witenagemot*, the gathering of the *witena* or *advisers*. The punishment they levied for crimes was a fine, called a *wite* – the *bloodwite*, for instance, was a price paid as reparation for injury or killing. It varied, according to the importance of the victim. In medieval England, a wite became the torture that souls in the afterlife would endure for their sins.

Wicca was the pre-Christian religion, the ancient wisdom practised by *witches*. *Wis* in Old English was *wisdom*, and those who possessed it were *wizards*. In medieval Dutch, a *wijssegger* was a soothsayer, but as the English dispensed with superstition it became a disparaging word – which is why nobody likes a *wiseacre*.

In Old French, **wid** gained a 'g' and became *guide*. In Latin, with the hard 'v', it was *videre*, to see – as in *veni, vide* and *vici*. *Viz* is an abbreviation of *videre licet*, meaning it is permissible to see, though when you see *viz.* in a written note now, it means namely or in other words.

253

Visibilis gives us *visible* and *invisible, visual, visionary* and even *visage* – the face, that bit of a body that we look at … unless it's covered by a *visor*.

Visere means to go and see, and *visitere* is going to see something often – doing this makes us regular *visitors*. *Revisere* is to go back to a place, the way a writer goes back to a page to *revise* it. In French, *visere* became *voir*, which in English turned into *view*: hence *review, interview, overview, purview* and so on. It is also the root of *purvey* and *revue*.

To keep an eye on things is *supervise* – that is, overlooking. In Old French, that was *sorveoir*, which we spell *survey*.

Videre also became *evidence*, the proof of your eyes. *Invidere* was to look intensely, which suggested *invidious*, tending to excite ill will and *envy*. Envy is *en + vy*, to look upon.

Providens, to foresee, becomes *providence* and, since it requires foresight to have a well-stocked larder, *provisions*. The adjectival form *prudens* is the root of *prudence*.

But it is in Greek that **wid** experienced some really profound changes. It started as *eidos*, a shape – if you have an *eidetic* or photographic memory, you can *visualise* exactly what you've seen. Because each *eidos* is unique, our looks give each of us an *identity*.

Idea was another Greek word for a shape, but this one meant a perfect form. In Platonic philosophy, an *idea* is an *ideal* pattern that exists eternally, beyond time and in some unreachable dimension. An *idyll* is a perfect place. The concept got watered down, though, and now an idea is just a notion. *Idealism* is belief in some perfect system, and it leads to inflexible *ideologies*. It also throws up spurious leaders, *ideopraxists* (acting on an ideal) who hide behind an *idealised* image.

Like wit in English, *istor* in Greek was knowledge. As with many Greek words, it was pronounced with an aspirate: *histor*. In Latin that became *historia*, and *estoire* in medieval French, until, as *historians* will have guessed, the English adopted it. And the rest is *history*.

Last Words

*H*istory never stops, of course … it just gets trimmed down, till all that's left is *story*. And the list of Indo-European root words never stops either, with more being inferred and deduced all the time. This book has listed 100 or so of the most pervasive roots in English, but there are scores more – some of them at the centre of sprawling families of vocabulary, others bequeathing us just a single word.

Take the syllable **i**, pronounced as 'ee'. It's surely one of the oldest, because it's one of the simplest, words in existence. It means to go – halfway between a grunt and a screech, it has the right, imperative sound for a command. **I** – go – get out!

To close the mouth, meanwhile, is **mom**. That's why people *mumble*. Sometimes it's better just to *keep mum*, or stay *mute*. *Mutire* in Latin is to *mutter*. In French, that became *mot*, the word for a word.

And finally … what about that word on the cover, **Halp**! It is an age-old cry of distress, more of a *yelp* than a word. In Old Norse it was *hialpa*, though surely the battle-hardened Vikings didn't use it very much. By the time Old English emerged in the fifth century, the word was *help*, and it hasn't altered since, although the past tense used to be *holp* instead of *helped*. Changing a distress signal is a dangerous business, after all; as Edward Smith, the captain of the *Titanic*, discovered. Instead of using the CQD emergency signal that was commonly used in 1912 when his ship hit that fateful iceberg, he broadcast the newfangled SOS, which simply wasn't recognised by the only ship close enough to rescue his passengers, the SS *Californian*. To radio users, CQD meant 'Cease transmissions; pay attention;

this is a distress signal' – though most remembered it as 'Come Quickly! Disaster!'

Still, we mustn't blame Captain Smith too harshly. While he might have steered clear of that iceberg, he couldn't prevent the language from evolving. It's been doing that since the Stone Age.

Acknowledgements

This book would not have been possible without the encouragement and support of many people. Heather Holden-Brown, my agent at hhb, has always been a tower of strength for me, and I am immensely grateful for everything she has done. The unflagging optimism of her assistant Elly Cornwall kept me going when the book was on the brink of imploding. Celia Hayley at hhb was the driving force at the beginning. Kate Moore provided her unparalleled skills as an editor, as well as encouraging me to write it in the first place. Kate was the original commissioning editor at Virgin, before handing over to the unflappable Elen Jones. Many thanks to them all.

Most of all, though, the superhuman patience and loving support of one person gave me the strength for the project – my wonderful wife, Nicola. I am grateful to her beyond all words … even Stone Age ones.

An Incomplete Bibliography

Anthony, David W. *The Horse, the Wheel, and Language: How Bronze-Age Riders from the Eurasian Steppes Shaped the Modern World*, Princeton University Press, 2007

Diamond, Jared. *Guns, Germs and Steel: The Fates of Human Societies*, Jonathan Cape, 1997

Diamond, Jared. *The World Until Yesterday: What Can We Learn from Traditional Societies?*, Allen Lane, 2012

D'Epiro, Peter and Mary Desmond Pinkowish. *What Are the Seven Wonders of the World? And 100 Other Great Cultural Lists*, Doubleday, 1998

Fiske, John. *Myths and Myth-Makers: Old Tales and Superstitions Interpreted by Comparative Mythology*, James R. Osgood & Co, 1872

Green, Jonathon. *A Dictionary of English Slang, Cassell, 1998*

Gutiérrez Pérez, Regina. 'A Cross-Cultural Analysis of Heart Metaphors', *Revista Alicantina de Estudios Ingleses*, 21, 25–56, Pablo de Olavide University, 2008

Hood, Bruce. *The Domesticated Brain: A Pelican Introduction*, Pelican, 2014

Jones, Stephen, Robert D, Martin and David R. Pilbeam (eds.). *The Cambridge Encyclopedia of Human Evolution*, Cambridge University Press, 1992

McArthur, Tom (ed.). *The Oxford Companion to the English Language*, Oxford University Press, 1992

Partridge, Eric. *Origins: A Short Etymological Dictionary of Modern English*, Routledge and Kegan Paul, 1958

Shipley, Joseph T. *The Origins of English Words: A Discursive Dictionary of Indo-European Roots*, Johns Hopkins University Press, 1984

Skeat, Walter William. *An Etymological Dictionary of the English Language,* Clarendon Press, 1888

Thackray Bunce, John. *Fairy Tales, Their Origin and Meaning,* Macmillan, 1878

Ukers, William H. *All About Coffee,* The Tea and Coffee Trade Journal Company, 1922

Word List

abandon 32
abduction 60
abolish 29
absence 66
absent 28, 66
abstain 227
accede 205
accept 97
accomplice 180
accord 102
accordion 103
accumbent 113
accumulate 114
accurate 21
acerbic 21
acid 21
acidulous 21
acme 20
aconite 20–1
acquiesce 108
acquit 108
acrid 21
acrimony 21
acrobat 20, 21
acrophobia 20
acumen 20
acute 20
adapt 28
addictive 54
adept 28
adjudicate 54
administrator 150
admiral 144
admire 144

admonish 147
adroit 193
advocate 249
affable 33
affiliate 49
affirm 51
affluent 39
affront 190
agnostic 83
alcazar 105
alchemy 79
allergen 81
alliteration 127
alone 159
along 126
Amazon 136
amoral 27
amortise 149
amphora 37
anatomy 222
ancestor 205
anchovy 26
anger 26
angina 26
angle 25
anglerfish 25
angling 25
anguilliform 25
anguine 25
anguish 26
animal 22
animalist 23
animate 23
animism 22

animosity 23
animus 22–3
anomaly 158
anticipate 97
antidote 58
antipodes 184
anxious 26
apart 27
apologise 28
apostrophe 27–8
appendage 173
applaud 28
application 180
apply 27, 180
apposite 27
appraisal 185
apprehend 27
apprise 185
April 28
apt 28
aptness 28
aqueduct 60
arable 13
argent 29
argentiferous 29
Argentina 29
argentometer 29
Argonaut 30
Argos 30
arguably 30
argue 29
argument 29
arrears 191
arrive 61

arse 217–18
Aryan 11–12, 50
ash 13
aspic 208
assailant 203
assault 203
assets 202
assiduous 205
assizes 205
astringent 211
astrolabe 123–4
atom 223
attention 227
attentive 227
attentuate 227
attitude 28
aureate 241
aurora 240
autocracy 100
avenge 54
avoid 244
away 27
axle 12
aye 88

babble 166
baby 166
back 190–2
bairn 36
balance 202
ball 38
balloon 38
ban 32, 33
banal 32